I0793760

# SPANISH PUNK

## SCREAMING FOR DEMOCRACY IN A POSTDICTATORIAL STATE

David Vila Diéguez

PM

*Spanish Punk: Screaming for Democracy in a Postdictatorial State*
This edition © 2025 PM Press

ISBN: 979-8-88744-104-7 (paperback)
ISBN: 979-8-88744-114-6 (ebook)
Library of Congress Control Number: 2024943054

All rights reserved. No part of this publication may in any form be reproduced, transformed, duplicated, or distributed without prior authorization from the publishers.

Cover by John Yates / www.stealworks.com
Interior design by briandesign

10 9 8 7 6 5 4 3 2 1

PM Press
PO Box 23912
Oakland, CA 94623
www.pmpress.org

Printed in the USA.

*A Lua.*
*Questiona tudo.*

Iros todos a la mierda,
de uno en uno o en mogollón.
Todos a la puta mierda,
valientemente y con decisión.
Iros todos a la mierda,
estamos hartos de corrupción.
Todos a la puta mierda,
estamos hartos, ¡me cago en dios!
*"Iros todos a la mierda," La Polla*

Acabar con lo establecido,
poner fin a la disciplina,
borrar más de mil normas sin sentido,
caminar sin dueños ni policía.
Rechazar cualquier forma de estado
ejércitos, jerarquías y mandos,
romper las barreras que han puesto en tu vida,
y quitarnos el peso de su justicia.
*"Que deje de ser una utopía," Disidencia*

# CONTENTS

# ILLUSTRATIONS

Figures

# FOREWORD

Spanish punk emerged directly as a transformative force amid Spain's volatile transition from dictatorship to democracy, in direct opposition to the repressive legacies left by Francisco Franco's fascist regime. It came from disenfranchised communities in peripheral Spain. Bands such as La Polla Records, Eskorbuto, and RIP voiced dissent against oppressive elements lingering from Franco's reign. Among other things they protested the 1977 Amnesty Law, which they believed perpetuated impunity for Francoist crimes, channeling their discontent into aggressive music and provocative lyrics that resonated with the marginalized. They also reflected the era's strife and crafted a form of defiance that still resonates with today's global struggles.

Through meticulous examination of fanzines, documentaries, song lyrics, and music structures, Vila Diéguez explains how the transition from dictatorship to a shaky democracy uniquely shaped this movement and turned it into a critical vehicle for activism, bridging generational gaps, and fostering a global network within the punk scene.

Vila Diéguez's engagement with diverse music genres extends beyond academic study into personal participation and creation. Growing up in the Basque Country—a storied hotbed for punk—and in a Galician household, he directly experienced punk's influence from the inside. His journey led him from studying flamenco with Spanish gypsies in London to immersing himself in varied musical genres in Nashville with his band while pursuing a PhD in Hispanic studies at

Vanderbilt University. His dissertation focused on Spanish punk, and he is now a university professor in California. This lived experience enriches his scholarly perspective, granting him a nuanced understanding of music's role in societal resistance and change.

There are complements here with my own career. As a media, culture, and communication graduate, I examined the complex narratives and political nuances of *corridos*, ballads, that address US-Mexico border issues. Now, as an editor at *Billboard Español*, I delve into how various forms of Latin music can both reflect and challenge sociopolitical realities, illuminating widespread struggles, hopes, and resistances—just as Spanish punk did.

As the leader of the punk flamenco group the Rumba Madre, Vila Diéguez actively participates in some of the scenes he explores in his book. Their 2020 track "La Rumba del Coco," for instance, describes a case of mistaken identity, singing, "*Parece mexicano, no puede entrar*" ("He looks Mexican, entry denied"), from the perspective of a border patrol agent. This narrative unfolds as the musician recounts an absurd arrest for allegedly attempting to trespass with a coconut while crossing from Tijuana to San Diego. The track's critique is later intensified with samples of the infamous audio clip of Trump labeling Mexicans as "criminals," "drug dealers," and "rapists." While the border is justified as a measure of national security, the song highlights the contentious and often unjust realities faced at this heavily militarized border.

Combining this real-world practice with analytical insight into how punk emerged in Spain, this book brings to light the untold story of Spanish punk for the first time, investigating a pivotal era ignited by the death of dictator General Franco in 1975 that sparked a radical cultural renaissance. Vila Diéguez's diligent research and unique insight give readers a groundbreaking narrative that redefines the historical understanding of this underexamined chapter in Spain's cultural history.

In contrast to the underground Spanish punk scene of the time, La Movida Madrileña—lauded for its gothic and flamboyant explosion of creative freedom—emerged as a highly visible cultural phenomenon in post-Franco Spain, showered in accolades from Spanish institutions and global media. Enrique Tierno Galván, the mayor of Madrid during this epochal period, praised the movement, declaring, "Bless the chaos, because it is a sign of freedom." In 2020, *The Guardian* wrote, "Formed after a free punk concert in 1980, an influential collection of musicians, artists, and filmmakers including Pedro Almodóvar exploded punk counterculture in Madrid—and changed their nation forever."

While La Movida, championed by figures like Alaska y los Pegamoides, Kaka de Luxe, and Nacha Pop, garners praise for its glammy cultural output, Vila Diéguez challenges this perspective, pointing out the overshadowed, deep-seated political engagement of the more grassroots side of Spanish punk movement, which flourished away from media attention. Despite its original rebellious intentions, La Movida morphed into a largely apolitical, hedonistic spectacle behind a rebellious façade. In juxtaposition, the Spanish punk community, firmly rooted in the working-class struggles and distinctly separate from La Movida, embraced a form of activism distinctly critical of the Transición, capitalism, and neoliberalism—elements often misinterpreted or overlooked by mainstream narratives.

As we navigate current political divisions in the US, the insights from Vila Diéguez's research are timely and vital. His book underscores how cultural expressions can serve as powerful tools of resistance and community-building and how to harness these dynamics in our advocacy and catalyzing change. The impact and influence of movements like Spanish punk in the country's tumultuous past demonstrates the enduring significance of cultural resistance and suggests parallels to our present.

**Isabela Raygoza**
January 2025

# ACKNOWLEDGMENTS

This work would not have been possible if my grandfather Antonio (aka "o Limiao") had been killed while serving in the Spanish Civil War. It would probably also not have been possible had the Guardia Civil caught him smuggling nuts, coffee, and various essential goods through the Galicia-Portugal border in Tamaguelos (Ourense) in the years following the Civil War. If it wasn't for my grandmother, Clotilde, who raised nine children and moved to the Basque Country with Antonio to work there for years, this work would have never happened. Do mesmo jeito, se meu avô Luis não tivesse trabalhado cerca de dez anos na Alemanha enquanto minha avó Camila criava seus seis filhos em Quintela, Junqueira de Ambia (Ourense), esta livro nunca teria existido. Junto com isto, se meu pai, Benjamin, não tivesse emigrado ao País Basco e trabalhado na indústria metalúrgica oito horas ao dia durante quase quarenta anos, este trabalho não teria sido possível. E por último, se minha mãe, Mari Carmen, não tivesse trabalhado outros mais de quarenta anos numa linha de montagem a fazer sargentos em Eibar, esta livro nunca teria sido escrita. Agradeço a todos eles, e especialmente aos meus pais, que tenham dedicado toda sua vida a que eu pudesse seguir meus sonhos musicais, literários, culturais, e artísticos em geral. Agradezco también a mi hermano, Óscar, que, aunque en la distancia, siempre estemos ahí.

Matiena eta Euskal Herriko lagun guztioi ere, eskerrik asko. Faltan botatzen zaituztet egunero. Ez dut izenik emango, zuek badakizue nortzuk zareten. Thanks to all my mates from the UK too. Many of the things I learned about music I learned from you. Thanks to all my friends in Nashville for making me feel at home during my years living there and thanks to the Rumba Madre for making my life in Nashville more meaningful. Thank you to my former colleagues at UTEP, where I spent two wonderful years. Thank you to all the musicians I've had the pleasure to play with since moving to California too. Thanks, também, al grande Juande por el trabajazo de ayudarme a plasmar en el disco *Apropiaciones Culturales V.2* todas mis excéntricas ideas musicales.

Muchas gracias también a Andrés por su ayuda y apoyo con todo durante mis años de doctorado en Vanderbilt University y por haber dirigido la tesis que fue el germen de este libro. Su honestidad y hacer intelectual carente de egocentrismos son un ejemplo de lo que un verdadero académico debería ser. Thanks to Jon Andoni Franco Elorza for helping me put up with all the bullshit surrounding academia. Our conversations about music, academia, and life are something I will forever cherish in my heart. Since you've been gone, academia has only gotten worse (but life has gotten much better). We need to catch up.

Thanks to Steve Wenz for having helped me edit the text of my dissertation before its final submission, and thanks to all my friends from the Department of Spanish and Portuguese at Vanderbilt University for all the time we spent together. Also, thanks so much to Edward Friedman, Neica Michelle Murray, and Luis Martin Cabrera for having been part of my dissertation committee and for all their generous feedback. Además de esto, agradecer también a Luis Moreno Caballud, Gareth Dylan Smith y Mike Dines por las lecturas atentas y tan generosas de la versión final de este libro.

Para concluir, e de jeito muito especial, obrigado a Kadiri, Lua e Galega por serem minha família e por me darem amor, apoio e ajuda constante e incondicional em absolutamente tudo o que faço. Só espero poder reciprocar isso durante o resto das nossas vidas.

Finally, thanks to you reading these lines too, in case I forgot your name.

# INTRODUCTION

May 12, 1986. Madrid is celebrating its annual San Isidro festivities. As part of this year's program, there is a rock concert going on at the recently inaugurated Casa de Campo auditorium. The acts performing tonight are the punk band La Polla Records (Cock Records) and the hard-rock bands Bella Bestia (Beautiful Beast) and Obús (Howitzer). It is almost nine o'clock and the members of La Polla Records are already on stage checking that everything is ready to kick off their show.[1] The drummer plays a few arrhythmic beats—showing his obvious lack of musicianship—and the rest of the band makes sure their instruments are tuned and working. Out of the blue, Evaristo Páramos, the singer of La Polla Records, grabs the microphone in the center of the stage and announces that they are going to start by singing a *jota*.[2] He then starts singing a few lines over a traditional jota melody: "Me cago en el coronel / y en toda la compañía / y me limpio con el culo / detrás de la sacristía."[3] These lines introduce their first number, "Todo por la patria" (Everything for the nation), a song in which the band denounces police brutality and political corruption, and criticizes the close ties between

1 For the entire La Polla Records concert, see "La Polla Records – San Isidro 1986 (Concierto Completo)," YouTube, uploaded by Víctor Hugo Calderon Brizuela, June 12, 2016, https://www.youtube.com/watch?v=R5rOlw7mk2I.

2 A Spanish musical style that has nothing to do with rock music.

3 I shit on the colonel / and on all the military / and I wipe my ass / behind the sacristy.

the Guardia Civil and Francoism.[4] After this first song, they move on to "Vuestra maldición" (Your curse), a song in which they denounce the indoctrination Spanish children endure at schools. Next, they talk about class inequality and working-class repression with "Es política" (It's politics), and they mock the nostalgic patriotism of those who still view Spain as "una, grande y libre"[5] (one, great, and free) with the song "Sin país" (Without a country): "Yo no debo nada / ni a Dios ni al gobierno / por haber nacido / por el coño de mi madre."[6] After this, they perform "Estrella del rock" (Rock star) and "Herpes, talco y tecno-pop" (Herpes, powder, and techno-pop), two songs in which, among other things, they criticize the music business, and "Tú seras nuestro Dios" (You will be our God), a song in which class inequality and the hypocrisy of the church and the police are the main themes: "Si convences de que lo deje a un madero / te daremos un caramelo / si convences a un rico para que ame a los demás / te daremos otro más [...] / si consigues que cualquier religion deje de mirar en su propio ombligo / te daremos un higo."[7] Then the band performs a few more songs until something unexpected happens.

"¡Oye! La policía que se vaya, que no soluciona nada,"[8] Evaristo shouts into the microphone. Apparently, while the band was playing "Demócrata y Cristiano" (Democrat and Christian), the crowd tried to jump over the fence separating them from the stage, and the police threw gas bombs and used force to repress them. The result is a heated confrontation between the audience and the police. From here on, jumping the fence seems to become a political statement, and the concert turns into a fight between the state's repressive forces and the crowd. After a couple of songs, the spectators not only manage to jump the fence and break it, but they even get up on stage. Despite the circumstances, La Polla Records goes on with their show while a voice coming from backstage begs Evaristo to calm down the crowd. The rest

---

4 A Spanish police corps that played a determining role in Francoist repression and is still in place.

5 One of the Franco regime's main patriotic mottos.

6 I do not owe anything / to God or the government / for having been born / through my mother's cunt.

7 If you convince a policeman to quit / we will give you a sweet / if you convince a rich person to love others / we will give you one more [...] / if you stop any religion from navel gazing / we will give you a fig.

8 Hey! Tell the police to leave—they are not helpful.

of the concert becomes a huge Bakhtinian carnival.[9] A stone that was probably aimed at a policeman hits the drummer of La Polla Records, people from the audience grab microphones on the stage to insult the police, and the organizers despair while trying to get the event under control.[10] As for the members of La Polla Records, they get upset when the rock hits their drummer or when the crowd interferes physically with their playing but, for the most part, they ignore the incident and keep performing while the audience dances on stage. In fact, when one of the organizers grabs a microphone to ask the audience to calm down, Evaristo keeps interrupting him, saying provocative things such as "se ha perdido un peine"[11] and "bueno ¿¡qué!? ¿echamos otra?"[12] As if this was not enough, while the organizer is still talking, La Polla Records starts playing the melody of "Cara al Sol"[13] (Facing the sun) over his voice as an introduction for their song "Cara al culo" (Facing the arse). By the end of the gig, the stage is completely packed with people dancing to the last La Polla Records song. Finally, shortly before everyone leaves the stage, someone in the audience grabs a microphone and shouts something that sums up the political and cultural relevance of the incident: "¡Y en la calle, igual que aquí!"[14]

What could that affirmation mean in 1986 Spain? Five years after the Francoist coup attempt by Antonio Tejero, two months after the referendum on NATO, three years after Lasa and Zabala's murders,[15] in the middle of ETA's continuous activity, and right when the country was going through one of its worst economic recessions. According to

---

9 In *Rabelais and His World* Bakhtin (2009, 10) states that in the Middle Ages the carnival "celebrated temporary liberation from the prevailing truth and from the established order; it marked the suspension of all hierarchical rank, privileges, norms and prohibitions." The crowd's actions during the La Polla Records concert described here seem to produce a very similar result.

10 In the video, we can clearly hear phrases such as "policía hija de puta, policía a tomar por culo" (police sons of bitches, police go fuck yourself), "madero bueno, madero muerto" (good cop, dead cop), and "picoletos, fascistas" (cops, fascists).

11 There is a lost comb.

12 So, should we play one more?

13 A Falangist (Fascist) anthem that everyone was forced to sing at school during Franco's regime.

14 And on the street, just like here.

15 Jose Antonio Lasa and Jose Ignacio Zabala were two twenty year-old members of ETA that were kidnapped, interrogated, tortured, and murdered by the GAL (Grupos Antiterroristas de Liberación), a paramilitary group part of the PSOE government that conducted several acts of state terrorism.

Madrid's council, it was La Polla Records who turned the concert into a huge war zone, and newspapers such as *El País* or *ABC* do not hesitate to back up this position. According to *El País*, a representative of Madrid's council stated that they would never deal again with "gente como esta, que no tiene ningún reparo en fomentar el desasosiego."[16] In addition, the journalist Gabriela Cañas echoes the words of Rafael Cana's—chief of security services—when saying that "últimamente hay un brote de violencia en los conciertos de rock porque 'ahora hay bandas que van a montarla'"[17] (Cañas 1986, 32). The truth is that the incident did not go unnoticed, and it even made the cover of the May 14 edition of *El País*—which, by the way, featured a picture not of La Polla Records but of Bella Bestia. In the inner pages, Cañas continues to describe the incidents of the Casa de Campo. Gabriela talks about La Polla Records by continuously referring to them as "grupo vasco" (Basque band)—while he did not feel the need to inform the readers of the origin of the rest of the bands he mentions.[18] Additionally, he even shares the opinion of one of the members of Siniestro Total—a band that did not even play at the event—who calls La Polla Records "un grupo vasco muy radical."[19] Similarly, *ABC*'s headline about the incident says that "Obús levantó un concierto arruinado por los 'punkies.'"[20] It is not until the second paragraph that the name La Polla Records appears to refer to the band as one that is "capaz de despertar, por igual, sentimientos de amor y odio, aunque los primeros derivan rápidamente hacia emociones cercanas a la repugnancia por todo lo que no sea la exaltación de su ego."[21] Then the author of the article continues to discredit La Polla Records by saying that "musicalmente ya se sabía que eran cero,"[22] since "cualquier labor creativa les importa bien poco; sólo buscan agresividad y violencia y en

16 People like these, who do not have any reservations in inciting uneasiness.

17 Lately there is a violence outbreak at concerts because there are bands that go to start riots.

18 By referring to them as "Basque," the journalist might be trying to suggest a certain connection between punk and ETA or Basque nationalism, especially considering that this was a time when ETA was especially active.

19 A very radical Basque band.

20 Obús makes up for a show spoiled by the "punks."

21 Able to spark, equally, sentiments of love and hate, although the first derive rapidly toward emotions closely related to repulsion for anything that is not the exaltation of their ego.

22 We already knew that they have zero musical skills.

# EL PAIS

DIRECTOR: JUAN LUIS CEBRIAN — DIARIO INDEPENDIENTE DE LA MAÑANA — MADRID, MIÉRCOLES 14 DE MAYO DE 1986

Redacción, Administración y Talleres: Miguel Yuste, 40 / 28037 Madrid / ☎ (91) 754 38 00 / Precio: 60 pesetas / Año XI. Número 3.325

El PCE se querellará contra tres jueces del Supremo

## Expulsados de la carrera los dos magistrados del 'caso Bardellino'

**El Consejo General del Poder Judicial sancionó ayer con la expulsión de la carrera judicial a los magistrados Jaime Rodríguez Hermida y Ricardo Varón Cobos, absueltos la semana pasada por el Tribunal Supremo. El acuerdo, que se adoptó por unanimidad, responde a la falta muy grave apreciada en relación con la puesta en libertad del mafioso italiano Antonio Bardellino, *rogada* por Rodríguez Hermida y dictada por Varón Cobos. El pleno del consejo rechazó, por 11 votos contra 9, la petición al fiscal de que instruyera acciones penales contra los magistrados que absolvieron a los dos sancionados. El PCE anunció que si no prospera su iniciativa parlamentaria en igual sentido, se querellará por prevaricación.**

El hecho de que la sanción de separación del servicio fuera acordada por unanimidad del pleno del consejo, al que pertenecen vocales de todas las tendencias de la magistratura, se valoraba ayer en medios jurídicos como una respuesta adecuada a lo que se ha considerado una sentencia escandalosa. La gravedad del asunto ha hecho que el interés se centre en este momento, más que en las sanciones a los dos magistrados, en las posibles acciones penales contra los tres jueces del Tribunal Supremo que les absolvieron.

Rechazada la propuesta de cinco vocales del consejo de instar al fiscal a que instruyera las posibles acciones penales, y considerando la posibilidad de que tampoco prospere la petición del PCE a la Diputación Permanente para que haga al Gobierno igual solicitud, el diputado comunista Fernando Pérez Royo anunció su propósito de interponer una querella por prevaricación en el ejercicio de la acción popular.

Juan Alberto Belloch, portavoz de Jueces para la Democracia, manifestó ayer que el consejo "ha cumplido con su deber". El presidente de la Asociación Profesional de la Magistratura (APM) —mayoritaria y conservadora—, José Gabaldón, no quiso pronunciarse, por su parte, sobre las sanciones por no conocer sus fundamentos. Sin embargo, en una reunión celebrada recientemente a propósito de la decisión jurisdiccional sobre los magistrados sancionados ayer, el comité ejecutivo de la citada asociación anticipaba su "sólida confianza en las instituciones del Estado de derecho, social y democrático", entre las que figura el órgano de gobierno del poder judicial.

**Página 13**

Editorial en la **página 10**

### HOY, EN EL PAIS

Tres militares muertos y otro desaparecido al chocar un helicóptero contra el 'Dédalo'
Página 19

La Llamada de Jesucristo iba a atentar contra intereses judíos y de EE UU en España
Página 14

Reagan y Gorbachov mienten, según el Instituto Internacional de Estudios Estratégicos
Página 2

Las organizaciones católicas de la enseñanza critican a los obispos por recomendar la firma de los conciertos
Página 26

Álvaro Pino ganó la Vuelta a España y la última etapa, contra reloj
Página 49

El IPC subió en torno al 0,5% en abril, según estima el INE
Página 53

Atracador muerto en Madrid en un tiroteo con la policía
Página 22

EL PAIS FUTURO

BERNARDO PÉREZ

**Incidentes en la Casa de Campo.** Ocho heridos leves y un detenido, que ya ha sido puesto en libertad, es el balance de los incidentes registrados anteanoche durante la actuación del grupo vasco de música *punk* La Polla Records en la Casa de Campo. El Ayuntamiento de Madrid, organizador de los conciertos de San Isidro, entre los que se halla el que se convirtió en batalla campal, culpa al grupo vasco de no intentar aplacar los ánimos de sus seguidores. El público derribó las vallas que dan al escenario, pero el concierto continuó con los grupos Bella Bestia —un momento de cuya actuación recoge la foto— y Obús, sin que se registraran nuevos incidentes.

**Páginas 32 y 33**

Editorial en la **página 10**

## El accidente de Chernobil no detendrá el plan soviético de construcción de centrales

Ivan Emilianov, uno de los diseñadores de la central de Chernobil, manifestó ayer que el reactor siniestrado quedará enfundado en hormigón durante siglos, pero que la central volverá a funcionar y que se construirán nuevas centrales de este tipo.

Paralelamente, los observadores subrayan que el líder soviético, Mijail Gorbachov, que acostumbra a pronunciarse en público sobre los grandes temas que afectan a su país, no ha hablado todavía del accidente de la central de Chernobil, ocurrido el pasado 26 de abril, y que pudo convertirse en una catástrofe de incalculables proporciones. Con todo, la televisión soviética comenzó su último telediario de ayer anunciando que Gorbachov aparecería hoy por la noche en el programa de mayor audiencia, el noticiario *Vremia*. Observadores occidentales en Moscú estiman probable que el líder soviético aproveche esta intervención para romper su silencio.

En medios intelectuales soviéticos se estima que el siniestro de Chernobil ha desencadenado la mayor crisis planteada a Gorbachov desde que subió al poder, hace algo más de un año. Las mismas fuentes señalan que existe un claro predominio de los defensores de la energía nuclear en el seno de la comisión designada por las autoridades soviéticas para investigar el accidente. No se cree, sin embargo, que lo ocurrido pueda contribuir a que la URSS modifique sus planes energéticos. Algunos dirigentes hablan ya de la reanudación de actividades en la planta de Chernobil, pese a que el reactor continúa emitiendo radiactividad a la atmósfera.

Emilianov, que es vicejefe del Instituto de Equipamiento Energético, ha manifestado que el modelo de reactor RMBK (a base de neutrones moderados por grafito y agua ligera) es totalmente seguro en su funcionamiento.

**Págias 3**

interviu

Nº 522
Del 14 al 20 de mayo

**Accidente nuclear en la URSS**

**Llevamos al médico a los españoles afectados**

- GUÍA PRÁCTICA PARA NO COGER EL SIDA.
- Bombas, sentencias, corrupciones... CERCO A LA JUSTICIA DEMOCRÁTICA.
- Entrevista con Monseñor Cirarda: "EL PSOE QUIERE DESCATOLIZAR ESPAÑA".

**Ya en su kiosco.**

## Los partidos cierran las listas con enormes dificultades

El cierre de las candidaturas electorales, cuyo plazo de presentación finalizó la medianoche pasada, se hizo con grandes dificultades para Coalición Popular, Izquierda Unida y el Centro Democrático y Social. A primera hora de la noche de ayer, estos partidos aún no habían presentado la totalidad de sus listas de candidatos en las juntas electorales provinciales correspondientes.

"Problemas notariales", según la versión oficial, retrasaron la prometida difusión de las candidaturas de Coalición Popular, en cuyo seno se registraron todavía ayer nuevas *rebeliones provinciales* debidas a la composición de las listas en Segovia, Toledo y La Rioja.

La coalición Izquierda Unida también tuvo problemas de última hora, al negarse a firmar la organización madrileña del Partido Comunista de los Pueblos de España (PCPE) la lista correspondiente, decisión que amenaza con provocar una escisión en el partido que lidera Ignacio Gallego.

Por su parte, el CDS, que lidera Adolfo Suárez, registró las ausencias en las candidaturas de algunos de sus más significados dirigentes. "Desmoralización personal" fue la causa alegada por algunos de los que se negaron a figurar en las listas.

**Páginas 15 y 16**

Figure 1. *El País* cover story about La Polla Records show during San Isidro festivities, May 14, 1986 busca de ello pasaron toda la actuación"[23] (Cuéllar 1986, 82). Could that be what that fan meant by "¡y en la calle, igual que aquí!"?[24] That they should keep rioting and creating altercations just for the sake of it while they are out in the street?[25]

The disdain for La Polla Records showed by the press makes one wonder what it is that makes this band so different from the other two that performed that night. A quick listen to Bella Bestia's 1986 album *Lista para matar* (Ready to kill) reveals a number of songs in which an extremely high-pitched voice talks primarily about girls, sex, and rock and roll, all surrounded by never-ending fast guitar solos. To be fair, there are a couple of lines that mention women fighting for equal rights and the idiocy of wars, but, even then, their lyrics are so vague and surrounded by such high-pitched vocals and guitar solos that the political message goes completely unnoticed. In the case of Obús, if we listen to their 1986 album *Dejarse la piel* (Give it all), we find a good number of songs that have a political or social content, such as "Crisis," "Spain is different" or "Líos en el congreso" (Trouble in congress), but the lyrics are still very general and lacking direct accusations to any specific centers of power. In fact, that might be the biggest difference with La Polla Records. As the journalist from *ABC* pointed out, the members of La Polla Records do not really know how to play their instruments, they hardly ever play solos, and the songs are normally around two minutes long. Yet in spite of the band's lack of musical skills, all their songs have strong and direct political content with which they point their fingers at very specific people.[26] They talk about the police, about the clergy, and they even mention the pope, the king, and several other politicians, and they blame them for the political and social problems of the time. Surprisingly, neither *El País* nor *ABC* noted this about the "Basque radical band." Perhaps the fight with the police at the Casa de Campo was not just a circumstantial confrontation but something that

23 They do not really care about any creative activity; they only seek aggressiveness and violence and they spent the whole show searching for both.

24 And on the street, just like here!

25 It is also worth noting that, as part of a long string of accusations, the author of the article calls the band "provincial," as if that were an insult—perhaps because they came to play at Spain's capital all the way from Agurain, a small working-class village in the Basque Country.

26 Dave Laing highlights the "finger-pointing exercises" (2015, 44) of punk as one of its main differences between it and other protest song styles.

needs to be understood within the context of the police brutality and governmental corruption La Polla Records were denouncing with their songs. Perhaps when that person in the audience shouted, "¡Y en la calle, igual que aquí!"[27] he was saying that confronting the police and the government is something they should continue to do also after leaving the Casa de Campo auditorium. Maybe it was not simply a violent and insignificant event, and the media only tried to decontextualize it and undermine it because it clashed with the government and the official narrative of an exemplary *Transición*.[28]

*Spanish Punk: Screaming for Democracy in a Postdictatorial State* sets out to understand the political relevance of the punk phenomenon in Spain and, especially, its connection with contemporary social/political movements and antiestablishment political identities in the country. To do so, I adopt a multiperspectivist scope and I explore punk through cultural artifacts such as music or fanzines, testimonies from different people involved in punk culture, and the analysis of the ways of life derived from it. The first chapter, "Making Sense of Spanish Punk," provides an overview of some of the fundamental concepts and scholarship in the field of punk studies and introduces the theoretical framework that guides this book. The chapter begins with testimonies from various people involved in Spanish punk culture attempting to define what punk is, and it moves gradually to a more theoretical discussion and the exposition of the concepts necessary to understand the Spanish punk phenomenon. The second chapter, "The Movida Madrileña Versus Spanish Punk Culture," conducts a comparative study of the *movida madrileña* (Madrilenian scene) and Spanish punk culture. The movida madrileña is a cultural movement developed in Madrid during the late 1970s and early '80s that has often been used to define all Spanish cultural production during the Transición. Additionally, it has been used to qualify the Spanish youth of the time as apolitical and hedonist. This chapter aims to demonstrate that the movida madrileña was simply a cultural movement among many others and that, if one looks beyond it and studies other movements such as punk culture, they will realize that there were indeed many youngsters who were extremely critical

---

27 And on the street, just like here!

28 *Transición* is the name given to the process through which Spain became a democratic country after Franco's death in 1975.

and politically involved. By doing so, I intend to draw a continuity in Spaniards' political activism from anti-Francoism to the emergence of the 15-M movement in 2011.[29] Ultimately, I seek to argue against the narrative of those who state that the Transición represented a process of depoliticization among Spaniards and that they all suddenly became politicized again almost forty years later during the 15-M. I believe that such a narrative implies that the youngsters who grew up during and after the Transición were somehow stupid and easily deceived by an intelligent political and economic elite, and it unfairly discredits everything they have done since Franco's death. The third chapter, "First Negationist Topos: Punk as Anti-Transición," focuses on one of the two fundamental negationist topoi around which Spanish punk culture needs to be understood: punk as an opposition to the idea of an exemplary Transición. The chapter is divided into two main sections. The first explores punk's rupturist discourse before the Transición, and the second studies its politics of memory regarding the Spanish Civil War and the Francoist dictatorship. The fourth chapter, "Second Negationist Topos: Punk as Anticapitalism and Antineoliberalism," pays attention to the second negationist topos: punk as an opposition to capitalism's and neoliberalism's ways of life. To do so, this time I focus on punk's do-it-yourself (DIY) ethos and the forms of life derived from it through a close reading of several of the chapters of *Hazlo tú mismo: Recupera tu vida* (Do it yourself: Get your life back), a DIY manual published by the Spanish FAP (Federación Anarco Punk). Finally, I close the book with a list of instances that demonstrate punk's influence on contemporary social/political movements and antiestablishment political identities. Ultimately, the goal of this book is to provide a comprehensive account of punk culture in Spain to establish an alternative narrative of the culture of the Transición and to explore its political repercussions in contemporary Spain.

Concurrently, I conduct a detailed formal analysis of a wide array of punk cultural artifacts throughout the book—especially those related to punk music. This endeavor aims to achieve two additional objectives: to build a comprehensive survey of punk cultural artifacts that can contribute to the creation of an alternative archive of the culture

29 The 15-M is the name given to the protests and occupation of public squares that started on the 15th of May 2011 and lasted for several months.

of the Transición; and to provide a more holistic way of studying music by overcoming the limited approach of scholarship that treats songs as poems by focusing exclusively on the lyrics. For this reason, when I look at punk music, I will pay close attention to its aural and musical characteristics.

CHAPTER 1

# MAKING SENSE OF SPANISH PUNK

Punk is quite a controversial topic in current scholarship. Some experts talk about punk as a philosophy of life or an attitude, others define it as a fashion or style, and many others focus on it exclusively as a musical genre. In the first part of this chapter I will focus on these three aspects to provide a preliminary and multichoral definition of punk through the voices of those who were involved in it when it first originated. In the second section I will discuss several approaches to the study of punk in current and previous scholarship. Finally, I will close the chapter by proposing an approach tailored to the specific historic and political context of Spanish punk. Ultimately, this chapter will serve as a foundation necessary to understand the rest of the book.

## 1. In Their Own Words: Punks Talking About Punk

An attitude, a style, and a musical genre: three different, but inseparable, ways of looking at punk if one aims to grasp it in all its complexity. In the documentary *Peligro social* (Social danger) Silvia Resorte, Último Resorte's singer, provides the following description of punks:

> Los punks somos carne de cañón. Porque somos viscerales. Porque estamos unidos. Porque somos únicos. Porque exigimos y valoramos nuestra libertad. Porque tenemos una utopía que crear. Porque tenemos un mundo viejo que destruir. Porque no creemos en la moralidad vigente. Porque no creemos en la división

> de géneros. Porque las mujeres conozcan su glándula de skene y eyaculen sin cesar. Porque nos dan por culo las religiones que llevan siglos manteniendo estos patrones de amor divino sobre la fe en uno mismo. Porque siempre estaremos solos al cabo de la calle. Por todo esto, los punks somos carne de cañón. Pero estamos locos, somos peligrosos, somos violentos y somos inmortales. Y además, es verdad, somos el peligro social.[1]

From this perspective, punk appears as a complex net of different elements articulated around a specific attitude toward the world, an attitude based on a visceral denial of all social norms that simultaneously enables us to imagine new and alternative ways of socializing.

Such attitude chimes with the way Greil Marcus understands punk in his work *Lipstick Traces* when he frames punk within the Frankfurt School's broader concept of "negative dialectics." Interpreting punk as "a voice that denied all social facts, and in that denial affirmed that everything was possible" (Marcus 1990, 2), Marcus agrees with Theodor Adorno, who says that "to proceed dialectically means to think in contradictions, for the sake of the contradiction already experienced in the object, and against that contradiction. A contradiction in reality, [dialectics] is a contradiction against reality" (Adorno 1990, 145). This way, when the members of the band Eskorbuto define themselves as "antitodo" (anti-everything) and say that "nada más nacer / comienzan a corrompernos / crecemos y envejecemos en absoluta sumisión"[2] ("Antitodo"), they are reflecting on life's contradictory social facts in order to liberate themselves from them and reframe their lives in a different manner. Denying all social norms, they reject the concepts through which they learned to function in society and seek an alternative way to make sense of the world—even if they die trying, which two

1 We punks are cannon fodder. Because we are visceral. Because we are united. Because we are unique. Because we demand and value our freedom. Because we have a utopia to create. Because we have an old world to destroy. Because we don't believe in the prevailing morality. Because we don't believe in gender division. In order for women to know their Skene's glands and ejaculate nonstop. Because we are fucking fed up with religions that have favored divine love over having faith in oneself. Because we will always be alone at the end of the street. Because of this, we punks are cannon fodder. But we are crazy, we are dangerous, we are violent, and we are immortal. And, in addition, it is true, we are the social danger.

2 Right after being born / they start to corrupt us / we grow up and get old in absolute submission.

of them actually did.[3] In Silvia Resorte's words, "un mundo viejo que destruir" and "una utopía que crear."[4] In this theoretical context, punk could be defined as a particular mindset that reads society against the grain through various cultural manifestations. Yet not everyone views punk's antisocial character as necessarily constructive, and Boliche, Subterranean Kids' drummer, reminds us of its deeper implications by comparing it to the subgenre of hardcore punk:

> El punk era una gente bastante más autodestructiva. El hardcore era una gente bastante más constructiva, que quería hacer cosas en comunidad, en grupo. Y en el punk pues bastante individualista y, a pesar de que cuando miras las cosas con el paso del tiempo sólo te acuerdas de las cosas buenas, había muchas cosas malas. Sobre todo con el punk, conocías mucha gente guay y también conocías mucha gente chunga. Mucha gente enganchada a las drogas. Muy mal rollo, muy antisocial. A pesar de que el punk es ser antisocial ¿no? El hardcore pues no lo veo de la misma manera. Entonces, claro, con el tiempo te acuerdas de lo bueno pero hubo de todo, ciertamente.[5]

In his statement, Boliche reflects on the dual character of being antisocial: questioning the establishment and the prevailing norm, but also potentially detaching oneself from the rest of society. In similar terms, Santi Ric refers to Eskorbuto's antisocial attitude as "politics of self-destruction" and "badly managed nihilism" and reproaches them for having been part of a sector of punk that contributed to "que seis generaciones de punkis hayan muerto antes de tiempo, unos por sobredosis, otros por SIDA y otros por sobrevivir a una reconducción

---

3 Eskorbuto's guitarist and vocalist, Iosu Expósito, and bassist and vocalist, Juanma Suárez, both died in 1992 after various health problems resulting from the use of drugs.
4 An old world to destroy / a utopia to build.
5 Punk was more self-destructive people. Hardcore was significantly more constructive people that wanted to do things together, as a team. And punk, well, more individualist and, even though with the passing of time you only remember the good things, there were many bad things. Especially with punk, you would meet many cool people and you would meet many lousy people. Many people who were addicts. Really bad vibes, really antisocial. Even though punk is being antisocial, right? Hardcore, well, I don't see it like that. So, of course, with the passing of time you remember the good things, but there were all kinds of situations, to be honest.

evangelista y volverse gilipollas profundos"[6] (Alfonso et al. 2007). An illustrative example of that antisocial and self-destructive attitude is Paralisis Permanente's famous song "Autosuficiencia" (Self-sufficiency) in which the band seems to celebrate suicide as a way to self-sufficiency. The lyrics include lines such as the following: "No pienso en nadie más que en mí [...] encerrado en mi casa todo me da igual [...] y me corto con cuchillas de afeitar [...] ahora soy independiente [...] ya no necesito a nadie [...] soy autosuficiente al fin."[7]

In 1977 TVE1 aired a short documentary on punk in *Informe semanal: Punk o cómo colgarse un imperdible de la nariz* (Punk, or how to hook a safety pin in one's nose). Many punk musicians such as Evaristo Páramos—singer of the bands La Polla Records, the Kagas, the Meas, and Gatillazo—or Santi Ric refer to this documentary as their first contact with punk (Alfonso et al. 2007). In this documentary we see a Spanish journalist who walks around London asking people about their opinions on punk. He interviews many different people and, again, they all define punk in many different but interconnected terms. A young English man defines punk as a musical movement against all the previous music styles and fashions, a Catalan punk talks about a cathartic experience to overcome the frustration caused by unemployment, and another English man frames punk within a movement against the previous generation, which seems to think that everyone has to live by the rules they established. Beyond their personal opinions, the most relevant aspect of this documentary is that, for the first time, people in Spain could see how the first punks lived and what they looked like. This fact, as the description of the video on YouTube reads, "hizo un click en la mente de muchos marcando un antes y un después en la evolución socio-musical española"[8] (Rioboo 1977). That same year, Producciones Editoriales, the publisher of the famous contracultural magazine *Star*, published Salvador Costa's book *Punk*. This book represents the first visual documentation of the British punk scene through over ninety

---

6 Six generations of punks having died before they should have, some due to overdoses, other because of AIDS, and others for having survived and followed an evangelist redirection and turning into complete arseholes.

7 I don't think about anyone except myself [...] locked up at home I don't care about anything [...] and I cut myself with razor blades [...] now I am independent [...] I do not need anybody [...] I am self-sufficient, finally.

8 Contributed to a mindset change that represented a before and after in Spanish sociomusical development.

pictures taken that year in London. Both *Informe Semanal*'s documentary and *Punk* portrayed people who, as Javier Sayes says when talking about Basque punks, "iba y vestía a su bola, no había el prototipo de uniforme punk"[9] (Pascual 2015, 17). Yet they all shared at least two things in common: They made or modified their own clothes with any accessories they found around, and they tried to defy the concept of good taste by intentionally tearing apart their clothes or getting eccentric haircuts, among other things. In the next picture, we see a young man wearing a shirt, black trousers, and a tie—quite an elegant look according to traditional standards. Yet his clothes are covered with handwriting, his trousers are dirty, and his tie knot is a mess. In the other picture, we see a band performing and the singer is wearing blue coveralls, as if pretending to be a construction worker—and maybe he is one indeed. In fact, scholars such as Dick Hebdige, in his *Subculture: The Meaning of Style* (1979), have interpreted such performative acts as the working class challenging symbolically, through style, the meanings imposed by the dominant class.

In other words, the singer in coveralls could very well be a construction worker and, symbolically through style, he is saying that he is as good as anyone from the upper class and that he can also play in a band or be on stage. As a quote from *Interviu* that Salvador Costa includes in *Punk* says:

> Los pobres trataban, antes, de esconder su condición. Esta vez la echan a la cara de la burguesía. Pelos perfectamente mal cortados y de increíbles colores: rojo, verde, amarillo, plata. Ropas destrozadas y manchadas. Por si fuera poco, muchos se maquillan, pero ojo, ni Mary Quant ni Margaret Astor han ayudado ni se aprovechan del caso, esto salta a los ojos.[10] (Costa 1977)

A few years later, in 1984, La Polla Records would record "Muy punk" (Very punk), a song in which they criticize the commercialization

9 Followed their own rules and dressed the way they wanted to, there was no prototype of a punk uniform.

10 Before, poor people used to hide their condition. Now they rub it in the bourgeoisie's face. Perfectly poorly cut hair with unbelievable colors: red, green, yellow, silver. Ripped and dirty clothes. As if this was not enough, many put makeup on, but don't be deceived by this, neither Mary Quant nor Margaret Astor have contributed or taken advantage of this situation, that is obvious.

Figure 2. Cover of *Punk* by Salvador Costa

Figure 3. Punk wearing coveralls in the inner pages of *Punk*

of punk and the attitude of those who turned a certain punk fashion or style into the new status quo: "ven con tu uniforme / y con tu mente deforme / Moda punk en Galerías ¡Muy punk!"[11] In addition to this, the following year they would also release "En Londres" (In London), a song that mocks the obsession that a part of Spanish youth developed for the culture and fashion coming from England. The song starts at a slow tempo with various vocals humming a soft melody in the background. This intro serves as background music for the first lines of the singer, Evaristo, who talks like a BBC radio announcer introducing a show: "Aquí la BBC, con lo último de lo último, lo muy muy y lo más, más. Y lo tope de lo tope ¡muñequitos!"[12] Then he makes a growling sound and the rhythm speeds up: "Si en Londres les pica un huevo / aquí todo el mundo se rasca / Si allí tienen a la Thatcher / aquí tenemos a Ardanza."[13] From here on, the lyrics keep juxtaposing Spain—or the Basque Country—with London, saying that people are more interested in what is going on in London than in their own country. Besides, at the end of the song, they make a reference to the famous children's TV show presented by singer Alaska, *La bola de cristal*, when they say that "preguntan los muy necios / a la bola de cristal / qué hacen ahora en Londres,"[14] perhaps criticizing the show for its commodified punk influenced aesthetics and topics—which, nonetheless, was extremely progressive for Spanish TV at that time.

As years went by, punk evolved in multiple directions. In *Que pagui Pujol! Una crónica punk de la Barcelona de los 80* (Let Pujol pay for it! A punk chronicle of Barcelona in the 1980s), Joni D includes a text posted by an anonymous person on Silvia Resorte's blog describing some of those changes in music. They say that, at the beginning, punk concerts were pretty relaxed and the music was more "poppy" and that now, in 1981, the music and dancing were more aggressive and that he did not like the new bands such as GBH, Discharge, or Crass. The first two were bands of the newly established "streetpunk" subgenre, and

---

11 Come with your uniform / and your deformed mind / Punk fashion in the fashion boutique, very punk!

12 Here is the BBC, with the latest, the very latest, the very very, and the most most. And the peak of the peak, buddies!

13 If London's balls are itchy / here everybody scratches / if they have Thatcher there / here we have Ardanza. (José Antonio Ardanza Garro was the president of the Basque Country from 1985 to 1999.)

14 Those fools ask / the crystal ball / what they are doing in London right now.

Crass were the founders of the anarcho-punk movement. The three of them revolted against the co-optation of punk by capitalism, each of them in their own way. Streetpunk bands would normally do so by fostering a working-class punk scene that did not seek to "make it" in the music business—as was the case with many of the new bands of the 1980s—and, hence, playing a style of music that avoided catchy melodies or any specific commercial form. For its part, while musically similar to streetpunk, anarcho-punk's main goal is to spread anarchist philosophy through punk music, and they discuss politics more explicitly in their lyrics. In fact, one of the main aspects of anarcho-punk is that bands tend to write very long lyrics in which they reflect on topics related to anarchism. Crass's song "Punk Is Dead" (1978) illustrates this characteristic and also the anticommercial punk attitude that distinguishes both streetpunk and anarcho-punk and connects with the La Polla Records songs discussed above: "Yes, that's right, punk is dead / It's just another cheap product for the consumer's head / [...] / But it ain't for revolution, it's just for cash / Punk became a fashion just like hippy used to be." As a reaction to this song, as well as to other voices claiming that punk was really dead, the Scottish streetpunk band the Exploited released an album and a song named "Punks Not Dead" in 1981.[15] Through both, they give a different answer to the co-optation of punk by capitalism by reaffirming that they are the ones who are truly punk, not the other new commercial bands, and that, therefore, punk is alive indeed: "Say to me that punk is dead / I wish you even more contempt / Don't like the music, don't like the words / You can all piss off that the punk's not dead." In the specific case of Spain, the band Sin Dios would be a great example of the anarcho-punk movement, and we could cite Kaos Urbano or Non Servium within Spanish streetpunk.[16]

---

15 As part of the complex multiperspectivism of punk and studies on punk, many people would refer to the Exploited as not streetpunk but UK82 (which is a more historical classification), hardcore punk or speed metal (which is a category based on their music style), and more. In the discussion here, I will simply use "streetpunk," which stresses their working-class and anticommercialization nature but without any specific ideology, as is the case with anarcho-punk.

16 As was the case with the multiple categories assigned to the Exploited, Kaos Urbano, and Non Servium are defined by many as Oi! or skinhead bands based on their style or political views. Once again, at this stage, and for the purpose of the discussion here, we will not go into further detail regarding the different categories and offshoots of punk music.

At this juncture, we are back at punk as a philosophy of life or an attitude. I started this chapter with punk as an attitude that seeks to subvert hegemonic social norms, then I discussed punk's implications with fashion and style, subsequently I talked about punk as music, and now we are looking at punk as an inherently philosophical movement again. In order to do so, I have relied on materials from the UK, Spain, and some that combined elements from both countries, such as *Informe Semanal*'s documentary and the book *Punk*. I wonder, however, is punk a coherent and homogeneous body all across countries? And, more importantly, if it is not, what would be the best approach to study Spanish punk in all its complexity and specificities? In order to answer these two questions, in the following section I will discuss several theoretical approaches to punk studies and then will finish the chapter by proposing my own personal approach to studying the specific case of Spanish punk.

## 2. Punkademics

The title of this section refers to a book edited by Zack Furness and published with the same title by Minor Compositions in 2012.[17] In this book, different authors reflect on the relationship between punk and academia from different perspectives. Some focus on the pedagogical possibilities of punk, some adopt a historical perspective, and others lean toward cultural studies or ethnography. Despite such diversity, they all share a common goal: to uncover ways in which punk can constitute a relevant field within academia. In this sense, *Punkademics* represents an attempt to establish the field of what we can now call "punk studies." Articulated around such a designation, in the last few years an active movement of scholars studying alternative and underground cultures has resurfaced. This occurrence has influenced the creation of collectives such as the Punk Scholars Network or the Subcultures Network, the emergence of international congresses such as KISMIF (Keep It Simple, Make It Fast), and the development at publishing companies such as Routledge or Palgrave MacMillan of specific series focused exclusively on punk and subcultural studies respectively. As part of this punk studies

17 Coherent with the anticapitalism inherent to punk, the publishing company offers PDFs of this and other books for free on their website. Minor Compositions, http://www.minorcompositions.info/wp-content/uploads/2012/05/punkademics-web.pdf.

"revival," new punk scholars—or *punkademics*, to use the term coined by Furness—have gone a step further than many of the previous scholars who viewed punk only as an academic topic, turning it into a whole way of life that affects their academic practices as well. Among other things, they are fostering collaborative and nonhierarchical publishing between students, professors, and nonacademic specialists, they are essaying alternative conference formats such as roundtables and seminars instead of just the traditional panel format, and they also tend to share their publications for free or at very low cost when possible. Nevertheless, they also continue to draw from previous literature dealing with punk and subcultures that will also be decisive in my study of Spanish punk. Consequently, and in order to understand Spanish punk in all its complexity, I will now turn to discussing classic and also more contemporary punk-related scholarship connecting it with the specific context of punk in Spain.

### 2.1. Subcultures as Social Deviance

In order to fully understand the concept of "subculture," one needs to start by going as far back as 1921 to talk about the Chicago School of Sociology. It was that year when Robert Park and Ernest W. Burgess published their groundbreaking work *Introduction to the Science of Sociology*, in which they introduce the concept of "human ecology"—a theoretical approach to studying social life through the lens of ecology. According to Park and Burgess, society works like biological organisms: Different social groups coexist and work interconnectedly to achieve the stability of society as a whole (Park and Burgess 1921, 667). But contrary to biological organisms, society's stability depends not on biological factors but on economic and social aspects and their "satisfactory co-ordination from the standpoint of the inclusive social organization" (664). In this way, when social stability is not achieved, we are, most likely, facing economic or social disadjustments that hinder an organic cooperation between the different groups in society. This structural perspective laid the foundations for other sociologists of the Chicago School to study how urban life is organized. In 1942, Clifford Shaw and Henry D. McKay published their groundbreaking work *Juvenile Delinquency and Urban Areas*. In it, they build on Park and Burgess's work and develop their "social disorganization" theory, which examined the influence of social disadjustments and the environment into which someone is born on whether they will commit any crimes in the future. A little over a decade later, Albert Cohen, another Chicago School scholar, published his work *Delinquent Boys: The Culture of the Gang* (1955). In this study, he takes a step further from individual deviance and discusses the formation of subcultural delinquent groups as collective deviance. According to Cohen, when individuals of a certain social sector have difficulties achieving success under the terms established by society, they become frustrated and tend to "gravitate toward one another and jointly to establish new norms, new criteria of status which define as meritorious the characteristics they *do* possess, the kinds of conduct of which they *are* capable" (Cohen 1955, 66). In other words, they establish their own definition of success and create their own alternative subcultural worldview and social rules. In such a situation, they might also naturalize crime as an acceptable solution to their frustrations.

Human ecology, social disorganization, and subcultural delinquent formations—these three ideas provided a preliminary frame to understanding the functioning of social groups that develop outside society's hegemonic norms. Yet none of them questioned these hegemonic norms' validity, failing to see their fortuitous nature as ideological constructs. In spite of their significant contribution to the study of subcultures, all members of the Chicago School seemed to agree that there is *one* right way to be part of society, and they viewed anything different as deviant, illegitimate, and outside the law. Consequently, such a perspective fails to grasp the complexity of noncriminal subcultures and provides for the criminalization of any alternative way of life, criminal or not. In 2012 the ETB2 (Euskal Telebista) aired a documentary showing footage from different festivities in Bilbao over time. As part of that footage, they showed an incident regarding various punks in 1985 ("Detención de punks en Bilbao"). According to some of the people interviewed, punks came to Bilbao festivities and stayed on the streets for several weeks and never showered, which, according to the interviewees' words, increased the citizens' risk of catching diseases. In fact, one of the interviewed people goes as far as saying that punks "contagian la lepra."[18] As a result of these perceptions, the council of Bilbao decided to force them to shower, cut their mohawks, gave them new clothes, and destroyed their old ones. But punks did not like their haircuts or

18 Transmit leprosy.

the new clothes they were given. As Julian Fernández, the councilor of festivities, explains, "Se les duchaba, se les daba ropa y decían que no, que querían chupas [...] y tú les dabas una camisa o un buzo."[19] *El País* also echoes the incidents with an article that opens with the following headline: "Limpieza corporal obligada para los punks en Bilbao."[20] In this case, the author of the article states that not everyone agreed with the "esquilaje forzoso de las tupidas crestas"[21] and that many citizens complained about the council's action. Additionally, *El País* echoes some shopkeepers who argue that punks "estropean el ambiente de las fiestas. Ya no se trata de que se meen en plena vía pública, sino que han llegado a pincharse delante de todo el mundo"[22]—somehow connecting punk, heroin addiction, and a specific uncivil behavior—but also asserts that this opinion "no era compartida por los encargados de otros chiringuitos, que aseguran que son gente pacífica"[23] (Etxarri 1985).

Ultimately, it all came down to punks' deviance through their eccentric appearance and way of life. In this sense, the council's action punished an alternative subcultural formation regardless of whether it had committed a crime. If any of the punks committed any crimes on the streets, they would have to face justice like any other citizen, but the incident had nothing to do with that; they were "cleaned" and they changed their clothes only because their deviance challenged the hegemonic social norms and made others feel uneasy. In cases such as this, it is necessary to proceed with a theoretical frame that can look at subcultural formations in a deeper way that goes beyond simply criminalizing them. In this sense, the approach to subcultures developed by the Chicago School urged a more positive and less stigmatizing renovation. This endeavor was conducted in the 1970s by several scholars working at the CCCS (Center for Contemporary Cultural Studies) at the University of Birmingham, who added a decidedly Marxist approach to the study of subcultures.

---

19 They were showered, they were given clothes and they refused to accept them, they wanted leather jackets [...] and they were given a shirt or coveralls instead.

20 Forced body cleansing for punks in Bilbao.

21 Forced shearing of the big mohawks.

22 Spoil the environment of the town festivities. It is not only about them pissing in the street, but they have even injected heroin in front of everyone.

23 Was not shared by the owners of the street stands, who assert that they are very peaceful people.

### 2.2. Punk as a Working-Class Subculture

The School of Birmingham inaugurated the field of cultural studies and introduced a Marxist perspective into the study of different subcultural formations in the UK. One of their most important publications was *Resistance Through Rituals* (2006). This work is a collection of essays on different subcultures that includes a chapter, "Subcultures, Cultures and Class," in which John Clarke, Stuart Hall, Tony Jefferson, and Brian Roberts lay out the theoretical foundation for a Marxist analysis of subcultures. In it, they reflect on the positions different cultures can occupy within the classic Marxist class structure. According to them, different cultures arise from different classes and, parallel to class struggle, one can also talk about "cultural struggle" between different classes and even between cultures originating within a single class. First, they define what they mean when they talk about culture. For the authors, culture is "the way, the forms, in which groups 'handle' the raw material of their social and material existence." Therefore, culture does not only refer to cultural artifacts but also to the "peculiar and distinctive 'way of life' of the group or class, the meanings, values and ideas embodied in institutions, in social relations, in systems of beliefs, in mores and customs [and] in the uses of objects and material life" (Clarke et al. 2006, 4). From here, they establish a classification that, albeit too determined by class, is still helpful for understanding the phenomenon of punk culture in Spain.

Following Marx's division of society between those who have control over the means of material and mental production and those who do not (Marx 1998, n.p.), the authors establish the categories of "dominant culture" and "subordinate culture." They observe that "a social individual, born into a particular set of institutions and relations, is at the same moment born into a peculiar configuration of meanings, which give access to and locate her within 'a culture'" (Clarke et al. 2006, 4) and, since the working class and the upper class establish different social relations determined by their specific place in the economic structure, the cultures into which the representatives of each class are born are always different from each other.[24] In addition, they argue

24 Other determinant aspects such as someone's gender, race, or nationality were still not too present in their discourse but were later developed by other CCCS scholars such as the Women's Studies Group (*Women Take Issue: Aspects of Women's Subordination*),

that, due to its economic superiority, the upper-class culture always tends to submit the working-class culture into its own way of understanding the world.[25] Based on this reflection, the authors categorize upper-class culture as "dominant culture" and working-class culture as "subordinate culture." In order to further explain this dichotomy, they proceed to connect the concept of "dominant culture" to that of "ideology": "Dominant and subordinate classes will each have distinct cultures. But when one culture gains ascendancy over the other, and when the subordinate culture experiences itself in terms prescribed by the dominant culture, then the dominant culture has also become the basis of a dominant ideology" (6). In this way, in their understanding, the dominant culture would also represent the means through which social consent for the upper class's domination is legitimated across classes.

Yet, drawing from Gramsci's concept of hegemony, the authors believe that culture is a field in which dominance can be challenged and the meanings and values imposed by the dominant culture can be subverted. While acknowledging the dominance of upper-class culture, the authors assert that there are different cultures that create different "meanings, values and ideas" even within a single class, and that not all of those originating in the working class are always simply absorbed by the dominant one. The authors refer to all these different cultures that can originate within a single class as "subcultures." According to the authors, those subcultures originating within the working class are not always so accommodating with the dominant culture and, as a matter of fact, many of them represent a direct challenge to the meanings and values created by the upper class's culture. This is precisely why one can talk about such things as skinhead culture, mod culture, or punk culture as working-class antihegemonic subcultures. Consequently, and following Gramsci's idea of each class having their own intellectuals, the authors present working-class subculturalists—often too optimistically—as organic intellectuals or proletariat hegemony fighters.

Another groundbreaking work published within the CCCS is Dick Hebdige's *Subculture: The Meaning of Style* (1979). In it, Hebdige relies on

---

Paul Gilroy and others (*The Empire Strikes Back* and *There Ain't No Black in the Union Jack*), and Paul du Gay, Jessica Evans, Peter Redman, and others (*Identity: A Reader*).

25 This connects with the way most scholars of the Frankfurt school view mass culture.

semiotics to interpret the meaning of several subcultures' dress codes, musical styles, and social practices. Drawing from the theoretical frame developed in "Subcultures, Cultures and Class," Hebdige views subcultural style as the field in which the working class's challenge of the dominant culture acquires its strongest effect and "the area in which the opposing definitions clash with most dramatic force" (Hebdige 1979, 3). According to him, "subcultures represent 'noise' (as opposed to sound): interference in the orderly sequence which leads from real events and phenomena to their representation in the media," and they also represent a "mechanism of semantic disorder: a kind of temporary blockage in the system of representation" (90). From this perspective, one can interpret the incident between Bilbao's council and the group of punks forced to shower and change their clothes under a completely different light. Following Hebdige's theoretical proposition, one could read those punks' look and lifestyle semiotically and see them as a compendium of signs that created a semantic disorder in the hegemonic representation of the Basque city and its dominant culture. In this sense, those punks' look and social practices represented a semantic opposition to the hegemonic meanings imposed by the dominant class in the Basque society, and it was such an opposition that caused the council's and people's uneasiness.

Ultimately, the CCCS conducted a crucial renovation of the theory on subcultures and provided for a more positive and, above all, destigmatizing approach to studying punk culture. Yet their class determinism is somehow limiting if one wants to study punk in all its diachronic variety, since punk eventually became a subculture in which not only working-class people took part. In the specific case of Spain, there is no agreement among scholars on whether punk was even originally a working-class phenomenon, since there is also no agreement on whether we can talk about a national punk scene or about different punk scenes, each with its own characteristics. Drawing from the latter perspective, part of the scholarship on Spanish punk tends to distinguish two main punk-influenced scenes: the so-called *rock radikal vasco* in the Basque Country and the so-called movida madrileña in Madrid. In the first case, we would be talking about a clear working-class movement originating around the economic restructuring of the 1980s and different proletariat movements of resistance (Pascual 2015, 91). In the second case, we would be talking about a cultural movement developed in the late 1970s and early ’80s by “jóvenes de ascendencia burguesa fascinados por la modernidad de Londres y su contraste con la cultura española”[26] (Fouce 2002, 59). In “El punk en el ojo del huracán: De la *nueva ola* a la *movida*,” Héctor Fouce illuminates such a distinction by comparing the Madrilenian punk band Kaka de Luxe and the Basque punk band Las Vulpess (Fouce 2004, 65–67). According to Fouce, the former approaches punk exclusively as an aesthetic or a style, while the latter has deeper social and political implications due to the band’s working-class origins (63). By extension, one could conclude that the whole movida madrileña adopted punk almost exclusively as a style, while rock radikal vasco represented the cultural opposition of the Basque working class.

Not everyone agrees with such a territorial distinction, however, and there are various scholars who view Spanish punk from several other perspectives. In his documentary *Lo que hicimos fue secreto*, for instance, David Álvarez shows that there is an alternative punk scene in Madrid, whose members—despite being contemporary with the movida madrileña—do not feel identified with the latter and have more in common with other punk movements such as that developed in the Basque Country. In fact, there is a section in the documentary devoted exclusively to discussing the connection between Madrilenian punk and Basque punk, in which key figures of the punk scene in Madrid, such as El Kurdo from Olor a Sobako, Javier Couso “Canino” from Sin Dios, Perico from 37 Hostias, and Manolo Uvi from La UVI, speak of Basque punk as a determining influence for them. In this same line, José Calvo, singer of Delincuencia Sonora, asserts that there is a clear distinction within Madrilenian punk between those who “quiere[n] ser realmente punk y militar con ello, e intentar cambiar las conciencias o hacer estructuras sociales completamente paralelas, fuera de lo que es la sociedad o lo que te imponen, o estar ahí más en la noche en tener tu look de puta madre y ligar un huevo ¿sabes? y ya ser más popular.”[27] This clearly resonates with the distinction Fouce makes between punk in Madrid

---

26 Youngsters of bourgeois background fascinated by London’s modernity and its contrast with Spanish culture.

27 Want to be really punk and have an active role in the subculture, change consciences through it or create alternative social structures out of our imposed society, or just be out there at night, have a fucking great look and get laid a lot and, you know, be more popular.

and in the Basque Country. In this sense, it is especially important to notice Calvo's choice of words when he says "really punk," which shows that there is a conscientious feeling of being part of an alternative punk movement that they consider is the real and authentic one in Madrid and which does not have much to do with the movida madrileña. This is also true if one listens to the Spanish bands that several punk musicians from Madrid cite in the documentary *No acepto* as the most influential ones in the country (Alfonso and Bocos Oyarbide 2007). Ixma, bass player from La Broma de SSatán, when asked about his favorite punk bands in Spain, says that he cannot choose because there are many great bands, but he ends up citing four: Código Neurótico from Catalonia, and Cicatriz, Eskorbuto, and RIP, all of them from the Basque Country. For his part, Manolo Uvi, La UVI's singer, asserts that punk in Spain was not taken seriously until the Basque band the Vulpess performed "Me gusta ser una zorra" (I like to be a whore) on TVE1's program *Caja de ritmos*, which resulted in a national scandal, the program's cancellation, its director's resignation, and a court case for the Basque band. They also cite bands from Catalonia such as L'odi Social, Decibelios, GRB, or Subterranean Kids and, when they talk strictly about Madrilenian punk bands, they mention bands such as La UVI, Olor a Sobako, Tarzán y su puta madre buscan piso en Alcobendas (Tarzan and his fucking mother are looking for an apartment in Alcobendas), Delincuencia Sonora, La Broma de SSatán, Espasmódicos, or TdeK, and almost none of the bands from the movida madrileña—with the exception of Paralisis Permanente. None of them cites Alaska y los Pegamoides, Almodovar y Mcnamara, Nacha Pop, Hombres G, or Kaka de Luxe. In the same vein, it is also important to note that not a single artist from the movida madrileña is interviewed in *No acepto*, which shows that they are also not really considered part of the Spanish punk movement by those who produced the documentary (Alfonso and Bocos Oyarbide 2007). Similarly, Tomás González Lezama excludes the bands from the movida madrileña altogether in his guide to Spanish punk *Punk, pero ¿qué punk?* and establishes a clear distinction between Madrilenian punk and the movida madrileña in the fifth chapter, titled "Madrid, punk en vez de movida" (González Lezama 2016).

Clearly, there is a conscientious feeling of belonging to an alternative punk movement that has nothing to do with the movida madrileña and much to do with other scenes, such as Basque punk. Yet this does not mean that there was an alternative working-class punk movement in Madrid either, given that many of the people involved in this movement, such as members of Olor a Sobako, Tarzán y su puta madre, or Larsen—Madrilenian punk bands closer to Basque punk than to the movida madrileña—were still not necessarily working class. Moreover, in González Lezana's approach, class does not even seem to be a determining characteristic since, in spite of stressing the crucial role played by Madrid, the Basque Country, and also Barcelona in the development of punk in Spain, he attempts a national definition of punk culture by providing a vast catalog of bands from all over Spain whose social class is not necessarily mentioned. The same thing occurs with those bands considered punk by the musicians interviewed in *Lo que hicimos es secreto* and *No acepto*. While a leftist political commitment seems crucial in their understanding of punk culture, whether the people involved in it came from a working-class background or not seems secondary.

Such perspectives defy the binary classification of Spanish punk into rock radikal vasco versus movida madrileña, as much as they escape the rigid class structure proposed by the CCCS. This makes it very difficult to determine whether a cohesive punk scene across Spain ever existed and whether, that being the case, such a punk scene could be considered a working-class subculture. At this juncture, and in order to overcome the CCCS's class determinism as well as the limitations present in its theoretical framework, I will now discuss the work of more contemporary scholars who look at subcultures from a less rigid postmodern perspective.

### 2.3. Punk as a Polymorphic Postsubculture

When the CCCS (Centre for Contemporary Cultural Studies) published *Resistance Through Rituals*, the scholars studying subcultures focused primarily on those that originated immediately after the Second World War. Newer studies, such as some of those included in *The Post-Subcultures Reader*, state that the model proposed then is exhausted and cannot explain the multiple profiles and social backgrounds of those who engage in subcultural activity in the "new millennium, where global mainstreams and local substreams rearticulate and restructure in complex and uneven ways to produce new, hybrid cultural constellations" (Muggleton and Weinzierl 2003, 3). David Muggleton and Rupert Weinzierl identify three main theoretical paradigms that have been crucial in further exploring subcultures from a less class-determined perspective than that proposed by the CCCS: Pierre Bourdieu's thought in *Distinction*, Judith Butler's concept of "performativity," and Michel Maffesoli's idea of "tribus."

Bourdieu's influence has been crucial in the introduction of concepts such as "taste cultures," "subcultural capital," and "subcultural distinction"—especially through Sarah Thornton's work *Club Cultures*. Borrowing Bourdieu's idea of "taste," Thornton coins the concept of "taste cultures" to explain that those who participate in clubbing cultures do so based on a personal preference rather than the influence of the specific class into which they were born. In addition, just as Bourdieu speaks of "cultural capital" as the knowledge accumulated through each person's specific upbringing that confers belonging to a specific social class, Thornton refers to "subcultural capital" as the accumulated subcultural knowledge (being "in the know") that confers belonging to a specific subculture. From this perspective, in order to become part of a subculture, Thornton asserts that one needs to accumulate sufficient subcultural capital that distinguishes them from the members of other subcultures. Consequently, Thornton questions the CCCS's notion of subcultures exclusively in terms of class, and she views style not as political opposition but primarily as an element for subcultural distinction.[28] Ultimately, the theoretical frame proposed by Thornton suggests that the process for someone to become part of a subculture—in an extremely simplified manner—would be the following: wanting to become part of a certain subculture, accumulating the knowledge necessary to distinguish oneself as part of it, and, as a result, being seen by other subculturalists as part of it. In this way, class ceases to be the determining factor in subcultural formation, and belonging to a subculture seems to be articulated more around leisure and personal preference. In the present study, such a perspective improves our understanding of the varied class backgrounds of those individuals who took part in the Spanish punk subculture, compared to the more working-class background of those who took part in the British one.

---

28 This perspective would explain the existence of an article in the US zine by Marliz titled *Punk Rock: How to Look Punk* (1977) that gives full instructions on how to become a punk. https://archive.org/details/howtolookpunk1977/page/n13/mode/2up.

Regarding Judith Butler, her concept of "performativity" applied to gender identities has also been decisive in understanding subcultural identities as performative acts. Just like gender identities, subcultural identities are constantly constructed and performed in everyday life—dressing and talking in certain ways, going to certain bars, and so on. There is no prior cohesive conception of "punkness" that punks adhere to. The category of "punk" is constantly self-defining itself by the "stylized repetition of acts" (Butler 1988, 520) of those individuals who become recognized by others—and themselves—as punks. Punks are not punks because they act as punks act; punk is what it is because those who are recognized as punks act in certain ways that come to be recognized by others as punkness. The defining moment of punkness is then reiterated when such acts are repeated, and it is by this repetition that punkness as a category becomes consolidated. However—and this is the important part—each performative act can always be different and, as such, each act holds the possibility of subverting or redirecting the ongoing definition of any subcultural category. In this way, Butler's idea of gender identities as performative acts enables us to question the CCCS's idea of a fixed system of stylistic codes prior to individuals' subcultural performances, in the same way that it helps us to further reflect on each subculture's "subcultural capital" as formed by nonfixed and potentially ever-changing content. It is precisely because of this that people define punk in various ways and find punkness in numerous things, especially when considering punk subcultures developed in different social contexts. At the same time, this is also why the meaning of punk is always subject to variations depending on the specific reality of each country and time in history. The third section of this chapter will propose a definition for punkness in the specific case of Spain, within a specific theoretical framework that applies to Spanish punk.

For his part, Maffesoli introduces the idea of subcultures as tribal formations. Just as humankind congregated in tribes since ancient times in order to survive, Maffesoli views subcultures as tribes that allow individuals to connect and overcome the alienation caused by contemporary capitalist societies. In this way, he believes that companionship is more important than class in subcultural formations and borrows Max Weber's idea of "emotional communities" to explain the functioning of subcultures. Through this idea, Maffesoli understands that subcultures are articulated around participants' shared emotions regarding different topics. Consequently, considering the unstable character of emotions, he views subcultures as "emotional communities" whose major characteristics are "their ephemeral aspect; 'changeable composition'; 'ill-defined nature'; local flavour; their 'lack of organization' and routinization" (Maffesoli 1996, 12). In this sense, he equates subcultures to group formations such as "friends from work," "friends from the gym," or "people from church." In all these cases there is an emotional connection that helps individuals avoid alienation, but the belonging to the group is rather circumstantial if compared to the CCCS's or Thornton's conception of subcultures. In this sense, Maffesoli states that "it is less a question of belonging to a gang, a family or a community than of switching from one group to another" and that "the person plays roles, both within his or her professional activities as well as within the various tribes in which the person participates. The costume changes as the person, according to personal tastes (sexual, cultural, religious, friendship), takes his or her place each day in the various games of the *theatrum mundi*" (76). Thus, someone could participate in a punk fanzine because they love drawing, go clubbing regularly on Thursdays because they love techno music, and wear very formal clothes the rest of the week because they are the mayor of their town representing an extremely right-wing political party. Therefore, Maffesoli would not view subcultural participants defined as punks, mods, or rockers but as individuals who can shift from one subculture to another without needing to define themselves in any specific way. Such a perspective keeps me from classifying subcultural participants merely as "real" and "fake" participants.

In addition to these three theoretical paradigms, Muggleton's work *Inside Subculture: The Postmodern Meaning of Style* and Ted Polhemus's concept of the "supermarket of style" have also been decisive in renovating the approach to style developed by Hebdige. In his book, Muggleton conducts an ethnographic study to assess the extent to which subcultural style coincides with Hebdige's Marxist interpretation. Based on his informants' statements, Muggleton questions the idea of subcultural styles as working-class opposition and proposes that, on the contrary, "contemporary subcultural styles can be understood as a symptom of postmodern hyperindividualism" (Muggleton 2002, 6). In this sense, not only do subcultural styles not function as symbolic working-class opposition, they are also not even articulated exclusively around a collective subcultural definition of style. In other words, while still feeling affiliated to a specific subculture, subculturalists do not regard their style collectively but rather in individual terms. In fact, Muggleton's informants "saw their own style as an evolving expression of a gradually changing self," and it was "through a comparison with a homogenized conventional 'Other' that [they] maintained their distinctive individuality and heterogeneity" (158). Additionally, Muggleton states that "attitudes were held to be more important than style" (158) and that "self-authentication was achieved by emphasizing how inner feelings were more important than appearances" (93). Consequently, one could wear very formal clothes and still be considered punk because of their antihegemonic values, as well as dress in the way Hebdige characterizes punks and be seen as a fake punk due to stylistic uniformity. Ultimately, Muggleton shows that subcultures are porous communities in terms of style and that subcultural style is a malleable subcultural statement that, while still containing certain holistic features, does not necessarily represent a collective working-class opposition but merely self-expression. Therefore, one cannot but take Hebdige's interpretation of subcultural style as working-class opposition with a pinch of salt.

For his part, Polhemus erases the connection between subcultures and their respective styles. Subcultural styles would not exist anymore; only individuals who wear clothes that have traditionally been regarded as belonging to certain subcultures exist. It is that precisely which Polhemus refers to when he speaks of the "supermarket of style": the possibility of any individual of picking, mixing, and modifying any subcultural style to express their individuality without necessarily being affiliated with any subculture whatsoever. Polhemus goes as far as saying that he believes we are facing a decline of meaningful subcultures and that the twenty-first century is "the age of individual expression for one and all via the medium of creative personal style" (Polhemus 2014, 214). This does not necessarily mean, however, that subcultures themselves do not exist. Polhemus shows that style does not represent "a genuine subcultural commitment" (209) anymore, but perhaps that only implies that style has become secondary—or even irrelevant—as an indication of subcultural affiliation. Maybe subcultural style did indeed need to become meaningless for other ways of subcultural implication to arise. Ultimately, bearing the considerations of Muggleton and Polhemus in mind, I take a broader scope and avoid overemphasizing style's relevance as indicative of subcultural affiliation in this book.

### *2.4. Punk as an Ethos or Philosophy*

An alternative way of looking at punk that escapes any class determinism or stylistic meaning is viewing punk as an ethos or a philosophy. In "The Death and Life of Punk, the Last Subculture," Dylan Clark asserts that "punk had to die so that it could live" and that "with the death of punk, classical subcultures died" (Clark 2003, 223). According to Clark "the classical subculture 'died' when it became the object of social inspection and nostalgia, and when it became so amenable to commodification" (224). Yet there is another kind of subculture, one that has been "articulat[ing] a social form that anticipates and outmanoeuvres the dominance of corporate-capitalism" and that represents "the invention of not just new subjectivities but, perhaps, a new kind of cultural formation" (224–25). Class background and style are irrelevant in this subculture, and the new subjectivities embody a polymorphous anticapitalist ethos that escapes any fixed definition because being indefinable—and therefore impossible to co-opt by capitalism—is at this subculture's core. This subculture is the new punk subculture that originated after the death of the stylized subcultures observed by Polhemus.

Clark distinguishes classical punk from contemporary punk in the way they exercise their political opposition. "Early punks were too dependent on music and fashion as modes for expression," and "these proved to be easy targets for corporate cooptation." As a result, "classical subcultures were deprived of some of their ability to generate meaning and voice critique" (Clark 2003, 227). Today, punk style is not a semiotic disruptive statement anymore; its original eccentric character is no longer shocking and it has become "normal." Clark argues that academics, among other people, have contributed to creating a hegemonic discourse around style that reduces subcultures to "little more than hairstyles, quaint slang, and pop songs" and that contributes to the "depoliticization of subcultures" by "mistaking style as the totality of [subcultural] dissent" (231). But the overemphasis on style is not something subculturalists ignore and, as a reaction to it, contemporary punk has found a different way of becoming unified by making an anticapitalist ethos its main defining characteristic. Clark goes even further and states that contemporary punk "is now almost synonymous with the practice of anarchism" (233) and that "by slipping free of its orthodoxies—its costumes, musical regulations, behaviours, and thoughts—punk embodied the anarchism it aspired to" (234).

A similar view is present in Craig O'Hara's *The Philosophy of Punk*. According to O'Hara, punk "has evolved past the 'shock tactics' of colored hair and dog collars to have a fairly cohesive philosophy with little or nothing to do with one particular style of dress. While useful at the time, and still fun today, shocking people with appearances has taken a back seat to shocking people with ideas" (O'Hara 1995, 34). In his book, O'Hara explores how the media has traditionally portrayed punk exclusively in terms of style and deviance and then discusses punk's underlying philosophy regarding topics such as anarchism, gender issues, or environmentalism and ecological concerns. Similarly to Clark, he connects punk's underlying philosophy primarily with anarchism. He states that "unlike other young or bourgeois countercultures, punks reject communism and the left wing of traditional democratic governments as well as capitalism" and that "punks have turned to anarchism as an alternative to the world's existing systems" (72). While true in many cases, saying that all bands are anarchists may be a bit of a stretch. Bands such as Crass, Sin Dios, or Los muertos de Cristo are definitely anarchist; others such as the Clash, Boikot, or Mencer Vermello, however, sympathize more with communism. In the case of Spain, one could even find punk bands with a nationalist orientation, such as the Basque bands Kortatu and Etsaiak, the Catalan bands KOP and Inadaptats, the Valencian band Obrint Pas, and the Galician bands Xenreira and Keltoi. Besides, we cannot ignore that, while extremely marginal, nowadays one can even find Muslim and Christian punk—which could not be further from anarchist philosophy.[29] The only thing that seems cohesive across the world is that there is hardly any evidence

---

29 It is worth noting that there are even a few marginal punk bands that, while anticapitalist, present political orientations aligned with fascism and Nazism. This branch will not be considered in my study of Spanish punk because, in addition to being extremely marginal, they are viewed by most punks as a sector of society that is trying to hijack and use the punk movement for their own political projects. An interesting article in this line is "La renovación de la ultraderecha española: Una historia generacional (1966–2008)" in which, among many other things, Xavier Casals Meseguer shows how in Spain extreme right-wing movements relied on punk for an aesthetic renovation that could make fascism more appealing to the youth.

of punks that support capitalism.[30] With this in mind, and in tune with Dylan's approach, I would suggest referring to punk's political philosophy—if we insist on defining it in any specific way—as *predominantly* anticapitalist, or as almost synonymous to "the practice of anarchism" but not to anarchism as a specific philosophical branch.[31]

Meanwhile, viewing punk as the negation of something (e.g., capitalism) instead of as the affirmation of anything (e.g., communism or anarchism) avoids having to define punk in specific political terms and connects with the way Greil Marcus understands punk culture in his work *Lipstick Traces.* Marcus views punk as the negation of all social facts, which, at the same time, "produced the affirmation that anything was possible" (Marcus 1990, 16). By negation, punk clears the way for other possible realities to be considered. "Damning God and the state, work and leisure, home and the family, sex and play, the audience and itself, [punk] music briefly made it possible to experience all those things as if they were not natural facts but ideological constructs: things that had been made and therefore could be altered, or done away with altogether" (15). Such constant questioning through negation is a powerful mindset that crosses most punk culture, early and contemporary. But the negation of hegemonic social facts would be useless if not combined with the proposition of new ones that could substitute those negated. In this line, Simon Reynolds establishes a distinction between two moments in punk: punk and postpunk. According to Reynolds, the punk that negated all social facts died in 1978, and it was after that that a new affirmative and polymorphous postpunk developed. At the beginning,

30 There are a few exceptions of punks who have connected with the economic libertarian philosophy of what has been defined as "anarcho-capitalism." This philosophy reinterprets anarchism's individualism and opposition to authority as a neoliberal economic system in which the state does not interfere in any way. Obviously, such a perspective conflicts with anarchism's goal of achieving an economically equal society, and it is rejected by most anarchists and punks. Former Misfits singer Michale Graves is a good example of this marginal sector.

31 Matthew Worley studies early British punk as a "contested site of political engagement" (Worley 2012, 334) and shows how both the left and the right tried to appropriate the movement toward their own political goals. Such a statement is insightful when talking about early punk and bands that originated with no specific political affiliation. However, if we were to talk about bands such as the Clash, one cannot speak of appropriation because the band itself showed a clear sympathy for communism. In the case of contemporary punk, the political spectrum is even broader, and talking about appropriation as if there was a "pure" punk and a partisan denaturalization of it is even more complicated.

"punk's simple stance of negation, of being against, briefly created unity. But as soon as the question shifted to 'What are we actually for?' the movement disintegrated and dispersed, each strand nurturing its own creation myth of what punk meant and pursued its own vision of the way forward" (Reynolds 2005, xxix–xxx). While Reynolds focuses on punk as an art form, such a reading can also be applied to punk as an ethos. After negating the current capitalist system, where should we go now? Should we turn to a socialist, Marxist-Leninist, Trotskyist, anarcho-syndicalist, Christian, or even apolitical ethos to build our new ideal society? The punk movement needed a more specific definition to understand its purpose and direction, and it is in this context that one needs to understand the great variety of philosophical perspectives that followed the first negationist period. In the specific case of Spain, such a distinction between negationist and affirmative punk is more evident in the late 1980s and early '90s, when punk bands such as Reincidentes, Boikot, Sin Dios, and Los muertos de Cristo made politics a decisive element of their discourse and practices.

Finally, it is critical to distinguish the ethos promoted in punk's discourse from that present in punks' specific ways of life. Through songs, fanzines, and other cultural manifestations, punks can advocate for specific ways of life, but it is through their everyday practices that punks can create an effective opposition to capitalism. It is common, for instance, to disregard bands that, while singing against capitalism, rely on multinational record companies to commercialize their work instead of producing and distributing it themselves or through an independent record label. In this sense, Kevin Dunn stresses the DIY ethos as punk's most radical contribution. According to Dunn, "DIY punk provides individuals and local communities with resources for self-empowerment and political resistance." He uses the term "DIY punk" precisely to "draw attention to the difference between the organic cultural products that emerge from a DIY punk community and those 'commercial punk' products sold by major record labels and trendy mall stores" (Dunn 2016, 20). In this sense, "DIY punk has little to do with what you are wearing or listening to and everything with how you choose to interact with the world around you" (12). According to Dunn, DIY punk helps individuals achieve self-empowerment and fight capitalism's alienation. In order to explain how DIY punk can help achieve such a goal, he refers to the different kinds of alienation that Marx noted in his *Economic and Philosophical Manuscripts of 1844*. According to Marx, there are four ways in which workers are alienated under capitalism. First, they are alienated from the production process. Workers become part of a production chain in which they become little more than tools that keep the chain running. Instead of feeling like an organic part of the process of creating a product, they become little more than "button pushers" or "lever pullers." Second, they are alienated from the product they create since they do not work to create things they need and keep but rather things that, once they are finished, the owner of the business sells to make a profit. Instead of working to create the product, workers work exclusively to receive a salary. Hence the irony of workers who can create specific objects that they cannot afford to buy. Third, workers are alienated from other human beings since the relations of exchange are completely directed by the product and not the people. The worker creates something that another person needs, not in order to satisfy this person but to receive a salary that comes from the money this person pays for the product. Finally, workers are alienated from themselves because they work under someone else's power and in order to satisfy this person's needs and not their own. The DIY ethos of punk culture aims to de-alienate individuals by fostering the independence from the modes of production under capitalism. In this way, DIY punk seeks to facilitate a system in which individuals do not work for a salary but to create those goods they need to survive, as well as a system in which mutual cooperation is the driving force toward a more egalitarian society. Therefore, squatting, independent record labels, fanzines, pirate radio stations, and self-publishing, but also community gardens, food centers, collaborative fundraises and more, can all be seen as part of punk's DIY ethos. Ultimately, the idea of punk as an ethos will be crucial to understanding the underground net of DIY practices that emerged in Spain parallel to the development of punk culture. Phenomena such as Centros Sociales Okupados and *gaztetxes* (Basque occupied social centers, literally "houses of the youth" in Basque); independent record labels such as Esan Ozenki, Spansul Records, and Basati Diskak; fanzines such as *Destruye!!!*, *N.D.F.*, and *Penetración*; and other DIY manifestations will all need to be studied within the frame of punk's DIY ethos. With this in mind, the most accurate and less exclusive definition of punk culture could be that provided by Zack Furness when he defines punk as a movement of "interwoven subcultures, and a broader . . . 'Do it Yourself'

(DIY) counterculture in which people put ethical and political ideas into practice by using music and other modes of cultural production/expression to highlight both the frustrations and banalities of everyday life, as well as the ideas and institutions that need to be battled if there is any hope of living in a less oppressive world" (Furness 2012, 10).

Next, before offering a final reflection on the recently developed field of global punk and proposing a theoretical approach tailored to Spanish punk's context and own specificities, I will discuss a theoretical frame to study punk culture's most defining element: punk music.

### *2.5. Punk as Music Genre*

There is abundant literature that documents punk bands or describes punk's different musical subgenres. Yet little attention has been paid to punk music and its specific musical language. Hebdige speaks of punk music simply as one more element in the stylistic cluster that makes up punk culture, but he never explains exactly what punk music is. In comparison with his detailed analysis of punk visual imagery, he seems to simply take music for granted. Dave Laing does a more illuminating job in *One Chord Wonders: Power and Meaning in Punk Rock*, although he focuses exclusively on early US and British punk. Laing studies how early punk music "generate[d] meanings, what were those meanings and which of them were consumed by listeners to the music and in what way" (Laing 2015, 2). To do so, he follows a semiological approach and observes the ways in which punk music generated its own discourse within the broader frame of popular music. The benefit of using semiology is that "it brings into equivalence all types of signs (written, spoken, sung, played, gestured)" (2), which provides a more comprehensive approach to studying punk than that conducted by literary, music, or sociology scholars, who tend to focus on only one aspect at a time. A similar approach is followed by Robert Walser, whose work *Running with the Devil: Power, Gender, and Madness in Heavy Metal*, although focused on heavy metal and not punk, is still quite informative for punk's case. For his part, Robert Christgau's detailed analysis of the New York Dolls' music in his chapter in *Stranded: Rock and Roll for a Desert Island* is also very instructive in how to approach the analysis of punk music. In it, Christgau explores the different elements that characterize the New York Dolls' protopunk sound and provides an analytical approach that can serve as a model to study future punk music. Next, having Laing's,

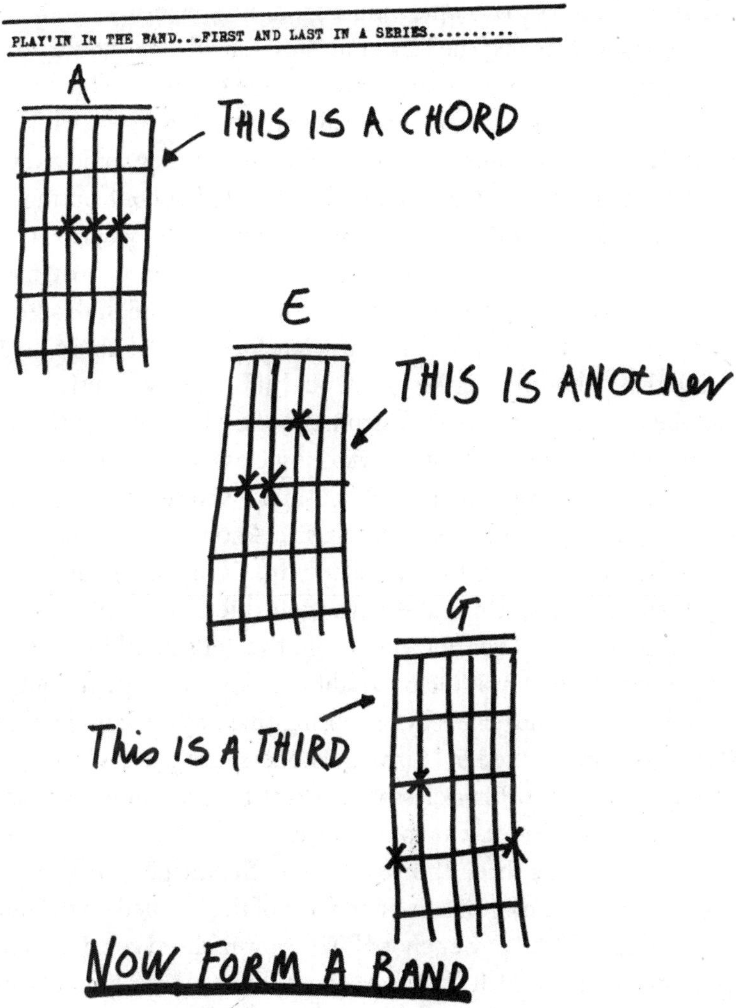


Figure 4. "This is a chord. This is another. This is a third. Now form a band." *Sideburns* 1

Walser's, and Christgau's works as a reference point, I will provide a preliminary analysis of punk's general musical discourse in order to establish the necessary musical concepts that I will be using when discussing Spanish punk in the following chapters.

A defining characteristic of punk musicians is making virtue out of simplicity—or even incapacity. A paradigmatic example of this is the classic image published in the fanzine *Sideburns* saying that only three chords are necessary to become a punk guitarist and form a band. Such a statement suggests that the lack of musical knowledge should not be an impediment to creating music and that one should be able to do it no matter what. In this line, Laing recalls an occasion when, while the Sex Pistols were performing, someone shouted that they could not play their instruments and, instead of feeling offended or confronting this person, one of the band members simply replied, "So what?" (Laing 2015, 33). By doing so, he questioned the notion of good and bad music and opposed the underlying classism of limiting someone's right to make music based on their lack of musicianship—as if all those British working-class youngsters of the 1970s could afford to take music lessons or had the time to master their instruments. Punk broke with that classism and allowed the voice of the working class to be heard through their own musical proposal in which music skills were irrelevant; there was no such thing as bad music, and musical knowledge was not going to keep the working class from speaking up. As Sham 69 said in their song "If the Kids Are United"—with their thick working-class cockney accent—in 1978: "For once in my life I've got something to say / I wanna say it now for now is today." Additionally, as Laing points out, the demystification of musicians by proposing that anyone could become a punk musician resulted in "turning listeners into players" (103) and encouraged many working-class youngsters to form their own bands and challenge the domination of upper-class culture.

In fact, even the three chords shown in the image were too many to learn for many punk guitarists, and most of them relied on the much easier concept of "the power chord." The power chord consists in playing only the first and fifth notes of a chord on the lower guitar strings. A chord needs at least three notes: first, third, and fifth. The third will normally either be a minor third or a major third depending on the key in which one is playing. In the key of C major, the C major chord is formed by the first, the major third, and the fifth, while the D minor chord consists of the first, the minor third, and the fifth. As is evident if one does not have any musical knowledge, this can be quite complicated. That is precisely why most punks will take the third out and only play the first and the fifth notes, considering that there is only one single position for every possible power chord on guitar. All you need to do is move that one position up and down the fretboard. Furthermore, the power chord is crucial to understanding punk music because, while it resulted from trying to find the easiest way to play, it marked punk's sound forever; the sound of the power chord became the quintessential element of punk music as well as one of the features without which most people would not define any music as punk.

In addition to the use of power chords, Christgau identifies another decisive feature of punk music when he describes the New York Dolls' guitar sound as "drone-prone guitar countertradition that was not only loud but tumultuous" (Christgau 2007, 136). The countertradition Christgau refers to is that developed by guitarists such as Wayne Kramer, Jimmy Page, or Pete Townshend. These guitarists' style is based on an extremely loud and distorted guitar sound that, as Walser points out when talking about heavy metal, communicates a sense of power. Such a guitar sound is immediately adopted by punk guitarists due to the fact that it provides an opportunity to show power through music without really needing to be a virtuoso; the sense of power does not rely on any musical skills but merely on an aural sensation caused by a loud, distorted, and, ultimately, "noisy" guitar. In tune with this perspective, most punk guitarists avoid playing any kind of guitar solos, since this would normally force them to play high-pitched melodic lines instead of loud-sounding power chords. The only occasions when they would play a solo are those in which the solo contributes to the general noise production by playing loud squeaks or unpleasant out-of-key noises. As a result, with the passing of time, making noisy music became another distinctive feature of punk music as a whole, influencing all the other instruments that would normally form a punk ensemble. In this manner, Hebdige's metaphor of subcultures as "noise (as opposed to sound)" (Hebdige 1979, 90) acquires in punk music its most literal meaning, and punk culture presents yet another questioning of the concept of "good" and "bad" music through its fundamental aspiration to creating noise.

Alongside the guitar, punk music ensembles are normally formed by three additional core elements: a bassist, a singer, and a drummer. Punk bassists' most distinctive feature is their tendency to play a continuous single-note line that tries to emulate the rhythm guitar instead of developing their own specific counter-rhythmic bass line—as any bassist playing in any other style would normally do. When Christgau talks about Arthur Kane, the New York Dolls' bassist, he states that "although the Dolls would have been tastelessly aggressive and urban even without Arthur, his inability to come up with a catchy counter-rhythm, to supply the kind of syncopation that sets the body swaying, left them no room to be anything else" (Christgau 2007, 138). That is a statement that can be applied to most punk bassists. In a similar way, Laing speaks of punk bass as "a monadic rhythm [...] anchored in a continuous and regular series of single notes which contradict the syncopations of the drumming" (Laing 2015, 79) and cites John Entwistle's bass line on the Who's "My Generation" as an example. In the case of Spanish punk, one could think of RIP's "No hay futuro" (There is no future), Eskorbuto's "Cuidado" (Watch out), or Cicatriz's "Horacio." These songs allow us to hear the bass alone at the beginning—which makes it easier to distinguish it from the other instruments—but one could virtually choose any punk song and the bass and the rhythm guitar would, almost definitely, be playing a very similar line. Eskorbuto's "Cuidado" is especially illustrative because, after the first chorus, the bassist plays a short line in which he does something different from what the guitar is doing and enables us to see how the song, suddenly, becomes less monotonous. But despite everything, and in tune with Christgau's definition of the New York Dolls' sound as "aggressive," punk bassists' usual tendency of keeping a monotonous single-note rhythm that tries to emulate the guitar results in greater bass frequencies and a stronger unison statement that gives the music a much more powerful sound. Anyone who has experienced loud music with great bass frequencies can identify the physical sense of power it conveys in the strong vibrations coming from the speakers.[32] Such a sensation is even stronger when both bass and guitar play almost the exact same line. If they play different lines, the ear will hear different parts working together, diversifying the aural message; if they play the same line, the aural statement is far more robust. It would be like listening to different people shouting different things or having one group of people shouting the same phrase. In the second case, the statement is much more powerful. In addition, connecting with Christgau's description of the New York Dolls' bass as lacking "the kind of syncopation that sets the body swaying" (Christgau 2007, 138), punk bassists contributed to keeping listeners from dancing, which, ultimately, forced them to pay more attention to the music and the lyrics.

32 Walser (2014, 48–50) makes a case for including the physical involvement of the body in the study of music, especially regarding rhythmic analyses.

In the case of punk singing, the most illustrative way of describing it would be to say that singers tend to shout or make random noises as much as they actually sing. According to Laing, punk voices "seem to want to refuse the perfection of the 'amplified voice,'" and "the homogeneity of the singing voice is replaced by a mixture of speech, recitative, chanting or wordless cries and mutterings" (Laing 2015, 70). In this way, if punk guitar developed from a former guitar countertradition, punk vocals present themselves as a great example of a contemporary counter-singing style. Laing states that "the implicit logic would seem to involve the conviction that by excluding the musicality of singing, the possible contamination of the lyric message by the aesthetic pleasures offered by melody, harmony, pitch and so on, is avoided" (71). Vomito's song "Las fuerzas de seguridad" (Security forces) is an excellent example of this singing style. The song begins with the singer simply saying the following lines: "Ellos siguen usando su violencia para mantener su orden / Ellos siguen usando su violencia para mantener su ley / Ellos te controlan, ellos te detienen, ellos te encierran, ellos son . . ."[33] Then he remains quiet for a couple of seconds and comes back furiously shouting—with an almost growling voice—that the people he was referring to were "*¡las fuerzas de seguridad!*" Then the singer keeps singing in a very recitative and shouting style until the chorus comes in. At that point, he is joined by the backing vocals, and they all chant the following lines with a very rhythmic staccato, as if they were at a protest: "Perros guardianes del orden y la ley / asesinos a sueldo, abuso de poder."[34] This kind of choral chanting is very common in punk music and is often based on singing such things as "lololololo" or "woaaaaaah," with no specific lyrics. In most songs, this wordless singing style would be used either as a chorus or to substitute an instrumental solo, while still singing actual lyrics in the rest of the song. There are numerous examples of such a characteristic. Just to cite a few, Piperrak's "Mi primer amor" (My first love), "Txus" by La Polla Records, and Reincidentes' "Odio" (Hate) all include wordless chanting parts. The advantage of this singing style compared to more "sophisticated" singing is that, just like the three-chord punk guitar

---

33 They keep using their violence to maintain their order / They keep using their violence to maintain their law / They control you, they arrest you, they lock you up, they are . . .

34 Guard dogs of order and law / hitmen, power abuse.

lesson in *Sideburns*, it encourages any listener to become a singer—since no real singing skills are necessary and practically anyone could do it. Additionally, the wordless chanting encourages the audience to sing along in a live performance context even if they have never listened to the band, since they do not need to know any specific lyrics. As with bassists playing in unison with guitars, such accumulation of voices singing the same thing provides punk vocals with a loud, noisy sound that makes the aural statement—and message when there are words—far more powerful. Moreover, as noted by Laing, when combined with the shouting, talking, and random noises, punk vocals are constantly calling the listener's attention to different elements that would often go unnoticed—such as an important political message in the lyrics—hidden in the aesthetic pleasure produced by melody and harmony. In addition to this, the diction and pronunciation of punk vocals are also important features, since singers always try to sing as the average person would normally talk in the street. In the case of the UK, for instance, it is common for punk singers to have a strong working-class cockney accent—as I briefly mentioned earlier with Sham 69's song "If the Kids Are United." In the case of Spain, it is common to contract words (e.g., "*pal*" instead of "para el") or shorten participles (e.g., "*acabao*" instead of "acabado"). No one wants to sound posh. In the same line, the choice of words used in punk lyrics also tries to reflect a certain oral quality, and lyricists tend to always dismiss any unnecessarily complicated language that could interfere with the message.

If bassists' lack of counter-rhythmic lines contributed to making punk an undanceable genre, drummers' steady and overloaded playing does not fall short in comparison. Christgau states that Jerry Nolan, the New York Dolls' drummer, "is an ordinary rock and roll madman [...] schooled in 1-2-1-2, with the jumbo-size panoply of rolls, cymbal accents, and crossbeats at his disposal" (Christgau 2007, 139). The "1-2-1-2" refers to a rhythmic pattern built around the binary 4/4 time signature and the accentuation of the second and fourth beats that characterizes rock and roll music. Laing goes even further by stating that often punk aspires to a 1-1-1-1 rhythmic pattern in which all four beats are equally accentuated (Laing 2015, 79). A quick comparison between a classic rock and roll tune such as Chuck Berry's "Johnny B. Goode" and the Sex Pistols' anthem "God Save the Queen" proves Laing's appreciation as an accurate one. In "Johnny B. Goode," on the first and third beats the bass drum is almost imperceptible, while the snare sound on the second and fourth beats is rather staccato. In "God Save the Queen," all four beats are almost equally accentuated and the bass drum on the first and third beats is very prominent. Walser refers to heavy metal's rhythm in similar terms when he states that its "rhythmic framework is organized more basically around a pulse than a meter" (Walser 2014, 49). Additionally, he draws special attention to the relationship between rhythm and the physical experience of the listener. In this line, he states that "rhythm in heavy metal often seems very simple; it appears only to rouse physical energy and cue collective participation in heavy metal's version of dancing, headbanging" (49). In the case of punk, the 1-1-1-1, constant pulse, does not result in any rhythmic way of dancing. While heavy metal drumming tends to stress the 1-1-1-1 pulse, avoiding the interference of other rhythmic contaminations and at a speed that allows the head to bang along, punk drummers like to fill in with as much noise as they can and tend to play as fast as possible. This is especially true in punk's subgenre "hardcore punk." The Catalan band Subterranean Kids is an excellent example of this kind of drumming. Songs such as "Amigo" or "Has llenado ese vacío" (You filled that void) attest to punk drumming's speed and general noise. This keeps the listener from experiencing any kind of danceable vibrations, which explains the nature of punk's typical "pogo" and "mosh." Pogo is the improvised and anarchic way of moving while punk music is being played, and mosh is the pushing and jumping against each other that is typical, especially, of song parts in which the drumming is extremely fast. According to Joe Ambrose, "Moshing is the combination of three main factors. Crowd surfing, stage diving, and the slam dancing of the original punks [pogo] taken to a new level of violence" (Ambrose 2001, 2). One could refer to pogo and mosh as punk dancing, but it seems a bit too bold since there is no correlation between any specific rhythm and the movements of the body. If anything, the bodies react to the aggressive and noisy sound being played but not to any specific rhythm. In fact, mosh is probably more connected to a necessary release of the tension caused by punk's aggressive sound than to an actual willingness to dance. The Madrilenian band Boikot shared a video of their concert at Rivas Rock festival on their official YouTube channel (2015) in which there is a good example of a mixture between pogo and mosh. Additionally, as

Laing notes, the tendency toward fast rhythms in punk "supported the connotation of urgency of utterance which declamatory vocals and their lyrics evoked" (Laing 2015, 80), gearing, once again, the listener's attention toward the message in the lyrics rather than solely enjoying the music's aesthetic components.

As far as harmony goes, punk music is usually based on both minor and major keys. A song in a minor key would be composed using the notes in the minor scale. The minor scale has seven different notes that are a whole tone apart except between the second and the third and the fifth and the sixth, which are a halftone apart. In the key of A minor, for instance, the song would be composed around the notes A, B, C, D, E, F, and G. In general, minor keys communicate a sense of sadness. In the case of songs in major keys, they would be composed around the major scale. The major scale has seven notes that are a tone apart except between the third and the fourth and the seventh and the repetition of the first. In the case of A major, the notes would be A, B, C#, D, E, F#, and G#. But punk's harmonic trademark lies in the tendency to alter both keys by adding random semitones or notes that are not part of the main key of the song. Remaining loyal to only the notes of the key in which the song is supposed to be composed would communicate too much harmonic consonance; it would sound just fine, and the average ear would simply find it harmonious. As part of punk's will to create noise, the incorporation of all these notes that are not part of key provide the sound with a certain dissonance that would clash with the harmonic expectations of the average listener. As with the vocals, this tension would call the attention of the listener toward different elements by not letting them simply enjoy the aesthetic pleasure that consonance and harmonious compositions communicate. Soziedad Alkoholika's "Nos Vimos en Berlín" (We saw each other in Berlin), for instance, begins with a verse based on D#, E, and C power chords, which suggests an E harmonic minor key—the same as the minor key but with a raised seventh note that adds an extra halftone between the seventh and the first notes. But after the first two verses, they play an F—which does not fit within the E harmonic minor key—and start playing guitar lines based on multiple notes that do not fit in any specific key. In connection with everything said previously, punk often seems to aim for dissonance or harmonic "failure." It seeks to avoid the peace created by a consonant harmony by keeping the average ear from placing the progression in any identifiable key. Ultimately, this contributes to adding more tension to that already produced by punk's general will to create noise and unpleasant sounds.

Finally, most punks' lack of musicianship was not just notorious for punk music's simplicity but also for the numerous "mistakes" punk musicians would make in their playing. Such mistakes provided punk's noisy character with an extra unpleasant element. Many bassists and guitarists would play wrong notes or forget to play specific parts here and there, singers would sing out of key or simply shout instead of singing, and it was not uncommon for drummers to miss quite a few beats in most songs as well. This resulted in a cacophony that could be interpreted also as disruptive noise and that became part of the general sound of punk music. In this way, dissonance and arrhythmia became just natural elements in punk music. Laing cites the Mekons' "Never Been in a Riot" as an example of a song with an "almost total lack of any rhythmic continuity" (Laing 2015, 77). In the case of Spain, Ultimo Resorte's "Peligro social" (Social danger) is a paradigmatic example. Throughout the song, both the instruments and the vocals sound as if they were all following different rhythmic patterns. Once again, this challenges the notion of "good" music and destigmatizes mistakes as something that could never happen in punk music.

### 2.6. Global Punk

The previous sections provided a general description of classic and contemporary punk scholarship. Yet it is all based primarily on British and US punk and, with the exception of Mafessoli, written solely by British and US scholars. The Anglo- and Western-centrism of punk studies—or simply academia as a whole—is notorious and reflects a specific battle for hegemony in the production of knowledge. This battle is widely dominated by a few rich and powerful countries that impose their specific ways of thinking onto the rest of the world. To avoid such domination, I find it extremely important to assess each punk scene in its own terms by exploring the particularities that make them unique instead of simply applying a foreign theoretical model. Galician punk, for instance, tends to include Celtic rhythms and instruments as well as Celtic-sounding modal melodies and chord progressions, something most punk music would not do (e.g., Os Resentidos, Os Rastreros, Xenreira, and Os Diplomáticos de Monte Alto).

In recent years, there have been notable attempts to overcome the US/UK domination of punk studies, including the tendency to apply US/UK-developed theories and concepts to *all* punk, hardly ever questioning their applicability. An important component of this work has been the emergence of what's become known as "global punk." Global punk represents an approach to punk studies in which punk scenes from all over the world are studied in their own social, cultural, historical, and philosophical terms instead of solely through the lenses and frameworks developed for US or UK punk. Two of the main avenues through which global punk scholars have been disseminating their work are the academic journal *Punk & Post-Punk* and, especially, the Global Punk book series—both developed by the Punk Scholars Network in collaboration with the independent academic publisher Intellect. As the name implies, the Global Punk book series has been especially important in developing global punk's academic oeuvre. In 2023, it consisted of nine books. The first three books published in the series are multiauthor volumes in which each chapter is either devoted to reflecting on the concept of "global punk" or to studying a specific non-US/UK punk scene (Bestley et al. 2019, 2021a, 2021b). The series also includes another multiauthor volume titled *Punk! Las Américas Edition* that explores, compares, and contrasts numerous aspects of punk developed across the American hemisphere. In addition to these, the series also includes *In Search of Tito's Punks*, a book in which Barry Philips tells his adventures traveling around Yugoslavia talking to Yugoslavian punks. The rest of the books focus on punk from a broader perspective that is not limited to studying one specific punk scene[35] or focus primarily on the UK.[36]

This burgeoning of work body represents an important—and long due—swerve away from US/UK monopolization of punk-related scholarship. Yet it is important to note that it still serves exclusively an English-speaking community and that multiauthor volumes with chapters that study multiple global punk scenes can only provide snippets of richer and much larger punk movements. Furthermore, not only would

35 *Punk Pedagogies in Practice* discusses specific ways in which punk can contribute to pedagogical practice in post-16 education, and *Punk Art History* discusses punk as an art movement and draws on interviews with punk art protagonists from London, New York, Amsterdam, Copenhagen, and Berlin.

36 *Throbbing Gristle* and *Blank Canvas* both focus exclusively on the UK.

they provide limited analyses of punk scenes from around the world, it would also be virtually impossible to cover every existing punk scene. The editors of the series are thoroughly aware of this, and they state that they "have always acknowledged the enormity of the subject (and make no attempt to detail every punk and punk-inspired scene around the world)" (Bestley et al. 2021a, 11). Be this as it may, what I believe is crucial to understand here is that a) punk scenes of the world do not necessarily need "global punk" to come and study them, since, in many cases, there is already a large body of academic scholarship in punk-related studies from scholars who do not necessarily publish in English or for the English-speaking academic market, and that b) perhaps a more anticolonial move would be for those who want to support the study of non-UK and non-US punk—as well as for those who oppose the tendency to use US/UK theoretical frameworks to study all punk without distinctions—to foster spaces in which the research is not always mediated by the mandatory use of English. In the case of Spanish punk, for instance, there are seminal works on Spanish cultural studies that have not been translated into English and that are essential for the study of Spanish punk—*El mono del desencanto* by Teresa Vilarós, *Culpables por la literatura* by Germán Labrador, and *Movimiento de resistencia* by Jakue Pascual, just to name a few. It is practically impossible to have conversations in which these works are considered when discussions happen in English and with monolingual English speakers or scholars who do not speak, at least, Spanish (let alone Basque, Galician, Catalan, and so on). Furthermore, many of the scholars dealing with Spanish punk might also not be as comfortable discussing their work in English and will, more often than not, retreat from participating in initiatives like "global punk" while maintaining participation in other spaces and publications in which discussions are held in Spanish, Basque, Galician, Catalan, or others.

This is something the Punk Scholars Network quickly understood and—I presume—one of the reasons why the idea of having different regional groups arose. The regional groups are the independent groups that run their own initiatives related to punk scholarship around the world and which, at the same time, are connected to the global network that the Punk Scholars Network represents. Some examples of these groups are PSN Iberia, PSN Colombia, PSN Brasil, and PSN Indonesia. Among other things, these groups run their own events, conferences, research projects, and publications. In what concerns me as a punk scholar who is part of PSN Iberia and also a scholar of Spanish popular music and cultural studies, I believe that one of the most important contributions of this group has been, precisely, creating a context for these various academic worlds to coexist. This book is in some way a result of this.

It is precisely for this reason that, in the third and last section of this chapter, I will establish a conversation between the previously discussed punk scholarship and some important perspectives on Spanish cultural studies. By doing so, I want to finish this chapter by proposing what I view as the most appropriate framework to study Spanish punk in all its specificities by both considering previously published punk scholarship from other latitudes as well as doing it in terms of Spanish punk's own cultural, historical, and theoretical discussions.

## 3. Punk in Spain: A Methodological Proposal

After this short introduction into the world of punkademia, it is time now to explore how the discussed theories interlace with Spain's particular context in order to achieve a deeper understanding of Spanish punk's specific characteristics. In order to do so, I will begin by discussing a crucial concept in Spanish cultural studies: the CT, or Cultura de la Transición. After that, I will examine the applicability of punk as negation in the context of Spain, and I will close the chapter by pointing out the main ideas that will guide my approach to Spanish punk in the rest of the book.

### *3.1. Cultura de la Transición*

After dictator Francisco Franco's death in 1975, Spain started the process of becoming a modern democratic state. This process is widely known as the *Transición Española*, or simply as the Transición. The Spanish journalist Gregorio Morán questions the exact date of its starting point and asserts that "la transición empezó el mismo día que Franco ya no pudo resucitar"[37] (Morán 1991, 41)—a statement in which Franco and Francoism are one and the same. By adopting such a perspective, Morán suggests that neither the members of the Franco government nor Franco's successor, Juan Carlos de Borbón, had necessarily any plans of

37 The Transición started the same day Franco could not be resuscitated.

moving toward a democratic state had Francoism not lost as many adherents as it did during the last years of the dictatorship and especially after Franco's death. In other words, Francoist politicians and Juan Carlos de Borbón were not necessarily democrats waiting for Franco's death to finally establish a democratic system; Franco's death coincided with the decline of the dictatorship and the government's realization that a popular demand for a political change was omnipresent, and *that* was the catalyst for them to enact the transitional project. As a result, after 1975, a slow process of negotiations and gradual democratization began.

As part of those negotiations, a fight to define the kind of democracy Spain should adopt arose between the main political figures of the time. Besides a marginal fascist sector in support of continuing with the dictatorship, there were two main political blocs: the reformists and the rupturists. The reformists were those politicians who thought that a clear cut with Francoism was too dangerous, considering that the military forces were still in the hands of the Francoists, as well as those members of the Franco government who saw their privileges threatened by the decline of the regime and thought that it was necessary to implement certain changes to maintain their power. Additionally, it can also be argued that there was an opportunistic sector that, while not having had any privileges during the dictatorship, approached the reformist bloc to gain privileges that they had never had. On the other hand, rupturists believed that a clear cut with all past Francoism was necessary for a real democratization to occur. Such a rupture would include the trial and sentencing of all the people involved in Francoist crimes, the confiscation of the goods Francoists obtained during the dictatorship, and the ineligibility of all the politicians involved with the dictatorship, among other things. Gradually, the reformist forces—with a significant part of the remaining Franco government at the forefront—either absorbed or pushed out the rupturists and took control over the transitional process. Paradigmatic in this regard is Santiago Carrillo—a historic communist leader—accepting Juan Carlos de Borbón as king of Spain, as well as the PCE's (Partido Comunista de España) incorporation of the current bicolored monarchic flag in addition to their traditional republican one.[38] Had they not done that,

38 "Republican" in the Spanish case refers to the nonmonarchic government established between 1931 and 1936.

however, they would have been pushed out of the reformist elite directing the Transición, as was the case with Izquierda Republicana, Esquerra Republicana de Catalunya, and Acción Republicana, political parties that remained illegal until the first democratic elections were over in 1977 due to their refusal to shed their republican ideas. The historian Julio Pérez Serrano explains that reformist leaning as the result of a "consenso de los débiles" (consensus of the weak) (Pérez Serrano 2004, 29). Through this expression, he explains that "tras la muerte de Franco la memoria histórica de las generaciones vivas, muy marcada por los traumas de la Guerra Civil y el franquismo, condicionó el proceso de toma de decisiones en el sentido de potenciar la alternativa reformista, entendida como la opción menos arriesgada"[39] and that the reformist option resulted from the weakness of a rupturist possibility rather than from the strength of the reformist option itself (29–30). Manuel Vázquez Montalbán argued similarly that during the Transición there was a "correlación de debilidades"—instead of a "correlación de fuerzas" (a correlation of weakness instead of power)—that made the reformist option succeed over the rupturist one.[40]

Victoria Prego, for her part, rejects the idea of the reformist option winning over the rupturist one, and in her documentary *La Transición*, she depicts the Transición as a complex process in which the main political forces of the time found a common ground by distancing themselves from their own particular concerns—republicanism in the case of Carrillo and the PCE—as a collective effort to move forward and leave the dictatorial years behind. By the same token, simply by excluding them from her documentary, she portrays rupturists as intransigents who would not contribute to this collective effort and, therefore, as a destabilizing force for the Spanish democracy. Yet such an interpretation assumes that reformism was the only possible way to achieve a democratic state, and it dismisses the efforts taken by rupturists to that same end. This assumption is one of the most repeated commonplaces regarding the Transición: Under a constant threat of a

39 After Franco's death, the historic memory of the surviving generations, very affected by the traumas caused by the Civil War and Francoism, conditioned the decision-making process by pushing the reformist alternative, which they viewed as the least risky/dangerous option.

40 https://web.archive.org/web/20200919121933/www.dos-teorias.net/2010/10/manuel-vazquez-montalban-epilogo-1-de-4.html.

new coup, rupture was an extremely risky alternative and reformism was the most sensible stance to take.[41] Whether that was the case or a clear cut with Francoism would have also worked, we will never know. Yet such an assumption resulted in the reformists designing one specific kind of democratic system that neglected the other possible scenarios that rupturists were imagining. In this way, Carrillo incorporating the bicolored flag was not simply a generous action to find a common ground with no further repercussions; it also resulted—at a symbolic level, at least—in creating a democracy in which republicans would not seem as relevant as they could have—something any rupturist would have fiercely opposed. In this sense, the concessions made by once-rupturist politicians such as Carrillo had a decisive influence on the kind of system being established and contributed to naturalizing the democracy that the reformists designed as the only possible outcome.

The culture produced during the Transición was decisive in this sense as well, especially after 1982 under the PSOE (Socialist Workers' Party) administration. In his inaugural speech after winning the 1982 general elections, Felipe González—president of Spain during the first PSOE government—asserted that "la cultura encarna nuestra concepción del mundo, nuestra escala de valores y nuestro sentido de la vida"[42] and stressed that he was going to devote special attention

---

41 In 2016, eldiario.es published an interview between Victoria Prego and Adolfo Suárez—a politician from the Franco government and the first president of democratic Spain (1977–81)—from 1996, in which he admits that most international leaders asked him to organize a referendum in 1977 asking whether Spaniards wanted a republic or a parliamentary monarchy with Juan Carlos de Borbón as the head. Immediately after this, Victoria Prego states, "Claro, y eso era peligrosísimo en ese momento" (Right, and that was extremely dangerous at that moment), to which Suárez responds that the truth was that polls showed that the republican option would win and that in order to secure the monarchy he included it as part of the constitution. In this way, when the Spanish citizens voted for the constitution to establish a democratic system, they also voted for establishing a democratic system *with* a monarchy. In another interview with Victoria Prego in 2016 regarding the interview from 1996, she mentions again that the referendum was impossible "porque la situación política no permitía esas alegrías" (because the political scenario didn't allow such boldness). The insistence on the dangerous character of rupturism is ever-present throughout materials regarding the Transición. See "Adolfo Suárez no sometió a referéndum la monarquía porque las encuestas le dijeron que perdería," *El Diario*, November 18, 2016, http://www.eldiario.es/politica/Adolfo-Suarez-referendum-monarquia-encuestas_0_581642259.html.

42 Culture embodies our perception of the world, our scale of values, and our sense of life.

to culture during his term.[43] Consequently, the PSOE government's cultural policies "asum[ieron] un rol fundamental en la socialización de los españoles, entendiendo por tal la voluntad de transmitir los valores democráticos consagrados por el nuevo Estado"[44] (Quaggio 2014, n.p.). In order to communicate such new values, the government "no dud[ó] en dar a conocer o propagar nuevos modelos y ejemplos de intelectuales u obras de arte mediante exposiciones, creando instituciones culturales específicas, o, en definitiva, a través de un calculado programa de conmemoraciones oficiales"[45] (Quaggio 2014, n.p.). As part of this effort, however, the government endorsed a significantly celebratory and nonconflictive cultural scene and ignored manifestations that questioned the nonrupture with the dictatorial past or how the transitional process was conducted. In this way, while the hedonism present in Alaska and los Pegamoides' song "Bailando" (Dancing) (1982),[46] Radio Futura's "Enamorado de la moda juvenil" (In love with the young fashion) (1980),[47] or Mecano's "Hoy no me puedo levantar" (I can't get up today) (1981)[48] enjoyed significant institutional and mediatic support, other controversial songs that questioned the Transición and its different governments were ignored, such as Eskorbuto's "Maldito país" (Damned country) (1983)[49] and "No somos nada" (We are noth-

43 "Discurso de investidura de Felipe González Márquez en el Congreso de los Diputados, 30 de noviembre de 1982," http://www.transicion.org/60hitos/1982-11NovDiscInvestGonzalez-VWEB.doc.pdf.

44 Adopted a fundamental role in the socialization of Spaniards, understanding that as the will to transmit the democratic values achieved by the new state.

45 Did not doubt about promoting new artistic and intellectual models through events, art exhibitions, creating specific cultural institutions and, ultimately, through a calculated schedule of official commemorative acts.

46 "Bailando, me paso el día bailando / y los vecinos mientras tanto / no paran de molestar. / Bebiendo, me paso el día bebiendo / la coctelera agitando / llena de soda y vermut" (Dancing, I spend the day dancing / and meanwhile the neighbors keep being annoying. / Drinking, I spend the day drinking / shaking the cocktail shaker / filled up with soda and vermouth).

47 "Y yo caí / enamorado de la moda juvenil / de los precios y rebajas que yo vi / enamorado de ti" (And I fell / in love with the young fashion / with the prices and sales I saw / in love with you).

48 "Hoy no me puedo levantar / El fin de semana me dejo fatal / toda la noche sin dormir / bebiendo, fumando y sin parar de reír" (Today I can't get up / The weekend really left me in pain / all night without sleeping / drinking, smoking, and laughing nonstop).

49 "Policia nacional, picoletos de mierda / Capitanes generales [...] Ministros, gobernadores [...] Este maldito país es una gran pocilga [...] Maldito país, España, maldito país" (National police, fucking shit cops / General captains [...] *Ministros*, governors [...] This damn country is a huge pigsty [...] Damn country, Spain, damn country).

ing) (1987) by La Polla Records.[50] In the case of Eskorbuto, the song was even censored, and due to this and other songs such as "Escupe la bandera" (Spit on the flag) and "ETA" they were tried for "apología del terrorismo" (advocacy for terrorism) in 1983.

As with the reformist measures that established the foundations of Spanish democracy, the PSOE's cultural policies were thought of as a part of a greater national project that aimed to leave the dictatorial years behind and avoid conflicts during the democratization process—a nonconflict preventive logic in the face of the ever-present fear of a new coup and fascist dictatorship. However, as with the rupturists during the first years of the Transición, it contributed to "la invisibilización de escenarios de producción y activación de otras memorias así como el desbaratamiento de la cultura como lanzadera de otros relatos que provienen de otras identidades colectivas y que se producen al margen del relato oficial"[51] (Martínez 2012, n.p.).

According to Guillem Martínez, the relationship between the state and culture during the Transición was the following: "La cultura no se mete en política—salvo para darle la razón al Estado—y el Estado no se mete en cultura—salvo para subvencionarla, premiarla o darle honores"[52] (Martínez 2012, n.p.). Furthermore, he asserts that during the Transición "un objeto cultural es reconocido como tal, y no como marginalidad, siempre y cuando no colisione con el estado"[53] and that, at the same time, the state "con su dinero, sus premios, sus honores, facilita la cosa y ahorra tiempo, al decidir lo que es cultura o no"[54] (n.p.). In this sense, the role played by the institutions for a specific kind of culture to succeed was crucial. This specific culture endorsed by the government, and the cultural hegemonic framework resulting from it, is what the concept CT or Cultura de la Transición refers to. In other words, using the framework provided by the CCCS, the CT is the dominant culture

50 "Somos los nietos de los obreros que nunca pudisteis matar" (We are the grandchildren of those workers you could not kill).

51 Making invisible spaces in which alternative memories could be produced or activated as well as deactivating culture as a means for alternative discourses constructed by other marginal collective identities to come into existence.

52 Culture does not interfere with politics—except to agree with the state—and the state does not interfere with culture—except to finance it, reward it, or give it honors.

53 A cultural artifact is recognized as such, and not as something marginal, as long as it does not collide with the state.

54 With its money, awards, honors, makes it easier to decide what is and what is not culture.

imposed by the ruling class of the Transición in order to naturalize their way of viewing the new democratic Spain.

Still, one should not conclude that alternative cultures did not exist or that their influence was irrelevant. While the CT attempted to normalize the reformists' democracy, there was a significant countercultural movement that opposed such normalization through alternative magazines, fanzines, pirate radio stations, music, and more. Punk culture was an important part of this countercultural movement. Furthermore, if the CT represents the dominant culture trying to impose the ruling class's worldview, punk emerged as a subculture that opposed that worldview by proposing alternative realities and ways of life. Consequently, the study of punk in Spain facilitates a completely new exploration of transitional subjectivities beyond the recurrent cliché of seeing the Spaniards of the Transición simply as depoliticized and conformist individuals.

### *3.2. The Negationist-Affirmative Character of Spanish Punk*

Punk's more immediate opposition to the ruling-class worldview during the Transición was carried out through the concept of negation. In this way, during the first years of democracy, punk was not only a countercultural movement but also a general oppositional attitude to the way the Transición was developing. Through the negation of the kind of democracy the reformists were establishing, punk contributed to the subsistence of rupturist views and the rise of other new ones. Furthermore, with the passing of time, punk extended its negationist attitude to other contemporary social injustices and established itself as a permanent cultural axis from which many of the new social movements and politics of the beginning of the twenty-first century emerged.

Juan Porras focuses on punk as negation in the case of the Basque Country in his work *Negación punk en Euskal Herria*. Drawing from Marcus's idea of punk as the negation of social constructs that allows for new worldviews to be considered, Porras presents a two-sided analysis of Basque punk. First, he explores how Basque punk's negation deconstructs these social constructs, and then he studies the affirmative alternatives it helps to construct, especially through its DIY ethos. To do this, he establishes two different sections under the names of EZ and BAI, "no" and "yes" in Basque. In this way, he begins by talking about Basque punk's oppositional character in terms of anti-institutionalism, anticommercialism, antimilitarism, antidiscrimination, anticapitalism, antibullfighting, and others. As he develops his argument, he discusses songs such as "No quiero cambiar" (I don't want to change) by Eskorbuto and "A la mierda" (To hell with it) by Piperrak, as well as numerous interviews with Basque punks. "No quiero cambiar" is a song in which the negation is expressed through the refusal to change one's beliefs no matter what: "Tengo heridas sin cicatrizar / de las últimas peleas / y a veces vomito sangre, / pero no quiero cambiar."[55] This determination is also present in the music, which is based on a single three-second melodic line in A minor that is repeated throughout the whole song with no changes whatsoever. In addition, the drummer plays the cymbals three times consecutively over the melodic line, providing the song with a heavy and monotonous ostinato. The only minor difference is that, while in the verses the guitar sounds muted, in the chorus they play open power chords, giving that section a slightly stronger character. In this way, even the music absorbed the change-resistant character expressed in the lyrics. "A la mierda," for its part, is a classic song composed by Piperrak in which they negate all sorts of things in a very disaffected way, combining the expression "a la mierda" (to hell with it) with a long list of elements they oppose: wars, prisons, Nazis, unemployed people, the working class ("Porque nunca han luchado para vivir mejor"[56]), the Vatican, the news, posh people, pills, and techno music. The music combines a very fast rhythm in the intro and the choruses, and a slower one in the verses. Such a combination allows for a better listing of the things they oppose in the verses and the stronger effect of the anomie expressed over the chorus, as if the slow listing reached a climax and exploded when the chorus comes in:

> Hoy es un día de los que sientes más las ganas de reventar
> Vas askeado eres un insocial, pasas de los demás
> Te preguntas porke los momentos malos duran más
> que los mejores y por esa razón está dispuesto a mandar: a la mierda . . .[57]

---

55 I still have wounds that have not healed / from the last fights / and sometimes I vomit blood / but I don't want to change.

56 Because they never fought to improve their lives.

57 Today is one of those days when you feel like you want to explode / You feel disgusted, you are an antisocial, you don't give a damn about anyone / You wonder why bad moments last longer / than the better ones and that is why you are willing to say: to hell with it . . .

Additionally, the fact that they repeat "a la mierda" constantly before each thing they oppose provides the whole song with a more robust oppositional character.

After this analysis of punk's negationist opposition, Porras proceeds to talk about its affirmative character, referring to alternative institutions such as gaztetxes (Basque squats or social centers), horizontal participation discussing each town's or neighborhood's matters through civic assemblies, counter-information through pirate radio stations or fanzines, and others. In this section, he cites songs such as "Okupación" (Squat) by Barricada and "Squatters" by MCD (Me cago en Dios), as well as fanzines such as *Destruye!!!* and pirate radio stations such as Hala Bedi Irratia or Txantxangorri. In "Okupación" Barricada advocates for squatting and rioting on the streets through the main vocals, "Monta jaleo en la calle / No van a darte la llave"[58] while the whole band shouts "Okupa / Okupa / Okupación"[59] in the background, as if they were chanting at a prosquatting demonstration. Similarly, MCD talks about squatting as a legitimate action for those who need it, considering the economic crisis of Spain during the 1980s:

> Controles policiales en medio de la ciudad,
> bastardos de azul nos quieren arrojar
> de casas ocupadas con nuestra dignidad,
> en nombre del alcalde y de la autoridad.
> No, no nos van a echar a los *squatters.*
> Si no tienes vivienda ni donde currelar
> móntate un *Gaztetxe* en tu propia ciudad.[60]

Similarly, in *Movimientos de Resistencia,* Jakue Pascual talks about Basque punk as part of a complex network of resistance movements that combine the negationist questioning of the status quo with an affirmative counterpart of creating alternative meanings and spaces against the privatization of the public sphere inherent to the advance of capitalism:

---

58 Make a racket on the street / They won't give you the key.

59 Squat / Squat / Squat it.

60 Police checkpoints in the middle of the city / assholes in blue want to kick us out / of houses occupied with our dignity / on behalf of the mayor and the authorities / No, they won't kick us squatters out. / If you don't have a house or place to work / organize a "young social center" in your own city.

> El discurso intuitivo de lo "anti" se traduce en consignas e himnos, algunos temas musicales de esta época son un claro ejemplo de ello, como los compuestos por La Polla Records, Hertzainak, Eskorbuto, Kortatu o Barricada. Un discurso negativo frente a lo impuesto que en sus inicios pocas veces profundiza en la alternativa (no solo en las letras musicales, tampoco en los fanzines, radios libres y comunicados que se emiten), pero que en una segunda fase—y con el surgimiento de grupos y movimientos con planteamientos político-sociales e ideológicos autónomos (no partidistas) en el seno de esta amalgama de expresiones sociales y juveniles—intentará superar la inmediatez del NO mediante el análisis y el establecimiento de acciones encaminadas a desarrollar alternativas sociales y comunitarias contrapuestas al proceso de privatización.[61] (Pascual 2015, 69)

With all the previous discussions in mind, I propose that if Spanish punk is to be understood in all its complexity, it needs to be studied as a movement articulated around two main negationist topoi: a) the negation of the Transición and b) the negation of the forms of life derived from capitalism and neoliberalism. In addition, I argue that it should be studied as a movement across the whole Spanish state due to the constant and uninterrupted relationship between the different punk scenes in the country. They all shared stages, collaborated with each other, and influenced each other in many ways all throughout Spain. Moreover, given that the whole country was affected by the Transición and that it is equally part of the same capitalist and neoliberal context, each punk scene throughout Spain will provide valuable perspectives on both topics. Consequently, I will study Basque, Catalan, Madrilenian,

61 The intuitive discourse of the "anti" translates into slogans and anthems, some of the songs from this time are a clear example of this, such as those composed by La Polla Records, Hertzainak, Eskorbuto, Kortatu, or Barricada. A negative discourse in relation to what is imposed that in its beginnings hardly ever deepens in the alternative (not only in the musical lyrics, neither in the fanzines nor the pirate radio stations nor the delivered statements), but that in a second phase—and with the emergence of groups and movements with autonomous (nonpartisan) political-social stances within this mass of social and youth expressions—will try to overcome the immediacy of the NO through the analysis and the establishment of actions directed to developing social and communal alternatives that opposed the privatization process.

and other punk scenes as different manifestations of a single punk culture within the Spanish state.

Along with this, in the rest of this book I will be looking at Spanish punk as a subculture—both a working-class subculture and a polymorphous postsubculture—a style, an ethos, and a music genre. I will assess each perspective in its own terms and will not discard as "not punk" a band that plays punk music but works with a multinational record or a punk-style painting made by someone who is not part of the working class. I will apply a very broad scope in order to achieve a more comprehensive view of Spanish punk culture. In spite of this, the clear political opposition of the majority of punk in Spain will be decisive in my selection of materials, since such opposition takes place across all the mentioned perspectives. There can be political opposition in style—as Hebdige pointed out—but also in the discourse put forward in fanzines or songs, or in the ways of life of those involved with punk culture. Consequently, I argue that most of punk culture in Spain is rooted in a political opposition that is constantly mutating to address the current affairs of the country, whatever these may be. In that sense, I regard the anti-Transición and anticapitalist/antineoliberalist character of Spanish punk as the two main frameworks in which this political opposition has occurred up until today.

Now, before exploring each of these negationist topoi in detail in chapters 3 and 4, in the next chapter I will conduct an extensive comparative study of the movida madrileña and punk subculture. By doing so, I aim to establish parameters to understand why they should be viewed as two different cultural movements—albeit ones that often cross paths—so that we avoid the common practice of defining all Spanish cultural production during the Transición solely through the artifacts produced within the movida. At the same time, I will also demonstrate that not all the youth of the Transición were apolitical or hedonistic and that there were indeed other critical and politically committed cultural movements and positions among young people.

CHAPTER 2

# THE MOVIDA MADRILEÑA VERSUS SPANISH PUNK CULTURE

## 1. The Movida Madrileña

The movida madrileña was an eclectic cultural movement that emerged in Madrid during the late 1970s and early '80s. It started as a "fenómeno underground y minoritario surgido entre gente muy joven, con inquietudes artísticas e intelectuales"[1] (Fouce 2004, 58), but it soon became the predominant cultural movement throughout Spain thanks to "una serie de estructuras productivas, industrias culturales y medios de comunicación, decisiones políticas, que catapultaron al movimiento hacia la masividad"[2] (58). Referring exclusively to its musical strand, Fouce and del Val go as far as saying that the movida "has been the most successful musical movement in Spanish popular music" (Fouce and del Val 2013, 130). Its great success resulted especially from the PSOE's commitment to financing a modern cultural movement that could "act as a metaphor of the changes that the country had experienced during the first decade after Franco's death" (130) and become "the image of the success of the Transition in Spain" (133). The movida was the perfect choice for both, since while it celebrated the freedom obtained after Franco's death by "embrac[ing] all the previously condemned social taboos" (Nichols and Rosi Song 2014, 2)—which

---

1 Underground and minority phenomenon that emerged among very young people, with artistic and intellectual inquisitiveness.

2 A series of productive structures, cultural industries and media, political decisions, that catapulted the movement toward massive popularity.

gave it a somehow radical and transgressive character—it lacked the critical attitude toward the Transición characteristic of punk bands such as La Polla Records or Eskorbuto.

The movida was highly influenced by two previous movements: the countercultural movement articulated around the Spanish "prensa marginal"[3] in the early 1980s and the glam, new wave, protopunk, and punk subcultural movements developed in the US and the UK during the 1960s and '70s. The former was crucial in the emergence of fanzines such as *La liviandad del imperdible* and *Kaka de Luxe,* whose combination of comics, opinion articles, and drawings showed great resemblance with fanzines produced within the prensa marginal such as *Premamá* or *Bazofia*.[4] The US and UK subcultural movements, for their part, had a deciding influence in the movida's aesthetic and musical eclecticism. Early bands such as Kaka de Luxe, which many consider the initiators of the movida, attest to such influence. If we listen to Kaka de Luxe's album *Las canciones malditas* (1983) we find songs, such as "La tentación" (The temptation) and "La alegría de vivir" (The happiness of being alive), that are based on a traditional rock and roll/doo-wop sound with almost no distortion. But they also recorded numbers such as "Pero me aburro" (But I am bored), which sounds more like the protopunk of the New York Dolls, and "La pluma eléctrica" (The electric feather), which is literally based on the guitar riff of "Blitzkrieg Bop" by the Ramones. Additionally, Kaka de Luxe's members mixed punk, glam, and new-wave aesthetics in their own personal style of dress as well.

Yet, despite these early influences, Spain's specific sociopolitical context shaped the movida's evolution, and it soon acquired its own distinctive character. Fouce identifies three defining characteristics in

---

3 The "prensa marginal" was a collective that "mezcla a personal muy diverso para crear un nuevo tipo de publicación alejada no solo de las revistas comerciales, sino también del tipo de fanzine politico y comiquero que se había hecho hasta ese momento. Los fanzines de PREMAMÁ se van a centrar más en la música, en las artes plásticas y en la vanguardia en general y van a ser la fuente para muchos otros fanzines que seguirán apareciendo, viviendo y muriendo desde entonces hasta hoy" (mixes very diverse people to create a publication that differs not only from commercial magazines, but also from the political and comic fanzines developed until that moment. The fanzines from PREMAMÁ are more focused on music, plastic arts, and vanguardism generally speaking, and they influenced many fanzines that will appear later on, that will keep being published and that will also disappear since then until today) (Lechado 170).

4 As a matter of fact, *Premamá* derived from the first syllables of "prensa marginal madrileña."

the movida: "a) Rechazo de la ideología de izquierdas y del compromiso político. Fin de la utopía y vivencia del presente. b) Nuevos referentes culturales, fuertemente internacionalizados. c) Nuevas estrategias y prácticas, marcadas por la amplia presencia de los medios de comunicación y las industrias culturales"[5] (Fouce 2002, 26). Here I want to stress the first and the third ones, which are both crucial to understanding the difference between the movida and the Spanish punk movement. Regarding the first characteristic, the movida established itself as a rejection of both Francoist and anti-Francoist movements, which tended to politicize most cultural manifestations. In this sense, people involved in the movida aimed to create art in the same way that Pedro Almodóvar understood his films when he said he made cinema "como si Franco no hubiera existido"[6] (Strauss 1994, 30). Speaking specifically about music, the movida rejected particularly the extremely politicized music of anti-Francoist singer-songwriters such as Raimon, Lluís Llach, or Paco Ibañez. For its part, regarding the media and cultural industry, it is important to refer again to the institutional endorsement from which the movida benefited and in which punk bands rarely ever had any space. In 1979 Radio 3 was created, TVE1 aired cultural programs such as *Popgrama* (1977), *La edad de Oro* (1983), and *La bola de cristal* (1984), among others, and the movida benefited greatly from these and other media, which led to the monopolization of the cultural production of the late 1970s and all of the 1980s.

Therefore, on the one hand, the movida presented an affirmative attitude that celebrated the recently acquired liberties, but, on the other, it became a fundamental part of the CT by contributing to making invisible the everyday problems that Spaniards were undergoing through its deliberate avoidance of political engagement and media monopolization. As a result, the movida became an important vehicle to disseminate the kind of culture Herbert Marcuse referred to when he spoke of "affirmative culture": culture whose most decisive characteristic is "the assertion of a universally obligatory, eternally better and

5 a) Rejection of the left-wing ideology and political commitment. The end of utopia and the importance of living the present. b) New cultural references, strongly globalized. c) New strategies and practices, characterized by a great presence of the media and the cultural industry.

6 As if Franco had not existed.

more valuable world that must be unconditionally affirmed: a world essentially different from the factual world of the daily struggle for existence, yet realizable by every individual for himself 'from within,' without any transformation of the state of fact" (Marcuse 2009, 70).

It is this "more valuable world" aloof from the everyday struggle that the movida is helping to construct during the Transición, a world in which sex, drugs, freedom of speech, and other individual liberties that were denied under Franco's regime are now to be celebrated but always at the expense of making invisible other less positive factors that could spoil the movida's illusion of plenitude—the general amnesty granted indistinctively to all crimes committed since 1936, or the economic crisis and high unemployment rates in Spain all throughout the 1980s, just to cite a couple.

In 2016, *El País* published an interview with Alaska, a classic icon of the movida madrileña still active today as the singer of Fangoria.[7] In addition to the interview, Alaska appeared on *El País*'s cover page next to the following statement: "Hicimos divertida la España de los 70 y los 80."[8] At first, it seems unclear who the subject of that statement is, but after reading the interview in the inner pages, one discovers that she is referring to her generation and those involved in the movida madrileña. A day later, Emilio Silva, founder of the ARMH (Asociación para la Recuperación de la Memoria Histórica), published an article in the online newspaper *Tercera Información* responding to Alaska's interview. In it, Silva questions Alaska's celebratory attitude by reminding her about the governmental inaction with the still-missing 114,226 bodies of people executed during the Civil War and the subsequent dictatorship, Tejero's coup in 1981, and the general violence experienced by a great number of people—regardless of their political orientation—during the Transición, among other things.[9] Additionally, he also refers to the movida madrileña specifically and states that "lo más conocido de ella, con todo su apoyo mediático, económico y político fue poco más que un disfraz, un gran disfraz para aparentar que en veinticuatro horas pasamos de un país en oscuro blanco y negro a una sociedad con el pelo de colores, y una especie de irreverencia estética que poco

---

7 Juan Cruz, "Hicimos divertida la España de los 70 y 80," *El País*, March 27, 2016, https://elpais.com/cultura/2016/03/23/actualidad/1458733323_500399.html.

8 We made the Spain of the 1970s and '80s more fun.

9 https://elpais.com/cultura/2016/03/23/actualidad/1458733323_500399.html.

tuvo que ver con un cambio en la ética."[10] This clash between Alaska and Silva illustrates the antagonistic interpretations of the movida as a celebratory and revolutionary cultural movement that broke with the past Francoist culture, and the movida as a depoliticizing and evasive movement endorsed by the governments of the Transición in order to establish a reformist democracy with as little opposition as possible. The official narrative constructed by the CT presents the movida only as the former; punk culture, on the other hand, sees it as the latter and establishes itself as a countermovement that contributes to keep the CT and the movida from naturalizing their view—as we already saw in the introduction of this book with the clash between the La Polla Records concert in the Casa de Campo auditorium and its media coverage.

## 2. Spanish Punk Culture

In the previous chapter we saw that, in the documentary *Lo que hicimos fue secreto*, Delincuencia Sonora's singer, Jose Calvo, distinguishes clearly between those who "quiere[n] ser realmente punk y militar con ello, e intentar cambiar las conciencias o hacer estructuras sociales completamente paralelas, fuera de lo que es la sociedad o lo que te imponen"[11]—as his own band—and those who merely want to "estar ahí más en la noche en tener tu look de puta madre y ligar un huevo ¿sabes? y ya ser más popular"[12]—which seems to be a reference to those involved in the movida madrileña, as Almodóvar's and Carlos Berlanga's pictures, shown while Calvo speaks, suggest. In this same documentary Manolo Uvi (La UVI's and Commando 9mm's singer) talks about Madrid and states that "por un lado estaba la movida, que era pop puro y duro, y luego estaba el rollo punk que éramos cuatro gatos"[13] (Álvarez 2017). Immediately after this, Alberto Eiriz, the author of the punk fanzine *Penetración*, states that in Madrid the movida was the primary

10 Its most famous part, with all its media, economic, and political support, was little more than a pretense, a big pretense to pretend that in twenty-four hours we moved from a dismal black-and-white country to a society with colored hair and an aesthetic irreverence that had little to do with an ethical change.

11 Want to be really punk and have an active role in the subculture, change consciences through it or create alternative social structures out of our imposed society.

12 Be out there at night, have a fucking great look and get laid a lot, and, you know, be more popular.

13 On the one hand, there was the movida, which was full-on pop, and then there was the punk thing in which there were only four of us.

movement, whereas in the Basque Country and Barcelona punk was far more predominant. In this regard, it is illustrative that when, in 1980, Silvia Resorte—punk singer from Barcelona—was asked whether her band, Último Resorte, had any similarities with Alaska's band, Alaska y los Pegamoides, she said that there was "una gran diferencia: las muñequeras de Alaska sólo sirven de adorno y las mías son para pegar"[14] (González Lezama 2016, 185). Similarly, in *No acepto*, Boliche, drummer of the Catalan band Subterranean Kids, states that

> a las bandas de Madrid no las aguantaba ningún punki de España. O sea, por ejemplo, les hubieran partido la cara a Alaska y los Pegamoides, a Siniestro Total y a cualquier otra banda de esta índole. Primero, porque no eran punkis, segundo, por la cabezonería de la época, porque luego igual los conoces y eran súper buenas personas. Pero por el hecho ya de salir en televisión, por cantar 'quiero ser un bote de Colón' y su puta madre, ya te los cargarías a todos uno tras otro en fila india.[15] (Alfonso and Bocos Oyarbide 2007)

Therefore, it seems that, as much as the movida might have had individuals who dressed in a punk style or followed early British or US punk bands, they were generally not considered part of the Spanish punk movement by Spanish punks, precisely because of their celebratory attitude, lack of political opposition, and participation in the mainstream media. Thus, I consider these last three to be Spanish punk's most crucial differences when compared to the movida madrileña. Punk in Spain was viscerally oppositional and politically engaged almost from the very beginning and, gradually, both became two of its main defining characteristics. Additionally, as a result of this political opposition, punk culture rarely had any institutional support or media exposure during the Transición and it developed primarily in a precarious underground and DIY context. In fact, as we will see later on when discussing punk

---

14 A huge difference: Alaska's bracelets are only fashion and I use mine to fight.

15 No punk in Spain could stand the bands from Madrid. I mean, for instance, they would beat the shit out of Alaska y los Pegamoides, Siniestro Total, or any other band like these if they could. First, because they were not punks, second, because of the stubbornness of the time, because then, maybe, you meet them and they were really good people. But just for the fact that they were on TV, and they sang "I wanna be a can of Colon [detergent brand]" and all that fucking shit, you would kill them all one by one in a row.

fanzines and fanzines from the movida, not being political or oppositional enough and taking part in the mainstream media even became, in the eyes of many punks, decisive elements for someone not to be considered part of the punk movement.

Spanish punk's politicization is partly a result of it being primarily developed in peripheral Spain and, with particular strength, in the Basque Country. In the documentary *No acepto* and the books *Punk: Tres décadas de resistencia* and *20 años de punk en España*, the authors establish four main punk scenes in Spain: the Basque Country, Barcelona, Zaragoza, and Madrid. For his part, in *Punk, pero ¿qué punk?*, González Lezama pays attention to different parts of Spain but stresses the scenes developed in the Basque Country, Barcelona, and Madrid. At the same time, and without belittling the rest of the scenes, they all agree on highlighting Basque punk's crucial role in the development of Spanish punk culture. Along the same lines, in the documentary about Madrilenian punk, *Lo que hicimos fue secreto*, there is even a whole section in which several punk musicians from Madrid discuss the influence that Basque punk had on them.

While in 1977 the movida was starting to bloom in Madrid, punk bands such as Escombro or Asco were also playing their first shows in the Basque Country. Additionally, during the following two years, bands such as Negativo, La Banda Sin Futuro (which would later move to Madrid, change their name to Derribos Arias, and become one of the most successful bands in the movida), Zarama, Tensión, La Polla Records, Odio, and MCD (Me Cago en Dios) were also formed. Another crucial band in the Basque punk scene—and in the Spanish punk movement as well—is Eskorbuto, which was formed in the 1980s and is probably, along with another Basque band, La Polla Records, the most international and best-known Spanish-language punk band. In this sense, Pascual asserts that Eskorbuto were decisive in the punk movement because they introduced "una crítica social tan radical y sin concesiones, que hasta entonces parecía impensable"[16] (Pascual 2015, 93). Other popular bands formed during the 1980s in the Basque Country were RIP, Kortatu, Basura, Las Vulpess, and Cicatriz. Additionally, it was also during these years that Javier Sayes printed the first issue of his fanzine *Destruye!!!* and

16 Very radical and uncompromising social demands that seemed unthinkable until that time.

that pirate radio stations such as Hala Bedi Irratia and Txantxangorri started broadcasting. This was crucial for the development of an alternative and counterinformative print and radio media in the Basque Country.

The political context in the Basque Country was also significantly different from other parts of the state, and this marked Basque punk's character to a great extent. With the celebration of the 1982 general elections in Spain, the democratic system established during the first governments of the Transición became consolidated. Most political parties of the time, as well as the king, seemed to agree unanimously that there was no turning back in the road toward democracy, and they asserted so repeatedly in their different statements during and after Tejero's coup attempt in 1981. Just to cite an example, in his response to the coup on TVE1, Juan Carlos I addressed the nation with the following statement:

> Para evitar cualquier tipo de confusión, confirmo que he ordenado a las autoridades civiles y a la junta de jefes de estado mayor que tomen todas las medidas necesarias para mantener el orden constitucional dentro de la legalidad vigente. Cualquier medida de carácter militar que en su caso hubiera de tomarse, deberá contar con la aprobación de la junta de jefes de estado mayor. La corona, símbolo de la permanencia y unidad de la patria no puede tolerar en forma alguna acciones o actitudes de personas que pretendan interrumpir por la fuerza el proceso democrático que la constitución votada por el pueblo español determinó en su día a través de referéndum.[17]

Therefore, there was a significantly widespread consensus among the political forces on the fact that democracy was there to stay. In this way, when the PSOE won the general elections in 1982, the fundamental

---

17 In order to avoid any kind of confusion, I confirm that I have ordered all civil authorities and the junta of chiefs of the state to take all necessary measures to maintain the constitutional order within the current legislation. Any military action that should be taken will have to be approved by the junta of chiefs of staff. The crown, symbol of the permanency and unity of the nation, cannot tolerate in any way some of the actions and attitudes of people who attempt to interrupt by force the democratic process that the constitution voted on by the Spanish people determined through a referendum. Casa de Mjestad el Rey, "Mensaje de S.M. El Rey a los Españoles en la noche del 23 al 24 de Febrero de 1981," https://casareal.es/ES/ArchivoMultimedia/Paginas/archivo-multimedia_archivos-videos-detalle.aspx?data=47.

structure of the new Spanish democracy was significantly well established, and the government focused on other endeavors among which—along with the already cited cultural one—we must highlight the changes conducted in the economic system. The 1980s were the years when Spain consolidated the adaptation of its economic structure to neoliberalism. This was not solely fostered by the PSOE government, and it had its roots in the late Francoist period of capitalist development and the economic measures developed by the previous governments of the Transición. Yet it was during these years that the great *reconversión industrial* (industrial restructuring) took place and that the government, instead of implementing measures to prevent the precarization of the working class's life, began to dismantle the Spanish industrial structure by shutting down numerous companies that, following a neoliberal logic, were considered unprofitable at a macroeconomic level. It is true that such measures aimed to renovate the Francoist economic structure, but it is equally true that such renovation followed a macroeconomic strategy that worsened many working-class people's lives in the process. Additionally, this scenario was also aggravated by the European Union's demands of efficacy in the economic area for Spain to be accepted as part of the union. Ultimately, this process of neoliberalization resulted in Spain going from 3.2 percent of unemployment in 1974 to 21.4 in 1985. The latter is almost twice as high as the European average, which rose from 2.9 in 1974 to 11.2 in 1985 (Petras 2018, 18), and it shows the exceptionality of the Spanish case. In this way, while the PSOE government tried to make the country more "efficient," during the 1980s the industrial working class of Spain faced the worst unemployment figures in years. In the specific case of the Basque Country, considering that this region is one of the most industrialized areas of Spain, the unemployment rates there were especially high. It is for this reason that these years in the Basque Country were characterized by huge demonstrations and confrontations, such as those developed in Bilbao in response to the closure of the Astilleros Euskalduna.[18] This scenario, in addition to the Basque independentist movements, the

18 There is a highly informative documentary that shows the ferocious opposition presented by the workers of the Astilleros Euskalduna called *Astilleros Euskalduna: Una guerra contra el estado*, produced for ETB and directed by Nuria Domínguez, YouTube, uploaded by EITB, October 28, 2010: https://www.youtube.com/watch?v=txeCkWhQuNA.

high activity of the separatist armed band ETA, the implementation of the ZEN plan by the government,[19] the activity of the GAL, and others, gave Basque punk an almost inevitable political character. It is in this context also that the media coverage of the concert by La Polla Records during the San Isidro festivities needs to be understood. Through their concert, La Polla Records represented the voice of many Basque citizens who—from various and different perspectives—opposed the PSOE government right in the main festivities of the Spanish capital. In this sense, their concert represented a threat to the democratic normality that the official narrative constructed by the CT and the movida were imposing in Madrid, and it is for this reason that making clear that they were a "Basque radical band" and, hence, something exceptional in Spain as a whole, became a crucial argument for the media.

Another determinant element in the politicization of Spanish punk was the emergence of anarcho-punk in the UK. While Basque punk provided Spanish punk culture with a social and political opposition derived from a general social disenchantment, anarcho-punk added a somehow specific ideology and a more conscious countercultural agenda. In other words, Basque punk presented a more visceral political and social opposition whereas anarcho-punk brought a more profound political consciousness. The same goes for the underground and DIY character of Basque punk compared to anarcho-punk. The former did not necessarily do it as a conscious political stance but out of pure necessity, while the latter's core values entailed avoiding the mainstream media and following a DIY ethos. Anarcho-punk originated in the UK in the late 1970s partly as a response to the rampant commodification of the punk movement, which had lost its revolutionary potential by becoming part of mainstream culture, and partly as the musical expression of various countercultural movements that were not necessarily connected to punk culture. The initiators of the movement were the band Crass,

> who were a radical anarcho-pacifist, anarcha-feminist, vegetarian collective, and the anarchism it espoused was not the anarchy

19 ZEN (Zona Especial Norte) (Special Northern Area) is a plan conducted by José Barrionuevo from the PSOE that aimed to fight ETA's terrorism by overfunding the police and giving them certain liberties over citizen's individual rights in the Basque Country while describing this part of Spain as a "special area" where terrorism needs to be defeated by any means necessary. https://borrokagaraia.files.wordpress.com/2013/08/plan_zen.pdf.

> of the Pistols ("Anarchy in the UK" begins with a frightening guttural laugh by Johnny Rotten and ends with the almost comic-book "Get pissed. Destroy"), but a lifestyle and worldview they developed through a combination of hippy idealism and resistance, punk energy and check, and some of the cultural strategies of the Situationists. (McKay 1996, 75)

In other words, a group of people who were not simply a punk band but a collective with a broader revolutionary agenda in which punk music played a decisive role within a complex net of other artistic influences. In this sense, it is in anarcho-punk that the DIY ethos and a lifestyle influenced by anarchism acquire their most definitive representation within punk culture.

Similarly, it is also important to refer to the Barcelona hardcore punk scene when talking about the politicization of Spanish punk. In *The Philosophy of Punk*, Craig O'Hara uses the term "hardcore" as "simply a synonym for Punk that Americans invented in the early eighties" and asserts that "hardcore music is usually faster than the Punk music of the seventies, but the ideas and people involved are virtually the same" (O'Hara 1995, 16–17). Such a statement is extremely vague and generalizing, especially if we think of the numerous differences between punk scenes around the world, but it holds true if we limit the comparison of hardcore exclusively to the more politicized branches of punk developed in the UK, such as streetpunk or the previously mentioned anarcho-punk. Along the same lines, one could say that hardcore punk in the US originates in similar terms as these two by trying to provide American punk with a countercultural and political significance that other protopunk bands such as the Ramones or the New York Dolls lacked. Additionally, the fact that hardcore is faster than other punk is also extremely important because it adds a far more aggressive sound to the music that produces different effects and reactions in its listeners when compared to other punk music. This is especially true in a live show context, as the development of the mosh pit within hardcore punk culture attests. In this way, the Barcelona punk scene was characterized by a faster and more aggressive sound than most of the punk coming from the rest of Spain. At the same time, since politics was another crucial element in hardcore punk, that also influenced Barcelona's punk politicization tremendously. According to the Subterranean Kids' drummer, Boliche, the concert played by the American hardcore band MDC in Barcelona in 1984 was decisive in the development of a local hardcore punk scene. In *Harto de todo* he states that in that concert

> Vimos una actitud mucho más politizada, más radical; una estética menos llamativa que la que llevábamos hasta el momento heredada del punk pero agresiva y muy de calle, y sobre todo por el sonido. [...] Ahí chocaba la actitud punki *destroyer* con la actitud de MDC, una banda de hardcore que entre canción y canción te explicaban de qué hablaba cada tema, contra qué iba dirigido ese tema. Los punkis decían "¡Que te calles y que toques!", pero a mucha gente nos marcó mucho y yo creo que de ahí salieron todas las bandas hardcore que ha dado Barcelona.[20] (Llansama 2011, n.p.)

Nonetheless, it is important to note that there were already Catalan bands that played very fast and politicized punk before 1984, such as, for instance, Último Resorte, L'odi Social, Frenopatics, and Kangrena.

In addition, as Delincuencia Sonora's singer, José Calvo, points out in *No acepto*, and due to Spain's strong anarchist culture all throughout the twentieth century, the influence of Spanish anarchist movements was also crucial in the politicization of many Spanish punks. Similarly, due to its fascist and dictatorial past, Spain had an already strong leftist and antifascist discourse of its own that also contributed to the politicization of the punk movement. Moreover, in *Antifa: The Antifascist Handbook*, a book about international antifascist movements, Mark Bray describes the strong connection between punk and antifascism while also referring to the Spanish Civil War and the republican resistance during Francoism as a deciding influence in the development of a global antifascist network. Such a connection is symbolically represented by the book's first chapter, which is about the origins of antifascist movements and titled "¡No pasarán!," a reference to the slogan used by the antifascist resistance in Spain during the Civil War. Ultimately, Spanish punk developed in a strongly politicized context, and that gave it a

---

20 We saw a far more politicized attitude, more radical; less striking aesthetics than the one we followed and inherited from punk, but aggressive and with a street attitude, and above all because of the sound. MDC, a hardcore band that between songs explained what each of the songs talked about, against what each song stood. Punks would say, "Shut up and play!" but many people were very influenced by that show, and I think it was from there that all hardcore bands in Barcelona emerged.

decisive political and oppositional character when compared to the more hedonist and apolitical movida madrileña.

## 3. Fanzines

If we take a look at one of the movida's most popular fanzines, *Kaka de Luxe,* and compare it to punk fanzines such as *Penetración*, *Destruye!!!*, or *N.D.F.*, the difference between both cultural movements becomes evident. *Kaka de Luxe* is a fanzine produced primarily by Fernando Márquez "el Zurdo," Alaska, and Nacho Canut. In it we find a mixture of comics, news, music reviews, and opinion articles. On the first page of the second issue there is a comic in which famous cartoon characters such as Tintin or Charlie Brown discuss what they think about a girl called Vitorichi. Tintin insists on saying that she is a "moñoña," while an unknown mysterious character refers to her as "pedorra." These two concepts are later discussed in a different article. According to this article, "las mujeres y los hombres se dividen en moñoñas y pedorras. Las moñoñas son de escasa estatura, de escaso peso, de escaso contenido y de escaso continente. Generalmente, poseen voz aguda (no aflautada, sino de pito) y parece que siempre están comiendo miel de abeja con delectación"[21] (Gara Jova and Canut 1977, 4). After this, the author of the article establishes a subclassification of the different kinds of existing moñoñas and then proceeds to define the pedorras. According to the author, the pedorras "se diferencian de las moñoñas en que, aún conservando todas las características físicas de escasez, son más feas que un pecado [y] su clasificación es inútil porque van a seguir siendo igual de callos"[22] (4). The article closes with the following moral: "Si eres, te consideras o te consideran moñoña, mándanos tu fotografia y te analizaremos fisiognómicamente para encauzarte en el porvenir y en la vida. Escribe al apartado 23029 de Madrid. Si eres, te consideras o te consideran pedorra mejor suicídate, chata"[23] (4).

21 Men and women are divided into "moñoñas" and "farty-pants." Moñoñas are not too tall, not too heavy, and don't have either much content or container. Generally, they have a high-pitched voice (not like a flute but like a whistle), and it seems that they are always eating honey with pleasure.

22 Are different from the moñoñas in that, even keeping all the physical characteristics of scarcity, they are uglier than a sin [and] their classification is useless because they will always remain equally disgusting.

23 If you are, consider yourself, or others consider you a moñoña, send us your picture and we will analyze you physiognomically to get you back on track in your future and life. Send a letter to 23029, Madrid. If you are, consider yourself, or others consider you a pedorra, it's best if you kill yourself, love.

In a similar tone but on a different page, we find an image of "Las aventuras de Mari-Tacones." In this image we see a woman who is presented almost as the villain of a Marvel comic. She claims that she wants to take over the world, and the image shows the different "weapons" she possesses to do so. She has "assassin metal chains," "the leather whip she uses with her lovers," and "high-voltage shoes," among other things. Additionally, according to the text at the bottom, she is fighting against the Vatican to make them canonize her as the "Patron of the High Heels."

A few pages later, we find "El caballero más romántico del espacio," a short comic in which all characters are naked at all times. In this comic, a nouveau riche named "Ruletto the Knight" travels to Saturn to talk to a woman called "Platinum Nipples." Once he gets there, he tells Platinum Nipples that he wants to buy some slaves for his new harem, and she takes him to her slave exhibition in a different room. When they get to this room, Platinum Nipples tells him that the problem with her current slaves—who are connected to several cables as if they were some sort of humanoids—is that they lost the "sexual button" and cannot be programmed for sex. It is worth noting that, while all this is happening, the images keep showing Platinum Nipples's breasts and nipples as well as Ruletto's intergluteal cleft, also known as "butt crack." Next, Platinum Nipples tells Ruletto that it was all Mr. S.'s fault—whom she defines as a repugnant lesbian—because it was she who stole the "sexual button." Then Platinum Nipples asks Ruletto if he could help her get the button back, and he says that he will try. While this conversation is happening, the image shows Ruletto inserting a sword up Platinum Nipples's anus. On the next page, Ruletto is at Mr. S.'s house. Mr. S. appears as a bearded person with big breasts and wearing a bikini. When Ruletto walks into Mr. S.'s room, he asks Ruletto to make love to him and informs him that he has something amazing called "the sexual button" in his anus. Ruletto starts having sex with him while trying to reach for the sexual button. After this, there is a cartoon in which a pen pretending to come from outside the page is trying to cross out the image in which the characters are supposed to be having sex, perhaps as a reference to Francoist censorship or making fun of Spaniards' puritanism. In the following cartoons, Ruletto goes back to Platinum Nipples's house and gives her the sexual button. Yet right before they install the button in the slaves, Mr. S. enters the scene to get back his/her sexual button.

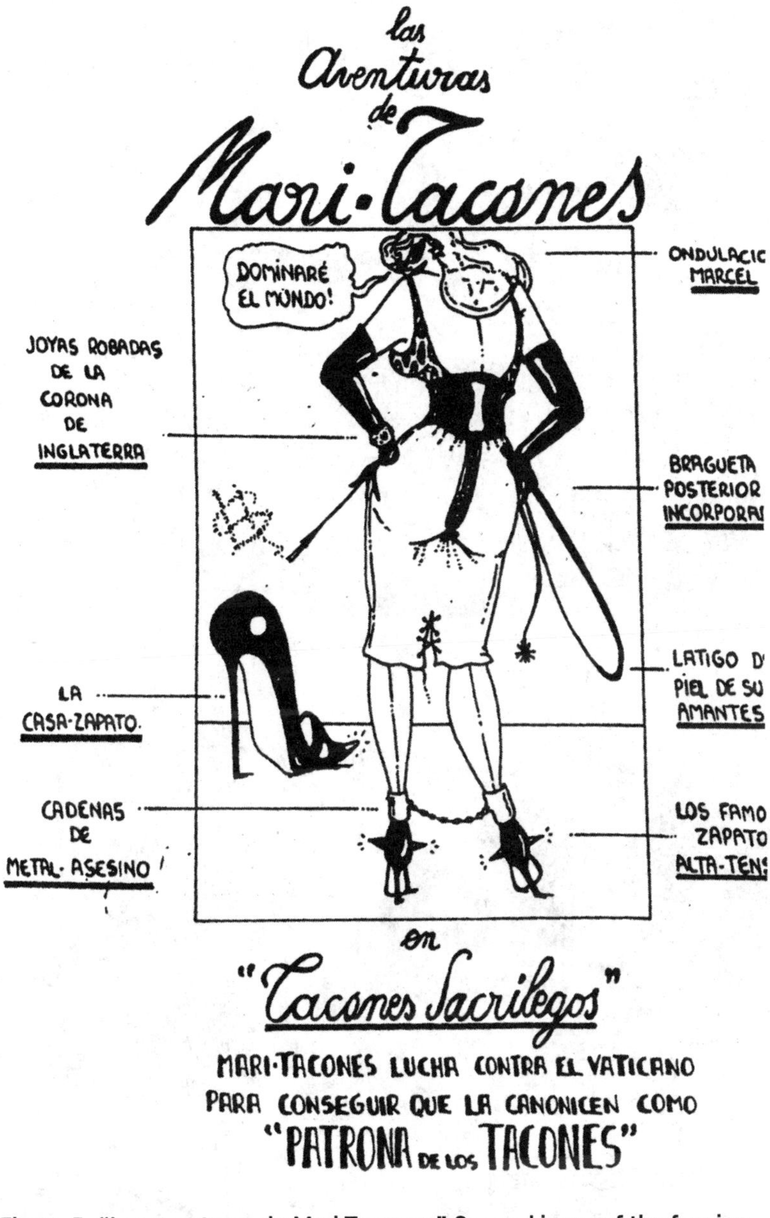


Figure 5. "Las aventuras de Mari-Tacones." Second issue of the fanzine *Kaka de Luxe*

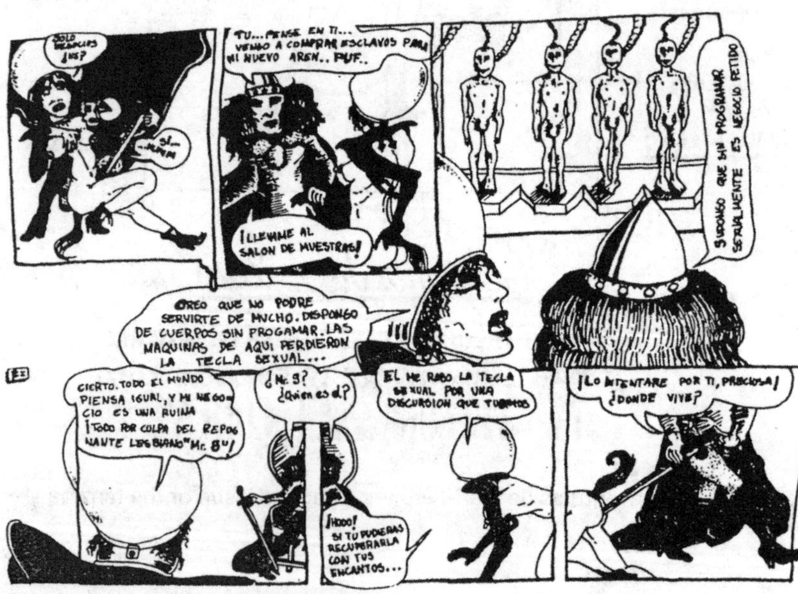


Figures 6–9. "Ruletto, el caballero más romántico del espacio"

RULETTO SE VISTIO DE MUÑECA LUJOSA Y TOMO EL CAMINO PARA LA MANSION DE "Mr. S" CUBIERTO SU CUERPO EN UNA NUBE DE CHANEL NUMERO DOS.
¡VAMOS! VEN A REVOLCARTE JUNTO A MI, SOBRE ESTOS MULLIDOS COJINES QUE SON LAS LATAS DE CERVEZA VACIAS. OLVIDA TODO PROBLEMA Y GOZA ¡MI NUEVO AMANTE!
HAZME SENTIR PLACER Y TE ENSEÑARE UNA MARAVILLA QUE TENGO: LA TECLA SEXUAL
JA, JA, JA, SE LA QUITE A UNA LOCA DE CELTIBERICOS OJOS.. Y JA, JA ¿SABES DONDE LA TENGO METIDA? EN EL CULO, JA, JA, JA, JA. ¡POR MI CULPA SE ESTA ARUINANDO!

PASADA LA BATALLA, RULETTO, ESCAPA CON EL PRECIADO BOTIN AL PALACIO DE PEZONES DE PLATINO, CONTANDO A ESTA TODO LO OCURRIDO...
JA JA JA
...LE QUITE EL AMOR CON EL TACON DE LA BOTA Y ¡NI SIQUIERA SE DIO CUENTA! JA, JA, JA
COMENZEMOS. COLOCA LA TECLA AQUI, DA A ESTA PALANCA, ESPERA QUE SE CALIENTEN LOS CIRCUITOS Y YA PUEDES PROGRAMAR
¡HOO, CIELOS, QUE NERVIOSO ESTOY!
PERO EN ESE MOMENTO ALGO OCURRIA EN LA PUERTA DE LA CASA...
¡Mr. 'S'!
¿COMO HAS CONSEGUIDO?? LLEGAR TAN PRONTO?
POR QUE SOY AMIGO DEL DIBUJANTE Y AHORA PREPARAROS PARA MORIR...
...PERO SIGUIENTE?

As we can see, for the most part, the content of the fanzine is extremely absurd—which is another major characteristic of the movida madrileña as a whole. It does challenge the prevailing morality and especially the sexual morality inherited from Franco's dictatorship, but in such turbulent and complicated times as were the years of the Transición it can also come through as trivial and evasive. Additionally, the lack of political content in the movida can also be seen as a class privilege of those involved in it since, as Fouce points out, the movida was a movement "composed of educated youngsters who came from families that were well connected to the new cultural establishment" (Fouce and del Val 2013, 125). In other words, youngsters who were not so affected by the growing unemployment and economic crisis that resulted from different decisions taken by the government during the 1980s.

In the case of the Madrilenian punk fanzine *Penetración*, the content is very different. The cover of the sixth issue (1985) shows three very illustrative pictures. In the left top corner, we see an old lady looking defiantly at a policeman. Next to this, there is a masked person throwing a stone while some random things burn in the background. Finally, at the bottom, we see a Spanish national policeman walking behind a civilian while he pushes him forward, grabbing him by his shirt collar and carrying a baton menacingly. Along with this there is a message in capital letters in the center of the page saying: RESISTIR! If we turn the page over and read the editorial piece, we learn that the authors of the fanzine are looking for people who could provide information about "luchas obreras, ocupaciones, movidas sociales variadas, presos a nivel oficial."[24] They explain that they are trying to gather more people to create a bigger and better magazine to "romper este jodido aislamiento al que nos somete el sistema."[25]

Then, at the end of the text, they say that they are going to stop talking because "ya va siendo hora de que la protesta, escrita o en canciones, dé lugar a la Resistencia, a la acción directa y eso sólo lo conseguiremos estando unidos, en solidaridad y con nuestra actividad."[26]

---

24 Working-class fights, occupations, varied social happenings, official prisoners.

25 Break this fucking isolation the system inflicts on us.

26 It is about time that the demand, written or in songs, changes into Resistance, direct action, and we will only achieve that by staying united, in solidarity and with our activity.

**Figure 10. Cover of the sixth issue of *Penetración***

The inner pages focus on describing different punk scenes around the world, promoting new bands or albums, or interviewing different punk bands. Additionally, there are a couple of news pieces about ecology, a protest in Copenhagen to support Nicaragua's Sandinista revolution, and the Stop the City movement in London.[27] There are no comics, and most of the drawings are there only to accompany the other materials. The only two drawings that stand on their own are one against heroin usage and another one in which the author criticizes different political ideologies and shows their sympathy for anarchism. In this drawing there are four different characters: Uncle Sam, a skull with a military helmet and swastika, a member of the Bolshevik Red Army, and a man wearing a traditional Basque *txapela* with a Basque flag in the background.[28] Above them all one can read the following text: "Wanted. Estos 4 peligrosos criminales, enemigos del hombre y de la naturaleza, dirigen esta sociedad. Aquellos que los destruyan colaboraran en la construcción de la nueva sociedad. La utopia. La Anarkia."[29]

Similarly, in the Catalan fanzine *N.D.F.* we find very explicit political content as well. On the first issue's cover (1983a), we see Uncle Sam's traditional image pointing his finger at us with a skull instead of his usual face. Considering that this image is traditionally used with the "I want you for U.S. Army" slogan, it could be connecting the US, capitalism, imperialism, and wars with death. Additionally, we see Crass's—anarcho-punk's founding band—symbol, and the symbol of peace and anarchy. There is also an E within a circle and a bird, both symbols of the band Flux of Pink Indians that refer to environmentalism and animal rights. Finally, there is also a dollar bill and a needle crossed out by a bar within a circle, as well as a few words saying "suicídate" (kill yourself), "hechos" (facts), and "lucha" (fight). In the editorial note, one can read that in "'NDF', que quiere decir algo así como 'Niños Drogados por Frank' y es una declaración de principios, estamos contra la droga y contra la gente que se enriquece gracias a los infelices que mueren

27 These movements involved several demonstrations against social topics such as war, oppression, destruction, and capitalism, generally speaking.

28 The image of the Basque man is probably a reference to Basque nationalism, which, from its predominant anarchist perspective and as with any other nationalism, punk would always oppose.

29 Wanted. These 4 dangerous criminals, enemies of man, direct our society. Those who destroy them will be collaborating in the creation of a new society. Utopia. Anarchy.

Figure 11. Cover of the first issue of *N.D.F.*

drogados"[30] and that they declare "ya de principio que somos anarquistas, pacifistas, ecologistas, anti-policiales, anti-nukleares, anti-racistas, etc."[31] (Destruye 1983a, 1). It is important to note the "etc." as if it was expected for a punk fanzine to already be opposed to some specific things everyone understands by simply saying "etc." In the rest of the fanzine we find reviews of albums and bands, interviews, and several opinion articles on topics such as the meaning of being a punk, drug use, or police abuse. In an article titled "¿Punk?" an anonymous author criticizes the attitude of those punks who have "mucha ANARKIA, muchas frases de NO FUTURE, pero nada más, no luch[an] por lo que qu[ieren], acepta[n] todo lo que se [les] dice"[32] (5). The author establishes a distinction between the first 1970s punk bands, whose most defining characteristic was their aesthetic opposition, versus those that resulted from the anarcho-punk and new streetpunk movements in the early 1980s, which have a more important ideological component. In "¿Punk Vegetal?" the author criticizes punks' use of hard drugs by saying that when someone takes hard drugs they become a "vegetable," referring to someone who cannot think or move and who becomes simply part of the system he is supposed to be fighting. Finally, in "¿Libertad?" (Freedom) the author questions the PSOE's government and talks about the increasing police presence in Barcelona. He goes as far as wondering whether "¿Es esta la nación libre que todos anhelábamos en época de Franco? Porque yo, la sigo anhelando."[33]

The same is true for the Basque fanzine *Destruye!!!* In its first issue's cover (1981), we find a picture of the Clash along with the following anonymous quote: "¿No nos han mandado a hundirnos en la mierda? Pues la mierda la tendrán en sus calles, en las entradas de sus casas, en las puertas del parlamento. Estaremos allí para recordárselo . . ."[34] In addition, in the editorial note we read that Javi, the author of the fanzine, "decidi[ó] sacar

30 "NDF," which means something similar to "Niños Drogados por Frank" (Children drugged by Frank) and is a statement of principles, we are against drugs and against the people who become rich thanks to the unfortunate people who died of drug abuse.

31 From the very beginning that we are anarchists, pacifists, ecologists, antipolice, antinuclear, antiracist, etc.

32 Plenty of anarchy, many, many phrases of NO FUTURE, but that's about it, they don't fight for what they want, they accept everything they are told.

33 Is this the free nation we all longed for in Franco's time? Because I am still longing for it.

34 Didn't they tell us to sink in shit? So, they will have shit in their streets, in the entrance of their houses, in the doors of parliament. We will be there to remind them . . .

este primer número de DESTRUYE!!! [...] porque cre[e] que ahora el punk es ese revulsivo que puede convertirse en arma de fuego"[35] and that, in his opinion, "es ahora cuando cargarse el sistema es deber de todos."[36] Along with this, and as we saw in *N.D.F.*, he questions the authenticity of those punks who are more focused on following a fashion than actually fighting the system. According to Javi, there are many bands that have contributed to corrupting the original spirit of punk as political opposition, and he cites the "nueva oleros"—a term that has also been used to refer to the movida—among them. In the rest of the fanzine we find several reviews and interviews with punk bands and a great display of photos from punk artists. Although this first issue is only twelve pages long, it is enough to see the common character with *N.D.F.* and *Penetración.*

Another illustrative comparative example that shows the difference between the movida and punk is how differently they talk about Swiss punk in *Kaka de Luxe* and *Penetración*. There is nothing especially relevant about Swiss punk, but, coincidentally, both *Kaka de Luxe* and *Penetración* have an article in which they talk about the punk movement in Switzerland, and the comparison of the way each of them covers the topic is an informative exercise to observe the differences between both movements. *Kaka de Luxe*'s page-long article has a picture of a young man dressed in a suit wearing sunglasses in the center. In addition, the text is handwritten, trying to emulate different fonts, bold, 3D letters, and other stylistic details. The content of the text is about some different places where you can go to experience Swiss punk in Switzerland. The tone of the text, however, is somehow silly and sounds as if the writer was attempting to be funny. For instance, the author says that a typical Swiss person is a "cabeza cuadriculada [...] y encima son banqueros"[37] and at the end of the text states that "pese a todo la mentalidad idiota del suizo adulto actúa de modo incomprensible y ya casi todas las familias que se precian tienen un jovencito punk en ella ¡¡tome ejemplo!!"[38] In *Penetración*, for its part, the text

35 Decided to publish this first number of DESTRUYE!!! [...] because he thinks that now punk is that revulsive thing that can turn into a firearm.

36 It is now when destroying the system is everybody's duty.

37 Square head [...] and, to top it off, they are bankers.

38 Despite everything the stupid mentality of the adult Swiss acts in an incomprehensible way and by now almost every respectable family has their own young punk, follow their example!

is all typewritten in the same font and has no other stylistic details. The article is also a page long, but the font is much smaller and has much more information. The author of the article starts with a long list of different punk bands from Switzerland. Then they list different Swiss punk fanzines and provides an address in case someone wants to order some. After this, they continue with a list of venues where bands can play as well as with a list of radios where they can send their works. The article closes by talking about several bands that have no recordings yet and provides an address in Switzerland where the readers of *Penetración* can write to establish connections. Through this address, bands from Spain can contact people involved in the punk scene in Switzerland and, among other things, go play there or send their own works to be played at Swiss punk or pirate radio stations. Additionally, it is important to note that the issue of *Penetración* in which this article was published also provides similar information about German, Swedish, Polish, Australian, Finnish, and Yugoslavian punk. Therefore, *Penetración* clearly aims to help develop the connections between different punk scenes and shows quite a different character from the tongue-in-cheek and humorous tone found in *Kaka de Luxe*.

To sum up: individual liberties, sexual liberation versus political commitment, network and community development. Punk stresses the importance of creating a network of counterinformation to exercise political resistance, while the movida seems to aim to provide an alternative entertainment for Spanish youth. This is why punk fanzines lack comics and have a reduced quantity of images, while the fanzines from the movida make comics and images one of their main features. Similarly, punk fanzines engage and discuss relevant topics of the time, such as police brutality, political repression, and drug addiction, while, for the most part, the fanzines from the movida limit themselves to showing an absurd and hedonistic perspective of life.

## 4. Music

In addition to the fanzines themselves, the bands mentioned in the punk and movida fanzines tend to also be very different from each other. In *Kaka de Luxe* we find a broad spectrum of styles ranging from David Bowie's glam rock to the Ramones' early punk, through Kiss's hard rock and Vainica Doble's pop-rock. Additionally, *Kaka de Luxe* includes a chart with the chords of the songs "Satisfaction" by the Rolling Stones and "The Kids Are Alright" by the Who. The former is a rock and roll song with a bit more distortion than one would expect from the Rolling Stones, and the latter is a pop song with backing vocals and melodies that resemble the early Beatles albums. This variety is another sign of the movida's decisive eclecticism. Another magazine from the movida, *Radical FM* (no. 2 1982), includes more Spanish bands, and we find names such as Alaska y los Pegamoides, Danza Invisible, Derribos Arias, and Gabinete Caligari, among others. These bands were very different from those in punk fanzines.

In the first number of *Penetración* they talk about the anarcho-punk British band Instigators, the American hardcore band Insanity Defense, the Catalan hardcore bands Antidogmatikss and GRB, and the Basque hardcore bands Tortura Sistematika and BAP! In the first issue of *Destruye!!!* we find bands such as the Clash, Sham 69, Crass, Discharge, and the American hardcore band Dead Kennedys. Additionally, after the sixth issue, published in 1982, we also start to see Spanish bands such as the Basque bands Basura, RIP, Optalidón, and Odio. Similarly, in *N.D.F.* we find bands such as Crass, Discharge, Dead Kennedys, the Madrilenian band Delincuencia Sonora, the Catalan band Último Resorte, the Basque band Cirrosis, and many more. The names of the punk bands alone demonstrate the noncelebratory attitude of punk music, with references primarily to dirt, hate, illnesses, and other negative characterizations. And when listening to all these bands, one realizes not only that the movida and punk cultures were different from each other in their explicit affirmative and oppositional attitudes, respectively, but also that this characteristic was present even in the sound of their music. In the rest of this section, in order to focus on this aspect, I will conduct a close reading of the music of two bands from the movida (Alaska y los Pegamoides and Danza Invisible), as well as that of two punk bands (Antidogmatikss and RIP), and I will compare them to explore their differences and similarities.

If we take a listen to Alaska y los Pegamoides' only album, *Grandes éxitos* (Greatest hits) (1982), we find their famous song "Bailando" (Dancing). This song begins with a bass drum beat and a funky/disco guitar riff in a minor key, using some reverb effect, both emphasizing the first and third beats of a 4/4 bar. The bass is playing a counter-rhythm responding to the guitar by accentuating the off beats of the first and third beats and using a slap technique.[39] Additionally, after a few bars, a horn section playing a funky-sounding pentatonic line joins in. The general sound of the song is very funk/disco and, as a matter of fact, a later version of this same song played by Alaska y Dinarama included an intro where they mixed the first few lines of James Brown's "Sex Machine" and the horn lines from his song "I Got the Feeling." Altogether, this makes the song extremely danceable—hence the title of the song, "Bailando." The second song of the album is "El plan" (The plan) a song in a 3/4 time signature emulating a waltz rhythm that, along with a descending melody on the keyboard, sounds similar to a circus song. The third song's title is "La tribu de las Chochoni" (The Chochoni tribe). This song starts with a few guitar chords with a reverb effect and, after a few bars, they are joined by a keyboard melody and some backing vocals that give the song a sound similar to bands from New York's new-wave scene such as Blondie or British postpunk bands such as Siouxsie and the Banshees. Additionally, there are a few songs such as "Vicky," "Secretos de belleza" (Beauty secrets), and "Rosa y verde" (Pink and green) that have a similar sound to the early protopunk sound of the Ramones. The rest of the album combines all these styles with more disco-sounding songs such as "Alta tension" (High tension), "La línea se cortó" (The line was cut off), and "¿Qué piensan de los insectos?" (What do you think about insects?) and more postpunk-sounding tunes such as "Estrategia militar" (Military strategy) and "Redrum."

Similarly, Danza Invisible is a band that has changed their style throughout the years, but most of their 1980s songs were in a postpunk and new-wave style as well. "Al amanecer" (At dawn) from their first album, *Contacto interior* (Inner contact) (1983), is a song that mixes synthesizers, keyboards, and a lot of general reverb. The song begins with a bass line and a mixture of keyboard, guitar, and synthesizer sounds with chorus and reverb effects. The vocals also have a lot of reverb. In the second song of the same album, "Tiempo de amor" (Time of love), the reverb, keyboard, and synthesizer-based background sound is pretty similar, but this time the guitar, bass, and drums play a more funk/disco-sounding rhythmic pattern that makes the song much

39 The slap technique is a technique developed within funk and disco music to reproduce a strong percussive sound on stringed instruments (generally a bass guitar) by hitting the thicker strings with the thumb.

more danceable than the previous one. As in "Bailando" by Alaska y los Pegamoides, in "Tiempo de amor" we also hear a slapping bass as a counter-rhythm responding to the guitar riff. Additionally, the keyboard plays various phrases mimicking the lines a horn section would normally play in funk music. This funky sound is even more obvious in the next song of this same album, "Mis ojos hacia ti" (My eyes toward you). This song begins with a bluesy-sounding pentatonic line and two guitars alternating full on funky rhythms with no added synthesizers or background keyboards with reverb. With the next song, "Ecos" (Echos), we are back to keyboards, synthesizers, and a general reverb sound with still funk/disco-sounding drums and bass. In "Así marchamos a la gloria" (This way we move toward glory), the reverb and chorus effects are much stronger than in any other song, and the drum pattern is very slow, giving the song a very psychedelic heavy sound. The rest of the album follows this same line, mixing more new-wave and postpunk-sounding tunes with a lot of reverb, effects, and synthesizers, such as "Contacto interior" (Inner contact) and "El legado" (The legacy), and more funk/disco tunes, such as "Arco iris" (Rainbow), "Gente especial" (Special people), and "Espiritu irreal" (Unreal spirit).

All these songs present a very different sound to that of most Spanish punk bands. Among the main differences, we could highlight the general "good" sound of the music from the movida. Alaska y los Pegamoides released their album *Grandes éxitos* (Greatest Hits) with Hispavox—the label of bands such as Nacha Pop and Radio Futura. Danza Invisible released their first two albums with BMG Ariola, and most of the rest with DRO—an independent record label that became one of the most successful of the movida. Generally speaking, the bands of the movida benefited from a powerful media industry and, sometimes, independent labels that became very successful in a short period of time, such as DRO, and that then became part of even more powerful labels such as Warner Music. In the case of these independent labels, Fouce states that they were "el reflejo de una modernización que ha sido entendida como ingreso en una estrategia macroeconómica"[40] and that "sólo la radicalización de las propuestas y la renuncia consciente a los grandes circuitos han funcionado como estrategias para mantener

---

40 The reflection of a modernization that has been understood as a way to enter a macroeconomic strategy.

la independencia"[41] (Fouce 2002, 113). In the case of Spanish punk, we would have to refer to a primarily independent and precarious circuit as well as to limited recording means, which made punk records, generally speaking, have a "worse" sound quality. At the same time, not only was the sound of the albums different, but also the sound of their playing. There are many bands from the movida that cannot play their instruments and that keep playing off key or off beat. But as the movida starts to benefit from institutional and media support, the musicians start to be more professional, and some bands would even hire session musicians for their recordings. This is precisely why in Alaska y los Pegamoides' album, for instance, one can hear very tight music when compared to Alaska's previous band, Kaka de Luxe. Punk, for the most part, will continue to sound "bad" in terms of both recording quality and music skills, because sounding "bad" became one of punk's most defining characteristics.[42] Hence the tendency to shout and roar in punk music and the ever-growing presence of melody and harmony in most of the movida's bands.[43]

If we now turn to the punk bands and start by focusing on the self-released album *Rompan filas!!!* (Break ranks!!!) (1984) by the Catalan hardcore punk band Antidogmatikss, we find an album in which one can hardly distinguish the instruments or understand the

---

41 Only the radicalization of the proposals and the conscious refusal to participate in the major circuits have worked as strategies to keep their independence.

42 This would change with the passage of time, and many punk bands would then sign with major record labels, which opened the never-ending debate about whether they "sold out" or were simply negotiating with the existing cultural market to gain more exposure and help spread their message. In any case, such change improved the recordings' sound considerably. Additionally, technological advances also allowed punk bands to keep self-recording and producing their own works with a much better sound quality, which posed a constant resignification of what punk sounds like. In spite of this, the simplicity and musical inaccuracy have always remained an important characteristic of punk music.

43 It might be relevant at this point to remember the incident between the band Kortatu and the sound engineer César Ibarretxe while recording their album *El estado de las cosas*. According to Roberto Herreros and Isidro López, when recording this album, Ibarretxe tried to convince the members of Kortatu to use less distortion in the recording to achieve a "better" sound. However, Kortatu not only wanted a distorted sound but even used the sound of Black Flag—one of the noisiest hardcore punk bands of the time—as an example of the sound they wanted for one of their songs. After listening to this and other sound examples the band showed him, Ibarretxe told the band that they were showing him examples of music that had all been recorded wrong. In these circumstances, Kortatu asked Ibarretxe to, please, record their album wrong too (Herreros and López 2013, 179).

lyrics. The album was self-financed and self-released by the band. In the first song, "Fuego en la Moncloa" (Fire in the Moncloa), there are very distorted guitars playing rapid power chords and drum patterns that, due to the high speed of the song, do not maintain a steady beat. Additionally, it is important to note that La Moncloa is where the president of Spain lives and that the first lines of the lyrics talk about "fuego en la Moncloa / aires de revolución / fuego en la Moncloa / anarquía en la nación."[44] The second song, "Religión," starts with a distorted bass line that is soon joined by also distorted guitars and very fast drumming. A few bars later, the singer comes in shouting and trying to fit long vocal lines within the fast music played by the instruments. The rest of the songs all sound very similar and are characterized by an extreme general "noisy" sound. There are songs against the US such as "Anti-USA," against Spain's treasury such as "Hacienda" (Treasury), and against the military such as "Campos de cruces" (Fields of crosses), among others. Additionally, there is also a song directly questioning the Transición, "El modelo de español" (The model of the Spanish), which opens with the sound recording of Tejero's coup attempt in 1981 and his famous line of "¡Se sienten, coño!"[45] Harmonically, they are all songs that escape any specific key with a strong tendency toward fast semitone movements, giving the songs a less identifiable and "pleasant" sound. Finally, another defining characteristic of Antidogmatikss's songs, and also of an important part of Spanish punk in general, is the short length of the songs. In *Rompan filas!!!* we find a paradigmatic example with "Ellos o tú" (Them or you), a song that is exactly nine seconds long. Such brevity, mixed with the general noise, makes the songs sound like short, cathartic rants resulting from social and political frustrations. Rants that could be cathartic not only for the musicians playing the songs, but also for those listening at home or attending a punk show.

In the case of the Basque punk band RIP, we find a combination of fast hardcore songs and other slower ones. In 1984 RIP published four songs in a shared project with Eskorbuto (*Zona especial norte*) for the Madrilenean independent record label Spansul Records. Two years later, in 1987, they recorded these songs and other new ones for their first LP, *No te muevas* (Do not move), which was released by

44 Fire in La Moncloa / airs of revolution / fire in La Moncloa / anarchy in the nation.
45 Sit down, damn it!

Basati Diskak—a Basque independent record label founded by Javi Sayes, also author of the *Destruye!!!* fanzine. The first song of this album is "Condenado" (Doomed), which starts with some slow melodic bars as an introduction before they speed up and play the rest of the song at a faster tempo. Unlike most of Antidogmatikss's songs, "Condenado" is in a clear major key that gives the song a more harmonic sound. Yet the guitars are still very distorted, the drum patterns are quite fast, and the singer shouts more than he sings. The lyrics of the song talk about a person who is in jail waiting to be executed. They do not mention why the person is going to be executed but, considering the recent fascist past and the actions carried out by the GAL throughout the 1980s even after the abolition of the death penalty, this song clearly had some controversial content. The following song is "Escoria" (Scum), which begins with a repetitive bass line in a minor key that plays throughout most of the song. The lyrics refer to the classic punk slogan "no future," but with an added twist: instead of simply presenting themselves as the ones with no future, they assume an active role and say that they will also destroy the future of those destroying theirs. The song starts with the following lines: "Nosotros somos escoria y escoria os vamos a dar / Nosotros sentimos odio y os vamos a hacer odiar / Vivís en colmenas tapizadas, soñáis con un sólido futuro / Escoria, vuestro futuro es."[46] In this way, the song seems to talk to those more privileged ones and tell them that their future is as uncertain as that of the band members and that they will make sure it is indeed that way. The next song, "Policía no" (No police), is one of the most hardcore-sounding songs—very fast with shouts in unison of "policía no" throughout the majority of it. After this, we find "Última generación" (Last generation), another fast hardcore song that revisits punk's "no future" topos. We find additional hardcore-sounding songs such as "Odio a mi patria" (I hate my nation), "Mundo muerto" (Dead world), and "Revolución" (Revolution) and other slower but still noisy and simple songs such as "Presos" (Prisoners), "Terrorismo policial" (Police terrorism), and "Enamorado de la muerte" (In love with death). Generally speaking, the RIP album sounds significantly better than the one by Antidogmatikss, but it is still a crude and down-to-basics sound. There are no keyboards,

46 We are scum and we will give you scum / We feel hatred and we will give you hatred / You live in upholstered hives / You dream of a solid future / Scum is your future.

effects, or synthesizers—as in most bands from the movida—and there are no complicated funk chords or bass-slapping sounds. As in the case of Antidogmatikss, all songs are dominated by the sound of fast and highly distorted power chords over which the singer shouts repetitive and off-key rants.

All in all, for the most part, Spanish punk music lacked the reverb, the echo, and the synthesizers, and it was a much cruder music than that being played by the majority of the movida bands. The quality of the playing was significantly worse, making out-of-tune notes and off-beat rhythms two of its most defining characteristics. Additionally, punk used a lot of distortion and power chords, which gave the music a noisier sound. Punk vocals were also very crude, with a lot of shouting and roaring, which provided the lyrics with rage and a ranting character that most singers of the movida lacked. Therefore, the aesthetic experience of punk was also more oppositional to the mainstream and the "high culture" of the time than that of the movida. The first remained hard to listen to, while the second became increasingly pop-sounding and commercial. Furthermore, most of the music produced within the movida was much more danceable than punk's arrhythmic and unstable beat. In this way, punk's noise and rhythm would normally agitate the listener, while the movida would most likely make the listener tap their feet and enjoy the music, which is one of the reasons why the movida became a decisive representative of the CT during the 1980s while punk developed in more marginal contexts. In this sense, following Hebdige's interpretation of punk as a "mechanism of semantic disorder" (Hebdige 1979, 90) and Laing's idea of punk music as dissonance, we can conclude by saying that, ultimately, punk music's "bad" sound became not only a challenge to the dominant culture's aesthetics but also a way to force the listener to acknowledge "that uncomfortable noise" that interrupted the omnipresent and more enjoyable music of the movida. By doing so, the aural characteristics of punk music could be interpreted as a symbolic metaphor of all the protests and mobilizations that are generally overshadowed by the pleasant sounds of the movida and the narrative of an exemplary Transición.

## 5. Spanish Punk and the Movida Madrileña as Subcultures

From the perspective of subcultural formations, there are also crucial differences between punk and the movida madrileña. In "The

Construction of Youth in Spain in the 1980s and 1990s," Mark Allinson states that in the 1980s and '90s "Spanish youth culture is distinct in that its emergence from the heady excesses of a suddenly liberated post-Franco Spain deprives it of the social signification as deviance or resistance often associated with youth subcultures" (Allinson 2000, 265). For their part, Graham and Labanyi speak of youth culture during the Transición as the "official image of Spain" (Graham and Labanyi 1995, 312). In a similar line, Núria Triana Toribio states that "movida or Nueva Ola, were the names given to Spanish punk" (Triana Toribio 2000, 275). All these perspectives fail to see the complexity of Spanish subcultural formations and focus exclusively on Madrid and the movida to define the whole of the Spanish state. As I have discussed, Spanish punk culture is indeed deviant and resistant compared to the movida madrileña, and it is definitely not the official image of Spain. These scholars focus on the movida and, due to its aesthetic resemblance to US and British subcultures, view it as the epitome of Spanish subcultures, to the point of considering it the Spanish version of punk culture. Such perspectives result from an approach that relies on mainstream media and, therefore, the dominant culture to define Spanish subcultures—which is a clear incongruence. Had they looked at the fanzines, squat concerts, pirate radio stations, and the punk music being played in Barcelona or the Basque Country beyond the mainstream movida madrileña, they would have obtained a very different picture. The movida madrileña can be considered a subculture only in its early stages, before it started to benefit from institutional and media support. After this support, the movida madrileña became part of the CT and the dominant culture and, therefore, no longer a subculture. Such perspectives as those presented by the scholars mentioned above have resulted in many people overlooking the relevance of subcultures that never became mainstream, such as punk culture, as elements of resistance during the Transición. At the same time, it has contributed to viewing all youngsters of the 1980s as depoliticized hedonists and to perpetuating the idea of a docile Spain that did not question the Transición in any way.[47]

47 In "Pasotismo, cultura underground y música pop: Culturas juveniles en la Transición española," Fernán del Val Ripollés (2011) explores the political engagement of youngsters during the Transición and argues against the commonplace of seeing the Spanish youth as depoliticized during this period.

Following the CCCS conception of subcultures as cultures developed primarily in a working-class context that originate as resistance to the domination of upper-class culture, we also need to consider a few more things regarding Spanish transitional subcultures. As Fouce points out, the movida madrileña was primarily formed by "jóvenes de ascendencia burguesa fascinados por la modernidad de Londres y su contraste con la cultura española"[48] (Fouce 2002, 59). In *Lo que hicimos fue secreto,* the pioneering radio and record producer Mariskal Romero speaks in similar terms and states that the movida was a movement formed by "una gente de clase alta, que los padres no sabían qué hacer con ellos. Los Berlanga, Olvido . . . Todos venían de familias de dinero, no querían estudiar y no sabían qué hacer. Ven a los Sex Pistols y dicen: 'Esto es lo mío. No sé tocar, no sé hacer nada, pero puedo coger una guitarra y armar una bronca.' Y es así."[49] Similarly, Kaka de Luxe's singer, Fernando Márquez, "el Zurdo," explains that, while he came from a middle-class family, the rest of the band was formed by the elite of the moment: "Estaba desde el hijo del dentista del rey, que era Nacho, a Berlanga propiamente dicho, la Olvido que también en aquel momento no le iba mal, su madre trabajaba en representación de cosméticos y tal, osea, que se movía. Y se iban cada dos por tres a Londres y volvían con todo el material"[50] (Álvarez 2017).

If we move away from the movida and Madrid and focus on punk, however, we can easily notice that the involvement of the working class was more decisive, especially in the case of Basque punk. Iosu (Jesús María Expósito López), Eskorbuto's singer and guitar player, was the son of Galician immigrants who moved to the Basque Country looking for work. He lived his entire life in Santurtzi, on the left bank of the Nervión River, in the industrial and one of the poorest working-class areas of metropolitan Bilbao. Jualma (Juan Manuel Suáres Fernández),

48 Youngsters of bourgeois background fascinated by London's modernity and its contrast with Spanish culture.

49 Some high-class people, whose parents didn't know what to do with them. The Berlangas, Olvido . . . They all came from rich families; they didn't want to study and they didn't know what to do. They see the Sex Pistols and say: "This is my thing. I can't play, I can't do anything, but I can pick up a guitar and fuck shit up." And that's it.

50 From the son of the king's dentist, Nacho, to Berlanga himself, Olvido, who at that time was not doing bad, her mother worked representing cosmetics and stuff, so, she was doing well. And they would go to London every other day and come back with all the materials.

Eskorbuto's singer and bass player, was also the son of Galician immigrants and lived his entire life in Kabiezes, a small working-class neighborhood in Santurtzi. Finally, Paco (Francisco Galán Portillo), Eskorbuto's drummer, was from Navas del Madroño (Cáceres) and was himself an immigrant in Repélega, also a small working-class neighborhood in Portugalete (10 Cerdán). Similarly, Evaristo Páramos, singer of La Polla Records, was born in Tuy (Galicia) and grew up in Agurain (Basque Country), where his parents moved looking for work. For their part, the band members of RIP were all from Mondragón, home of the famous worker cooperative Mondragón Cooperative Corporation. Catalan punk band La Banda Trapera del Río were all from Cornellá, a working-class village on the outskirts of Barcelona, and the members of Barricada were from Txantrea, a working-class neighborhood in Pamplona known for its strong political activism during the dictatorship and the Transición.[51] For all these people, punk served as the vehicle to express their social and political disenchantment as well as to create an underground cultural scene that helped develop alternative cultural institutions such as occupied social centers, gaztetxes, pirate radio stations, independent record labels, and more. In this sense, even if there were also punks who were not necessarily from the lower strata, the working class's involvement shows that punk culture did provide important cultural possibilities for people who in the past were primarily consumers of upper-class culture.

Consequently, the importance of Spanish punk as a subculture relies not merely on whether it was purely a working-class culture but also on the doors it did open for the working class. For someone from the upper class, it might have been just a fun cultural movement and not necessarily an empowering tool—because they did not need to be empowered—but for those in the lower strata it was indeed a class "revolution." In this sense, it is not so much a question of whether subcultures presented resistance, because they were solely developed

51 In a 2015 interview on ETB, Barricada's bass player, "El Drogas," stated that he "[viene] más de los años 80, de las peleas callejeras, donde en la Txantrea la policía, para entrar al barrio, se las veía y deseaba, y una vez que entraba se las veía y deseaba para salir." (His background was the 1980s, street fights in which, in the Txantrea, it was almost impossible for the police to come into the neighborhood and, if they did come in, it was almost impossible for them to leave.) https://www.youtube.com/watch?v=LlGA9TuypWU.

by the working class, but of how subcultural practices such as a DIY ethos or the class opposition represented by unskilled musicians putting out their self-financed albums and competing with major record labels while spreading alternative social messages contributed to an oppositional movement of resistance for those in the lower strata. Therefore, stating that youth subcultures in Spain lacked "a social signification as deviance or resistance" by only looking at the movida madrileña is extremely inaccurate and undermining.

CHAPTER 3

# FIRST NEGATIONIST TOPOS: PUNK AS ANTI-TRANSICIÓN

In *El mono del desencanto*, Teresa Vilarós seeks an explanation for the alleged depoliticization and disenchantment of the Spanish population after Franco's death. In order to do so, she first identifies Franco and the Francoist regime as the centre around which all social events intrinsic to Spain's historic narrative were symbolically organized during the dictatorship. Some people opposed Francoism, and some were in favor of it, but Franco was nonetheless the center around which the narrative of their lives was symbolically organized. Then she proposes an understanding of the left's utopic post-Francoist Spain as an addiction that fueled the anti-Francoist leftist resistance and the nonmaterialization of this utopia as the reason why this leftist resistance vanished during the Transición. In her own words:

> Quiero proponer aquí la adicción como metáfora para la utopía más o menos marxista que alimentó a la izquierda española desde el final de la Guerra civil. La utopía fue la droga de adicción de las generaciones que vivieron el franquismo. La muerte de Franco señala la retirada de la utopía y la eclosión de un síndrome de abstinencia. [...] 1975 representó el fin de la utopía, la constatación del desencanto y el advenimiento del Mono.[1] (Vilarós 2018, n.p.)

1 I want to propose addiction as a metaphor for the more or less Marxist utopia that fed the Spanish left since the end of the civil war. Utopia was the drug of the addiction of

According to Vilarós, therefore, once Franco died and the Transición showed that a rupture with the previous Francoist government that would allow the materialization of that utopic Spain was impossible, the Spanish left collapsed into profound disenchantment. As a result of this, the Spanish population entered that postmodern stage Jean-François Lyotard referred to as "the end of grand narratives." There was not going to be any Marxist revolution that would create a utopic Spain, and all those leftist grand narratives dealing with human emancipation seemed more exclusively theoretical than ever. With this in mind, Vilarós portrays the movida madrileña as the cultural evidence of the ending of all grand narratives and utopias and the shift to hedonism and enjoyment of the present. At the same time, she explains that the movida is not simply the result of a nonmaterialized utopia, but also the youth's rejection of the grand narratives in which an older generation that grew up fighting Francoism believed. Therefore, the depoliticization of Spaniards during the Transición would also be the result of a profound generational clash and disconnection.

Having shown in the previous chapter that this alleged depoliticization is the result of a very limited analysis of the culture produced in Spain at the time, here I would like to propose an alternative response to the unsuccessful utopic Spain and the end of the grand narratives by looking at punk subculture's political resistance instead of at the movida's hedonism. In order to understand that alternative response, it is helpful to look at Raymond Williams's concepts of archaic, residual, and emergent cultures, as well as at Stuart Hall's idea of parent cultures. According to Williams, "Any culture includes available elements of its past, but their place in the contemporary cultural process is profoundly variable" (Williams 1977, 122). In this sense, he defines "archaic culture" as that "which is wholly recognized as an element of the past," and "residual" as that "which has been effectively formed in the past, but it is still active in the cultural process, not only and often not at all as an element of the past, but as an effective element of the present" (122). Additionally, he defines "emergent culture" as the "new meanings and values, new practices, new relationships and kinds of relationship [that]

---

those who lived during Francoism. Franco's death signals the removal of utopia and the outburst of the withdrawal syndrome. [. . .] 1975 represents the end of the utopia, the confirmation of the disenchantment and the emergence of the withdrawal.

are continually being created" (123). For his part, in the introduction to *Resistance Through Rituals*, Hall identifies working-class culture as the parent culture of which subcultures are a subset (Hall and Jefferson 2006, 7). He also states that, while there is a wider working-class parent culture to which subcultures are connected, "sub-cultures must exhibit a distinctive enough shape and structure to make them identifiably different from their 'parent culture.' They must be focused around certain activities, values, certain uses of material artifacts, territorial spaces etc. which significantly differentiate them from the wider culture" (7).

Punk inherited elements from its working-class parent culture that remained as residual culture, such as the neighborhood assemblies, the *ateneos libertarios* (infoshops), or the more general fight against capitalism, but it also differentiated itself by the incorporation of a new emergent culture that fostered a nonpartisan DIY ethos and that unified a larger correlation of forces that did not want to depend on institutional solutions to their problems. Therefore, punk did not simply fall into disenchantment and indulge in hedonism but continued to be politically engaged and showed a rupturist continuum. It simply did so through new practices and meanings that were different from those of the Spanish anti-Francoist left. Thus, common to both the movida and punk was a rejection of the grand narratives in which anti-Francoism believed; the former's response to it was to indulge in hedonism, while the latter's was to look for alternative ways of staying politically committed. Punk did not originate simply as an abandonment of the grand narratives that anti-Francoism believed in but rather as an active negation of them that allowed for new practices and ideas to emerge. In other words, while the movida was apolitical through lack of concern about any political narrative, punk was apolitical insofar as it rejected all previous political narratives in order to remain political in its own new, emergent ways. A tangible example of this is how punk's distrust toward institutional politics and the hierarchic structures of most anti-Francoist parties allowed for a strong and more hands-on DIY culture to develop. In this sense, the refusal to collaborate with traditional anti-Francoist parties, rather than the abandonment of politics, represented an alternative stance through which punk was able to develop a DIY culture that empowered individuals and effected an immediate change without having to wait for the grand narrative's revolutions to take place.

Similarly, the fact that punk would hardly ever explicitly align with any specific political orientation allowed for a more unified working class to develop, in which ideological confrontations ceased to be rooted in right versus left, or republican versus Francoist, dividing binaries. In fact, it is here, to a certain extent, that one can find the seeds of the 15-M's famous expression of not being "ni de izquierdas, ni de derechas," which allowed for a great number of people with different political backgrounds to come together in the 2011 protests. As La Polla Records stated in the song "Odio a los partidos" in 1987:

> Tío Marx está podrido, tío Mao está cagao
> Jesucristo está en mi culo y Buda en mi oreja
> Hitler tiene sucesores y nadie los ve
> […]
> En el nombre de una idea yo no me quiero morir
> Pensadores en sillones no me van a dividir
> Y tus bonitas banderas a mi espalda quedan
> […]
> A la mierda ideologías, ideólogos también
> No me sigas ni me adores que yo no te sigo a ti
> Allá tú y tu ideología … yo tengo la mía
> ¡Odio a los partidos, fuego a las banderas!
> ¡Odio a los partidos!
> Fuego, fuego, fuego, fuego, fuego[2]

Now, keeping in mind punk's continued political engagement and its visceral opposition to the different governments established after Franco's death, in this chapter I will explore Spanish punk's anti-Transición character from two different perspectives. Through a close reading of different albums and songs, in the first half of this chapter I will concentrate on exploring Spanish punk's rupturist discourse and the ways it has contributed to the development of anti-Transición and

2 Uncle Marx is rotten, Uncle Mao shat himself / Jesus Christ is in my ass and Buddha in my ear / Hitler has successors and nobody sees them / […] / On behalf of idea I don't want to die / Thinkers in armchairs will not divide me / And your beautiful flags stay behind me / […] / To the hell with ideologies, ideologists too / Don't follow or worship me, I don't follow you / I don't care about you or your ideology … I have my own / Hatred for the political parties, fire for the flags! / Hatred for the political parties! / Fire, fire, fire, fire, fire.

more general antiestablishment identities among Spanish youth. In the second half, I will focus on punk's politics of memory regarding the Civil War and the subsequent dictatorship.

### 1. Spanish Punk's Rupturist Discourse

In 1985, the Basque band Kortatu released their first album, *Kortatu*. The cover of the album portrayed a man holding an axe with his eyes covered as if they were trying to hide his identity. This man is dressed as an *aizkolari*, an athlete of the traditional Basque sport *aizkolaritza*. In this sport, each aizkolari competes to be the first to cut a set of logs. In addition to this, it is important to highlight that, in Basque, the ending *-atu* is the imperative form that many Latin verbs take—*deribatu, pintatu, akabatu, pentsatu*—and it is a common practice to add this ending to Spanish words to use the imperative when speaking Basque as a result of living in a permanent diglossic context.

For instance, instead of using the Basque verb *itzali* (turn off), many people would say *apagatu*, from the Spanish *apagar*. Taking this into account, and considering that *cortar* in Spanish means "to cut," for those familiar with Basque language, the word *kortatu* sounds like the imperative form of "to cut" (you, "cut!")—which could also be read as an order. At the same time, for those Spaniards not familiar with Basque language, the word *kortatu* would also resonate with the imperative form of "to cut" plus the personal pronoun "you" in Spanish: "corta tú." Thus, one could interpret the picture of the aizkolari and the band's name as an invitation or, more precisely, as an order for us to metaphorically cut or break with something. Along the same lines, the fact that the identity of the aizkolari is hidden could also be interpreted as a universalization of the aizkolari, telling us that anyone can go ahead and break with whatever we want. In the context of the Transición, and taking into account the songs on the album, it seems that this "cut" could also be interpreted as a "clear cut" or rupture with Francoism as an opposition to the reformist stance taken by the transitional governments, or even a rupture with the transitional process as a whole. Similarly, considering the specific references to Basque culture, this cover could also be interpreted as a rupture with Spain or the Spanish state from a Basque nationalist perspective.

This album includes songs such as "Tolosako Inauteriak," "Sarri Sarri," "Hernani 15/6/84," and "Sospechosos." "Tolosako Inauteriak"

Figure 12. Cover of *Kortatu*

starts with an *alboka* melody—a traditional Basque wind instrument—and a tambourine, both playing a traditional Basque song. After the intro, there is a short jazz/blues-sounding progression right before they move onto the ska rhythm that characterizes the rest of the song.[3] The lyrics talk about a carnival festivity in which a violent police charge occurred, and the music is based on a major key, which gives the song an unexpectedly cheerful character. Similarly festive in sound but this time also in lyrics, we find the song "Sarri Sarri," a cover of "Chatty Chatty" by Toots and the Maytals. Kortatu's version is slightly faster and is based on happy-sounding ska in a major key. As far as lyrics go, "Sarri Sarri" celebrates the 1985 prison escape of Joseba Sarrionandia, a Basque poet

3 It is important to note that Kortatu is known for being the first band in Spain to mix punk and ska music.

who had supposedly collaborated with ETA. "Hernani 15/6/84," for its part, is a song about the action conducted by the police in Hernani in 1984, when they killed two members of ETA by first throwing a grenade into a house and then shooting them. This was a controversial event in which some argued that the police tried to defend themselves—since the suspects also shot one of the police officers—while others, as is the case with Kortatu, state that the action was conducted specifically to kill them. Up until the 1:47 mark, the song follows a slow rhythm with an unusual echo effect in the lyrics, giving it a somewhat dark sound while the singer describes how the police entered the house: "Un horrible sueño mi cuarto en llamas / una granada todo lo incendiaba. / Entre las llamas yo disparaba / sombras verdes acechaban."[4] After this, the song speeds up, acquiring a more hardcore sound while the singer calls the police "asesinos a sueldo"[5] and says that they got a "buena recompensa por un etarra muerto."[6] This song connects with the criticism toward the GAL and Spain's state terrorism during the 1980s. Finally, the song "Sospechosos" refers to the ZEN plan implemented by the PSOE minister of the interior, José Barrionuevo. The song is based on a major key progression, and the lyrics are short and very direct:

> Lo siento, no lo puedo remediar
> Tu cara de culo nunca puedo aguantar.
> Barrionuevo y su plan Zona Especial N.
> Nos trae por fin La "seguridad."
> Sospechosos. Sospechosos.[7]

Finally, *Kortatu* includes other numbers that focus on more international issues, such as "Nicaragua Sandinista," dealing with the revolution against Somoza in Nicaragua, or "Desmond Tutu," a song about the famous priest and Nobel Prize winner Desmond Tutu, who fought against apartheid in South Africa.

If in this album we find songs that are critical of the political affairs of the time along with others that have a more festive tone, with their

4 A horrible dream, my bedroom on fire / a grenade set everything on fire. / I was shooting within the flames / green shadows lurked.

5 Hit men.

6 A good reward for a dead ETA member.

7 I'm sorry but I can't help it / Your arseface I could never stand / Barrionuevo and his Zona Especial N. plan / Finally brings us safety / Suspects. Suspects.

next album, *El estado de las cosas* (1985), Kortatu achieves a sharp critical and political character that became the definitive trademark of the band. In the book *El estado de las cosas de Kortatu*, Roberto Herreros and Isidro López include an interview with Kortatu's bass player, Iñigo Muguruza, in which he states that when they released the album *El estado de las cosas* "la actividad del GAL era terrible. Estabas acabando un concierto y te comunicaban que habían matado a cuatro refugiados mientras tu tocabas ska. A mí, personalmente, cosas como esta me quitaban las ganas de hacer canciones festivas"[8] (Herreros and López 2013, 157). The first song, "En la línea del frente" (On the front line), is a power-chord-based punk song in a major key with no ska sections. The lyrics are an invitation to fight in "batallas que no aparecen en los mapas."[9] In other words, social conflicts untouched by the mainstream media. In another interview included in the book, the band's singer, Fermin Muguruza, states that during the 1980s they lived "en la línea del frente" because they would go out "a la calle y te estaba buscando la policía, te estaban deteniendo, te estaban chequeando, te llevaban a comisaria . . . era todo así"[10] (Herreros and López 2013, 160). In this way, the song seems to be an invitation to all people who were suffering from police repression to get together and fight back. Next, we have the song "El estado de las cosas" (The state of things). This song is a clear declaration of intent of Kortatu's role as musicians: "Pero no importa, aunque me digas / que estoy metido en una causa perdida. / Como ves mi guitarra no dispara / pero sé dónde apunto, aunque no veas la bala."[11] Therefore, they see their musical activity as a way to fight against the current "state of things." Musically, the song is based on a straightforward major-key power-chord progression with significantly high levels of distortion. The chorus is based on a riff that stresses every downbeat in a 4/4 time signature, giving it a strong chanting/marching continuous rhythm. Along with these we also have "Hotel Monbar," a song based on an incident that occurred in Bayona (France) in which four members of ETA were shot

8 GAL's activity was terrible. You were finishing a concert and someone would tell you that they killed four refugees while you were playing ska. In my case, personally, these things killed my desire to write festive songs.

9 Battles that do not appear on maps.

10 To the street and the police was looking for you, they would arrest you, search you, take you to the police station . . . it was all like that.

11 But it doesn't matter, even if you tell me / that I am in a lost cause. / As you see my guitar doesn't shoot / but I know what's my target even if you don't see the bullet.

to death by some strangers. Further investigations discovered that those involved in the shooting were some men from Marseille hired to do so by the GAL. This song is in a minor key, and the vocals have a considerable amount of reverb effect, which gives the whole song a dark and sinister sound. In addition to this, the drums play a fast pattern and there are screaming backing vocals supporting the singer throughout the whole song. The song closes with a sample of Lluís Llach's bells in his song "Campanades a morts" (Strokes for the dead). Llach's song talks about the assassination of three demonstrators in the "sucesos de Vitoria" (Vitoria events) by the police.[12] Through this sample, Kortatu establishes a connection between two different events that had occurred already in democracy in which the state's force killed several people. Similar to "Hotel Monbar," they also included "9 zulo" (Nine holes) a song written by writer and later ETA member Mikel Antza, in which they talk about a young Basque man killed by the police. Additionally, in this song there is an invitation to resist with armed violence: "Mendiko bazterretan ba da 'zulo' ugari, handik armak hartuta, tira etsaiari!!!"[13] Finally, we also find the atypical "Esto no es el oeste pero también hay tiros" (This isn't the West but there are also shootings), a song in which they play a Tex-Mex-sounding punk/corrido and praise Billy the Kid and the Mexican Revolution for their armed struggle against the government, perhaps as an example of what they thought people should do in Spain.

The album's cover and inner booklet are as important as the songs. The front cover of *El estado de las cosas* features a picture of several anti-Francoist militants holding a shotgun next to the following line: "Irún (1936). Milicianos antifascistas defienden . . ."[14] Additionally, on the back cover we can also read the following sentence: "Bajo el fuego enemigo y alrededor de la *ikurriña* (bandera vasca), unos gudaris . . ."[15] By doing so, Kortatu seems to identify with the anti-Francoist sector of the Spanish population. Similarly, looking at the inner booklet, we find a drawing with the silhouette of a person who seems to have been

12 The "sucesos de Vitoria" refer to the events that occurred in Vitoria in 1976, when the police opened fire on a demonstration in which six thousand workers were demanding better working conditions, killing five people and injuring a hundred and fifty.

13 There are many holes in the mountain's corners, take the arms from there and go get the enemy.

14 Irún (1936). Antifascist militiamen defend . . .

15 Under the enemy's fire and around a *ikurriña* (Basque flag), some *gudari* (Basque anti-Francoist militia) . . .

**Figure 13. Cover of *El Estado de las cosas***

erased or covered with black ink. This person is Juan Carlos, the former king of Spain. It is unknown whether covering his image was the record label's idea or due to pressure by institutional means.[16] A couple of years later, in 1988, they published a short demo in Switzerland, *Unzensuriert*

16 It is important to remember that, even today, insulting the monarchy or the Spanish flag is a felony that can be punished with jail. In 2010, the punk band Ardor de Estomago released the single "Una historia real," in which they talk about Juan Carlos I's ties with Francoism and call him a "hijoputa" (son of a bitch), and they were taken to court and each of the band members was sentenced to pay a 900-euro fine. The magazine *El Jueves* also had a similar experience in 2007. When President Rodríguez Zapatero approved a 2,500-euro payment for every child born in 2007, this magazine published a drawing of Prince Felipe [soon to be King Felipe VI] having sex with his wife, Letizia, and the following phrase: "Te das cuenta? Si te quedas preñada . . . ¡Esto va a ser lo más parecido a trabajar que he hecho en mi vida!" Not only was the issue censored and the police confiscated copies from newsstands, but the cartoonists were fined 3,000 euros each.

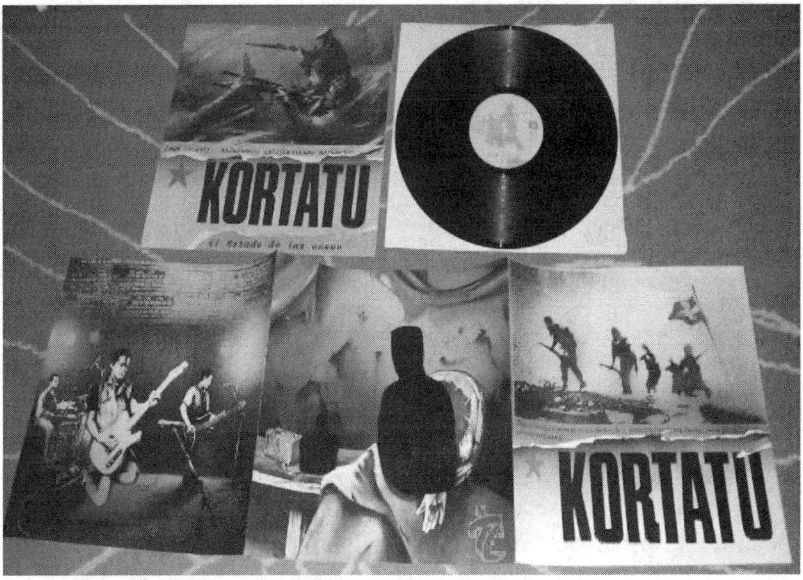


Figure 14. Inner booklet of *El Estado de las cosas*

(Uncensored), in which they used this same drawing without the black stain covering it—hence the title of the demo. In this image, we can see the king with half his head cut off and several cables coming out of his skull. These cables take the place of where one would expect the brain to be, somehow suggesting that the king has an electronic circuit instead of a human brain. Meanwhile, the head's top part is on a table connected to an electronic device as if being charged. This could be interpreted as the king having no brain and having to recharge it to think, or perhaps as a metaphor of how the transitional government is implementing a monarchic system that needs to be connected to a battery for extra energy due to its lack of popular support. In the inner booklet of the demo in which the image appeared without the black stain, we can also read that the money collected from its sales would be sent to the Salvadorean clandestine station Radio Farabundo Martí, which was part of the leftist armed band FPL (Fuerza Popular de Liberación) that fought several dictatorial governments in El Salvador during the 1980s.

Next, I want to propose that, through such a multiperspectivist and polymorphous rupturist discourse, Kortatu contributed to the development of anti-Transición and more general antiestablishment identities in at least two ways. The first is by engaging in a semantic

Figure 15. *Unzensuriert* 1

Figure 16. Cover of *Unzensuriert* 2

fight in which the Basque band and the CT dispute the definition of the Transición. The second is by making many of their political ideas become an intrinsic part of what it means to be a punk in Spain. If, with Marx, we understand that those who own the means of material production own the means of mental production as well (Marx 1998, n.p.) and that, as pointed out by the Birmingham School, upper-class culture always tends to subject working-class culture into its own way of understanding the world, Kortatu's discourse of rupture represents a short circuit in the CT's process of defining the Transición as peaceful and exemplary. Just as punk music represented a disturbing noise that interrupted the pleasant sounds of the movida, Kortatu's rupturist discourse falls like a lightning bolt that prevents the CT's definition of the Transición from becoming established. This does not necessarily mean that one needs to agree with Kortatu's viewpoints or opinions. It means that there is a different discourse from that constructed by those who own the means of mental production that is resisting the process of defining the Transición as peaceful and exemplary. As a result, alternative perceptions of the transitional process develop, and the ideas about the Transición through which upper-class culture would have subjected the working class are not as dominant as they could have been. Ultimately—and regardless of one's personal political ideas—what we have here is a semantic fight to define the Transición in which Kortatu, with its against-the-grain reading, is opening the possibility for more anti-Transición identities to develop.

In addition to this, Kortatu's work projects a fairly chaotic political identity that has often become synonymous with being a punk in Spain. Through the images of the anti-Francoist militia, for example, Kortatu seems to align with antifascism and suggest certain continuity between the fight against Franco and their own alleged fight during the Transición. At the same time, however, they seem to connect antifascism exclusively with the Basque Country when in one of the images we read that the militiamen are holding a Basque flag. In a similar way, they also connect Billy the Kid, the Sandinista revolution, and the antiapartheid movement in South Africa with the armed activity of ETA and fighting the government in Spain. Such random and, in several cases, rather arbitrary connections project a chaotic political identity that is susceptible of absorbing almost any social issue it encounters in its path. In this sense, anti-Fascism, anti-Francoism, Basque nationalism, anticolonialism, antiracism, and others all seem to come together as part of a single struggle in Kortatu's discourse. Additionally, Kortatu does not have a monopoly on presenting such chaotic political identities, and other bands such as Ska-P, Reincidentes, and Boikot could also belong in this same group. Bearing this in mind, what is truly important here is to realize how these political identities have, because of their recurrent repetition of themes, allowed for many of these issues to become intrinsic to what it means to be a punk in Spain. In this sense, borrowing Sarah Thornton's concept of "subcultural capital," we could say that in Spain being anti-Francoist, being in favor of the Sandinista revolution, supporting the independence of the Basque Country, and others have all, to a certain extent, become part of the "subcultural capital" one needs to acquire to be perceived as part of punk subculture. Moreover, if we establish an analogy with the way Butler understands gender, we could even say that several of the issues discussed in Kortatu's work have become a decisive part of the ongoing definition of "punkness" through a very particular "stylized repetition of acts" (Butler 1988, 520) regarding the performance of a specific Spanish punk identity. As a consequence of this, it would not be too far-fetched to state that all those individuals involved in punk subculture in Spain have probably been susceptible to agreeing with the political ideas presented by Kortatu and many other bands as part of their subcultural affiliation. To a certain point, this could explain the sympathy for the Basque Country's independence that many punks throughout Spain share or the reason why some non-Basque punk bands emulate Basque spellings in their writings, substituting *ch* for *tx*, *b* for *v*, *c* for *k*, and *c* for *z*.[17] Therefore, ultimately, rupturist discourses like Kortatu's present an opposition to the Transición not only because of the specific content of their lyrics but because they contribute to creating multiple political identities that, regardless of whether one agrees with them, do not align with those the CT and the government of the time aimed to foster in the new democratic Spain.

Although less diverse than Kortatu ideologically, the Catalan band L'odi Social also exemplifies a clear rupturist discourse. The cover of their first demo, *Que pagui Pujol*[18] (Let Pujol pay for it) (1986), shows four young men jumping over the metro barriers instead of paying to go through them. This image, in combination with the title of the demo, seems to be an invitation to social disobedience as a response to the wealth accumulated by the political class of the Transición and, perhaps, also the alleged impoverishment of the working class. Additionally, the people in the picture having their eyes covered in a similar way to that of the aizkolari on Kortatu's first album cover can be interpreted as an invitation for anyone to do it, as they will remain anonymous. The first song of the album, "Busca, busca" (Search, search), talks about unemployment and unfulfilled social promises: "Has de buscar curro / has de buscar una casa / has de buscar una novia / has de buscar un local / Sin curro no hay dinero para poder buscar."[19]

We must remember that this album was published in 1986, four years after the PSOE's victory in the general elections and right in the middle of the deep industrial reconversion conducted by this political party. At this time, youth unemployment rates in Spain were very high, and those young people who were told that a new and better democratic Spain was being born after the dictatorship discovered that, as a matter of fact, there were more job opportunities during

---

17 The names of the following bands can be a good example of this phenomenon: El Último ke Zierre, Konsumo Respeto, Manolo Kabezabolo, Envidia Kotxina.

18 Jordi Pujol is a Catalan nationalist politician who was the president of Catalonia from 1980 to 2003. In 2014 he admitted to having kept nondeclared money he inherited from his father in foreign banks for years. He then gave his children this money and they were able to develop different businesses with it. His son has been sentenced to jail for corruption, and many of his direct family members have been investigated for corruption due to large undeclared amounts of money.

19 You have to look for a job / you have to look for a house / you have to look for a girlfriend / you have to look for a rehearsal space / Without a job there is no money to look for them.

**Figure 17. Cover of *Que pagui Pujol***

the last years of Franco's regime than in the new democratic Spain. Such disenchantment connects with Albert Cohen's concept of "status frustration" (Cohen 1955, 131–32). According to Cohen, subcultures emerge as a response to the frustration caused by the deprivation of the social status we have learned to aspire to. From this perspective, subcultures would emerge as a reaction to the frustration at not being able to achieve this status and can result in illegal conduct to acquire that denied social status. In this sense, we could understand the call for social disobedience in Spanish punk culture during the Transición as a way to protest the youth's impossibility of achieving the great life that democracy seemed to promise them—one in which they would have a house, a job, and a partner, as L'odi Social's song says.

The feeling of frustration is even more evident in "Busca, busca" when they say that "te dirán con una sonrisa / que tienes que tener esperanza / que sigas buscando trabajo / que pronto lo encontrarás."[20] Musically, the song begins with a slow melody in E minor involving several semitones and fourth notes, which, along with the distorted tone, gives it a dark and slightly dissonant sound. After this, it speeds up gradually with a significantly inconsistent arrhythmic drumming. When the singer comes in, the song is already very fast and the singing becomes almost mumbling due to the difficulty of matching the lyrics to the speed of the music. All in all, the general vibe of the song is one of rush and anxiety, which could be viewed as an aural representation of the frustration showed in the lyrics as well. As usual, this sound also allows the band and the audience to shout and mosh in what could be seen as a cathartic experience. The next song on *Que pagui Pujol* is "La Fiesta Nacional" (The national celebration), a number in which the band denounces the brutality of bullfighting. This song features a similar vibe to that of "Busca, busca": fast and arrhythmic drumming, distorted guitars, and long singing lines that struggle to follow the rhythm of the music. The lyrics denounce the cruelty of bullfighting, something that would later become a common demand in Spanish punk culture as part of a broader fight for animal rights: "No es un deporte / no es una ejecución / no es un crimen / es el arte de matar."[21] Additionally, they emphasize bullfighting's character as the "Spanish national celebration"—as bullfighting is popularly known in Spain—which is also, to a certain extent, a questioning of the Spanish national identity.

After this, we have "Los cara de culo" (The arse-faces), a song dealing with torture techniques used by the police to obtain information in interrogations: "La bañera ya está llena / de todo lo peor / para sumergir la cabeza / del que ose protestar."[22] "La bañera" (The bathtub) is a torture technique in which one would be submerged intermittently in a bathtub often filled with feces, urine, and other substances, to cause a sensation of drowning. Such a technique is one of several used by the government during the 1980s in many of the investigations related to ETA—as the Basque government's study *Proyecto de investigación de la*

20 They will tell you with a smile / that you have to have hope / that you have to keep looking for a job / that you will find it.

21 It's not a sport / it's not an execution / it's not a crime / it's the art of killing.

22 The bathtub is full / of all the worst / in order to submerge the head / of those who dare to complain.

*tortura y los malos tratos en el País Vasco entre 1960–2014* directed by the forensic anthropologist Francisco Etxeberria attests.[23] (Etxeberria et al. 2017). In L'odi Social's case, however, they are not establishing any connection with ETA, and they seem to refer to this torture only as a metaphor for the different punishments any deviant attitude suffers, as the line "desprecian nuestra iniciativa, intentando dirigir tu vida"[24] shows. This song features the same fast drumming, distorted guitars, and almost mumbling lyrics to fit the speed of the song that we find in the previous ones. The following song, "Autobus nº 13," is thematically connected to the cover of the demo. In it we hear L'odi Social present themselves as "offenders" because they ride the bus without buying a ticket. It is at the end of the song that we see the connection with the name of the album, when they all shout, "Que pagui Pujol!" telling Jordi Pujol—president of the Catalan parliament during the Transición and until 2003—to pay for the bus tickets. Additionally, immediately after this, a single voice says, "Pujol, hijo de puta."[25] Finally, the last song of the album is "Gossos de cuadra." In this song, they insult the Catalan police and say that all they do is serve the interests of the Catalan political class. In regard to music, we still find the same style as with the previous songs: significantly noisy music, arrhythmic drumming, out-of-key singing, and a lot of shouting.

As was the case with Kortatu, L'odi Social's rupturist discourse provides an alternative narrative of the Transición that disputes the CT's definition of it as an exemplary process. Contrary to Kortatu, however, L'odi Social's discourse concentrates on the everyday battles of the working class of the time and does not project such a broad, all-encompassing, and multiperspectivist political identity. Before Kortatu's references to armed revolutions and antifascist resistance during the Transición, L'odi Social presents a discourse that complains about unemployment

---

23 To cite an example: "El juez ordenó que se realizara una prueba pericial... al comprobar que el relato del detenido sobre el lugar donde le practicaron 'la bañera' coincidía con un lugar donde . . . se encontraban las marcas de los utensilios que se habían utilizado para colocar una barra . . . para ser balanceado e introducido su cabeza en agua sucia y producir asfixia como forma de tortura" (385). (The judge ordered a forensic examination to be carried out . . . after confirming that the detainee's account of the place where he was subjected to "the bathtub" matched a location where . . . they found marks from tools used to set up a bar . . . used to make him swing and submerge his head in dirty water, causing asphyxiation as a form of torture.)

24 They despise our initiative, trying to direct your life.

25 Pujol, son of a bitch.

or not having enough money to pay for public transportation. In this sense, L'odi Social's rupturist discourse articulates an opposition to the Transición based on a chain of common working-class daily struggles rather than on remote political connections like those presented in Kortatu's discourse. As stated in "Busca, busca," L'odi Social's members want a job, a house, and to be able to have a worthy life with their partners and families. They are, therefore, less worried about Nicaragua's revolution or the racism in South Africa. In this sense, I want to propose that the discourse created by L'odi Social, in which they make specific references to several different problems regarding the working class of the time, has helped to give a stable anchoring point to the flux of possible social demands working-class punks could have had. Put differently, if, as is the case with Mikhail Bakhtin's idea of the novelist,[26] we understand that L'odi Social could never be a monoglossic voice that sends an original message but instead was merely a group of individuals selecting from myriad discourses and combining them in specific ways, one could view their songs as selections through which they bundle the issues their followers will eventually concentrate on. In this sense, L'odi Social's engagement primarily with materialist issues and the immediacy of their surroundings has probably been a deciding factor in their followers' avoidance of developing such all-encompassing and multiperspectivist political identities as the one presented in Kortatu's work. This could, for instance, explain the fact that, unlike in the Basque case, Catalan punk has seldom shown any sympathy for Catalan nationalism. By the same token, it could also explain the reason why Catalan punk has always been so explicitly close to anarchist collectives in Catalonia.[27] Ultimately, as far as punk's rupturist discourse is concerned, we could anticipate that this kind of materialist/everyday-struggle discourse—also shared

26 According to Bakhtin, in an environment of social heteroglossia, the novelist can choose the materials with which they assemble their novel "for the orchestration of his themes and for the refracted (indirect) expression of his intentions and values" (Bakhtin 1981, 292).

27 The fact that L'odi Social uses the Catalan language in the title of their album, in the acknowledgments, and in several of their songs, while also discussing anarchism and making its symbol an intrinsic part of their logo, substituting the "A" in "Social" for an "A" in a circle, is a good example of this. Another excellent example could be Joni D's fanzines (*N.D.F.*, *Melodias Destruktoras*, *Barnarock*, and others), as well as his book *Que pagui Pujol! Una crónica punk de la Barcelona de los 80*, which lacks the slightest reference to Catalan nationalism or any remote political causes but in which anarchist collectives and ideas appear constantly.

by bands such as Cicatriz, La Polla Records, Eskorbuto, Barricada, and others—would contribute to the development of a more profound working-class consciousness among their listeners and, consequently, to a stronger opposition of punks to the industrial and economic restructuring developed during the Transición by the government of the PSOE. Among other things, and contrary to Kortatu, L'odi Social's discourse would not result in micronationalist demands like those articulated by many Basque punks, contributing, in this way, to creating a stronger working-class bloc.

Moving away from northern Spain, even as far as the Canary Islands, we also find a strong rupturist discourse, as the band Guerrilla Urbana attests. Guerrilla Urbana released their first album, *Razón de estado* (National interest), in 1989 but had been active since 1983. Because of this, *Razón de estado* includes songs they had already been performing for several years prior to their album release. One of these songs is "Nemesio el mono" (Nemesio the monkey), a punk cover of the opening theme of the animated series *David el Gnomo* (David the Gnome) that denounces police brutality. The original chorus of the cartoon is as follows: "Soy siete veces más fuerte que tú, muy veloz, y siempre estoy de buen humor."[28] Guerrilla Urbana's version says, "Soy siete veces más chulo que tú, y un cabrón, y siempre estoy de mal humor,"[29] referring to policemen. In regard to the music, this song is in a happy major key, trying to emulate the original harmony and melodies in the cartoon's opening theme. Alongside this, we also find songs in which the band speaks of the Canary Islands as a Spanish colony. In "Canarias es una estafa" (Canarias is a fraud), for instance, we find a song that starts with a reggae-sounding intro and the singer saying the following lines:

> Canarias es una marca en un mapa militar
> un sin dios para el disfrute del turismo internacional
> un lugar de esquizofrenia y paranoia general
> hoteles, playas, sol y un puro,
> pero tú no vas a ver ni un duro.[30]

---

28 I am seven times stronger than you, very fast, and I am always in a good mood.

29 I am seven times more arrogant than you, and a bastard, and I am always in a bad mood.

30 Canarias is a mark on a military map / a great mess for the enjoyment of international tourism / a place of general schizophrenia and paranoia / hotels, beaches, sun, and a cigar / but you won't see a penny.

After this, the song speeds up and they play a fast hardcore-sounding second part in which they shout that "Canarias es una estafa" and they state that Canarias is "una colonia de un imperio de carton."[31] Along with these, *Razón de estado* includes songs about the Dirección General de Seguridad[32] such as "D.G.S.," more songs about the police such as "Seguridad Ciudadana," and various songs about state repression from many different perspectives such as "Muertos de asco" (Bored to death), "Con la mierda hasta el cuello" (Up shit creek), "Occidente agoniza" (The West agonizes), or "Estado Militar" (Militarized state). As was the case with Kortatu and L'odi Social, all these songs show an alternative reading of the Transición that challenges its definition as exemplary or peaceful. But regarding punk's rupturist discourse and its influence on the emergence of anti-Transición and antiestablishment identities, there are two songs in *Razón de estado* that I want to especially highlight now. These songs are "Enemigo interior" (Interior enemy) and "Transición mierdocrática" (Shitocratic Transition). In what follows, I will use these two songs and some from other bands to explore the last rupturist discourse I aim to discuss. This discourse is characterized by the articulation of a nonspecific "us versus them" dichotomy that, following a populist logic, allows for more people to come together and oppose the CT and the different governments of the Transición.

"Enemigo interior" speaks of several Francoist elements that, in Guerrilla Urbana's opinion, are still very much alive in the new democratic Spain. In this song, they speak about the repression used against "us"—referring, perhaps, to the Spanish youth, those dissident with the new democratic government, punks, or others—and they state that the repression occurs because "they" are the remaining enemies of a still-Francoist government. Then they speak of those who repress them, saying that "son los que antes apoyaban al general / y ahora se llaman demócratas / Son los mismos perros con distinto collar / Vosotros sois los terroristas / militares, jueces, políticos, fascistas."[33] After this,

31 A colony of a cardboard empire.

32 The Dirección General de Seguridad was an institution within the Spanish government in charge of ensuring the country's safety. However, "safety" is a relative concept, and this institution often repressed those who would oppose the government at the time, or young people who in their eyes look dangerous, such as, for instance, punks.

33 They are the same that supported the general / and now they call themselves democrats / They are the same dogs with different collars / You are the terrorists / military, judges, politicians, fascists.

they say that "we need to get rid of these people" and they shout that it is precisely because they want to get rid of these "militares, jueces, políticos, fascistas" that "we"—again referring to the band, punks, the Spanish youth, or others—"somos su enemigo interior" (We are their interior enemy). In "Transición mierdocrática," for its part, they denounce a direct connection between Franco's coup in 1936 and the governments of the Transición:

> Hace medio siglo que ocurrió
> que un general fascista lió la de dios
> ahogó al pueblo en sangre y de cadenas lo cargó
> Pues el leal caudillo, por la gracia de dios
> al fin le llegó la hora y como un perro murió
> rodeado por los buitres a los que él amamantó
> La transición a la democracia una estafa colectiva fue
> porque aún mandan los mismos que se alzaron en el 36
> Los que con las armas en la mano defendieron nuestra libertad
> fueron llamados terroristas enemigos de la sociedad
> y los que asesinaron al pueblo por gritar libertad
> son llamados los garantes de nuestra seguridad.
> ¡Que asco me dan![34]

In this song, Guerrilla Urbana questions the legitimacy of those politicians in charge of the transitional process because of the Francoist ties of many of them, something that became a trademark of Spanish punk during the Transición and later on. Yet contrary to the usual finger-pointing attitude of punk, these two songs are full of imprecisions, and it seems as if Guerrilla Urbana were avoiding certain references. Instead of clearly speaking of Franco and Francoists, for instance, they use expressions such as "los que antes apoyaban al general," "un general fascista," "el leal caudillo," and "los que asesinaron al pueblo por gritar libertad." In a similar way, instead of referring explicitly to the

34 It happened half a century ago / that a fascist general fucked it up really badly / He drowned the people in blood and covered them in chains / Well, the loyal *caudillo* (Franco), by the grace of god, finally reached his end and died like a dog / surrounded by all the crows he'd breastfed / The transition to democracy was a collective fraud / because the ones that conducted the coup in 1936 are still in power / Those who fought for our freedom with arms in their hands / were called terrorists, society's enemies / and those who killed the people for having shouted "freedom" / are called the guaranty of our security / They make me sick!

republicans, in "Transición mierdocrática" they speak of "los que con las armas en la mano defendieron nuestra libertad." Such imprecisions allow the singer to close the verse by referring to a nonspecified "they" that makes him sick, as well as to establish a vaguely defined "we" under expressions such as "nuestra libertad" and "nuestra seguridad." In the case of "they," and even if we lack an explicit reference, it is obvious that they are referring to the Francoist army. But who is the "we" they refer to? Considering their independentist stance, are they referring to the colonized citizens of the Canary Islands?

Still more abstract than in Guerrilla Urbana's case, in RIP's song "Escoria," on the album *No te muevas*, we find a very similar construction: "Nosotros somos escoria y escoria os vamos a dar / Nosotros sentimos odio y os vamos a hacer odiar" (We are scum and we will give you scum / We feel hatred and we will give you hatred). But who is this "you" and who are they referring to when they say "nosotros" (we)? The same goes for La Polla Records and their 1982 song "¿Y ahora qué?":

> Toda la vida comiéndome el coco
> pero ya veis que os sirve de poco
> no habéis conseguido prepararme
> para poder manipularme.
> ¿Ahora qué? ¿Ahora qué?
> ¿Ahora qué me vais a hacer?
> No podéis hacer nada contra mí
> queréis anularme, pero yo estoy muerto
> y sabéis que un muerto no puede morir
> ¿Ahora qué?[35]

Let's imagine a punk shouting that in the middle of the town square in 1982. Who are they referring to when they address that unidentified "you?" Is it the people in the town? What if they said that at an Apple Store today? What if they said it in a classroom? Moreover, what if they said it in a classroom in 1982 when the song was released? Finally, let's also take a look at Eskorbuto's song "Cuidado":

---

35 All my life you've tried to brainwash me / but you see you've achieved so little / You weren't able to prepare me / so that you could manipulate me / Now what? Now what? / what are you gonna do to me now? / You can't do anything against me? / You want to annul me but I am already dead / and you know that a dead man cannot die / Now what?

Gentes ignorantes que antes nos tenían miedo
cogen confianzas que nunca les dimos.
Cobardes, que van de valientes
hablando de nosotros mal ante la gente
Vuestro entorno huele a podrido,
vuestras palabras son ladridos
¡Cuidado! ¡Cuidado! Os avisamos,
somos los mismos que cuando empezamos[36]

Similarly to RIP's song, here we have not only a nonspecified dichotomy but a clear threat from the "we" to some other group we know nothing about. Therefore, the question remains the same: Who is "we" and who are they talking to?

Considering all the previous analysis, I would like to introduce my last idea describing the "us versus them" dichotomy as a twofold populist discursive mechanism. Taking this into account, I will look at both pronouns separately, focusing first on the "we" and then on the "them." In order to do so, I will borrow various ideas from Ernesto Laclau's conceptualization of "populism." According to Laclau, there are three preconditions for populism: "1) the formation of an internal antagonistic frontier separating the 'people' from power; 2) an equivalent articulation of demands making the emergence of the 'people' possible [...] 3) the unification of these various demands [...] into a stable system of signification" (Laclau 2005, 74). With this in mind, I suggest that the undefined "we" in punk is a substitute for "people," through which the frustrations of a sector of Spanish youth are unified under a single identity, creating a chain of equivalent complaints/demands. As a result, "we" establishes an "antagonistic frontier" separating these youngsters from power and creating a common popular/punk opposing identity.

As in Laclau's populism, all these demands will become part of a stable system of signification through "empty signifiers" such as "freedom" and "democracy." In this sense, young people with different frustrations such as not having a job, not earning money to rent a house with their partner, or having to work excessive hours would all

36 Ignorant people that were afraid of us before / take liberties we never gave them / Cowards that pretend to be brave / badmouthing us in front of people / Your environment smells rotten / your words are barks / Watch out! Watch out! We are warning you / We are the same as when we started.

agglutinate under the "we" through empty signifiers such as "justice." And here is where the "them" comes in. If there is an empty signifier that characterizes punk more than any other, it is "the system." "The system" can refer to the capitalist system, to the monarchy, to the patriarchy, to a colonial government, and more. As such, each punk with their own frustrations is able to identify in "the system" the alleged causes of their problems. Thus, I suggest that the "them" present in Spanish punk's discourse refers always back to this idea of "the system." In other words, "them" configures an undefined subject that can take the form of any of the demands punk youth might have and that equal the empty idea of "the system." In this same vein, I would further suggest that during the Transición "the system" would almost always refer to the different institutions included within the idea of the CT: the media, the government, the banks, the economic elite, the intellectuals of the Transición, and more. This could be an especially strong discursive mechanism if we consider how hundreds of people at concerts would sing together things such as "¡Cuidado! somos los mismos que cuando empezamos" (Look out! We're the same as when we started), all becoming part of one same group, even if in each case the "them" they are referring to is a different one. In fact, this could also be another way of explaining the confusion and transfer of concepts between punk and Basque nationalism in the context of Spain. At the end of the day, whether the system is the Spanish government, the police, or others, they could all easily fall under the undefined "them." Moreover, this could also explain the fact that neo-Nazi bands like Arma Blanca have Eskorbuto's song "Cerebros destruidos" as part of their repertoire. These are the last lines of the song:

> Perdida la esperanza, perdida la ilusión
> los problemas continúan, sin hallarse solución
> Nuestras vidas se consumen, el cerebro se destruye
> nuestros cuerpos caen rendidos, como una maldición
> El terror causando hábito, miedo a morir
> Ya estás muerto, ya estáis muertos
> ya estás muerto, ya estás muerto
> ya estáis muertos, muertos, muertos, muertos
> ¡Cerebros destruidos![37]

---

37 Lost hope, lost illusion / the problems continue / with no solution in sight / Our lives are consumed / our brains are destroyed / our bodies collapse, as if under a curse /

There is no way to tell who Arma Blanca were thinking about when they decided to play this song, but the "we" and the "them" are probably quite different to those imagined by Eskorbuto. In any case, it is the undefined quality of the "us versus them" dichotomy that enables them to appropriate and reinterpret the lyrics in their own way.

In this section we have considered four main ideas: a) punk as an alternative narrative of the transitional years that avoids the CT's definition of the Transición from becoming established; b) the projection of certain chaotic political identities that allow for specific ideas to penetrate the definition of punk in Spain; c) punk bands and their contribution to providing a stable anchoring point to the potential flux of demands working-class punks might have; d) punk's "us versus them" populist discursive mechanism and its role in creating a unified "us" and a vague "them" that can take almost any referent. All of them point to not only ways in which Spanish punk has opposed the Transición but also ways in which punk has influenced a more continuous emergence of antiestablishment identities. Next, I will focus on punk and its politics of memory regarding the Civil War and Franco's fascist dictatorship.

## 2. Spanish Punk and Its Politics of Memory

According to many scholars, discussing the Civil War and Franco's regime was seen as a destabilizing threat by different sectors of society during the Transición, and a will to forget the past and to move on impregnated politics, culture, and general life. In *Memory and Amnesia*, Paloma Aguilar states that "throughout the Spanish Transition a tacit pact was formed among the most visible elites in order to silence the bitter voices of the past which caused such unease within society" (Aguilar 2002, xx). In her work, Aguilar studies the importance of collective memory in processes of social change. Among other things, she states, "Individual and collective memory coexist, and, although they do not always coincide, the most important aspect for the stability of a regime is that they should not seriously contradict each other" (2). From this perspective, one could think that the confrontations between Francoists and republicans could have evoked contradictory

---

Terror becomes a habit, fear of dying / You're already dead, you're all already dead / You're already dead, you're already dead / You're all dead, dead, dead, dead! / Destroyed brains!

memories and made it impossible for a common collective memory to succeed and that, therefore, forgetting each sector's specific memory was considered a necessary sacrifice by many during the Transición. It is precisely for this reason that, as Aguilar states, although Francoism first proudly legitimised the dictatorship as the "reward" for having won a war, during the Transición, Francoists started to refer to the war as a fratricidal conflict in which both nationals and republicans were partially guilty (266–67). Through this change of discourse, Francoism tried to participate in a new collective memory that would ignore the fact that the Republic was based on a legitimate and democratically elected government and that Franco had conducted an illegitimate coup that was decisive in the development of the Civil War and the subsequent dictatorship.

Along similar lines as Aguilar, Salvador Cardús i Ros states that the Transición "depended on the erasure of memory and the invention of a new political memory" (Cardús i Ros 2000, 19) and claims that, in this sense, memory "is not so much the interpretation of the past as a justification of the present in terms of certain expectations about the future" (24). From this perspective, overlooking the specificities of the past and pushing forward an idea of collective guilt in relation to the Civil War and the dictatorship can also be seen as a strategy for a future Spain in which "old confrontations" cease to exist. In fact, for a long time, this has been the argument used by the Spanish right, represented in parliament by the Partido Popular, to justify its opposition to changing the names of streets named after Francoists, or to stop the unearthing of executed people still buried across over 2,500 mass graves, among other things. It is always relevant to remember that, according to the association Juezas y jueces para la democracia, Spain is the country with the second-largest number of mass graves and disappeared people, exceeded only by Cambodia (Junquera 2013). Yet despite how hard the architects of the Transición may have tried to create a peaceful collective memory by forgetting past frictions, there are individual memories and memories that dissent from official memory, which will always challenge the collective narrative of a shared guilt if there is no complete reparation and all wounds are not properly closed. Simply forgetting the past leaves many unresolved issues, and it is a matter of time until those same problems return to the forefront—as the current discussions regarding peripheral nationalisms, the republic versus monarchy debate, or the recent trials of policemen who tortured anti-Francoists still alive today, among others, attest.

From a cultural perspective, Jo Labanyi refers to these unresolved and partially forgotten issues as "ghosts" because she believes that, while buried in the past, they keep appearing in some writers' and directors' works, even if only in "spectral form" (Labanyi 2000, 65). Labanyi states that "in many respects, contemporary Spanish culture—obsessed with creating the image of a brash, young, cosmopolitan nation—is based on a rejection of the past," but she also suggests that "the current postmodern obsession with simulacra may be seen as a return of the past in spectral form" (65). She relies on Freud and Derrida to explain this idea, borrowing from Freud the concepts of "melancholia" and "mourning" and from Derrida that of "hauntology." "Melancholia" is when the unresolved past "take[s] over the present and convert[s] it into a 'living death,'" in a painful pathological process, and "mourning" would be when one offers the past "habitation in order to acknowledge their presence" in a healing way by "lay[ing] the ghost of the past to rest by, precisely, acknowledging them as past" (65). In this way, we can acknowledge the past of the dictatorship and the Civil War, pay homage to the affected people and provide the deserved reparation, and then move on and look forward (mourning), or we can try to forget everything without resolving the issues and freeze the pain forever (melancholia). The latter would result in the past lingering on in the present and, while the issues might not persist in their full form, they will still be present as the traces of "living death." Through the concept of "hauntology," Derrida refers to the return of the ghosts of the past and to the past itself "as that which is not and yet is there" (66). Labanyi connects these three ideas with the way in which the past manifests itself in contemporary Spanish cultural production. She speaks, for instance, about the "oppressive silences" in *El espíritu de la colmena* (1973) and *El sur* (1983); about "the image of snow blotting out the traces of landscape and with it memory" in *Luna de lobos* (1985) and *Escenas de cine mudo* (1994); and about "the traumatic crisis of memory related to a geographical displacement or 'loss of place'" (Labanyi 2000, 67) in Antonio Muñoz Molina's *Beatus Ille* (1986) and *El jinete polaco* (1991). Similarly, she also cites *Caudillo* (1977) and *Canciones para después de una Guerra* (1976) as films that "construct an alternative history through the articulation of popular memory, combining voice-over personal memories with a varied range of cultural trivia" (71). In all these cases, Labanyi argues that the past manifests itself even if it is in its absence. Leaving aside this postmodern take, I will now argue that, in Spanish punk culture, the past is not forgotten, and issues of the past do not appear as ghosts but in their full presence.

In 1987, a year after the incidents in San Isidro's festivities, La Polla Records put out their album *No somos nada* (We are nothing). In it they included a song with the same title. This song represents one of the most powerful exercises of historic memory in all of Spanish cultural production since Franco's death until that moment. The song begins with a smooth harmony in a major key in 3/4 time. After a few instrumental bars, Evaristo starts speaking in a very soft voice as if he was talking to some children: "Queridos amiguitos, en este mundo todo está bajo control." Then he asks sarcastically, "¿Todo?" and answers, saying, "No!" with a growling voice.[38] Immediately after this, he recites almost the exact same lines from the opening of the *Asterix* animated films: "Una aldea poblada por irreductibles galos resiste ahora y siempre al invasor con una poción mágica que les hace invencibles: el cerebro."[39] In the cartoons, Asterix was part of a Celtic village in France that resisted the invasion of the Romans during the expansion of the Roman Empire, using a magical potion that gave them incredible strength. In the song "No somos nada" it is their mind that allows the village Evaristo is talking about to resist the invader, not a magic potion. The listener cannot tell yet whom Evaristo is talking about, but they will soon find out that he is talking about the descendants of the republicans resisting the remaining Francoism in Spain. After this short waltz-sounding introduction, a melodic arrangement played by some bagpipes and some distorted guitars comes in. Bagpipes are traditionally viewed as a popular instrument and have a strong connection with the lower strata. They are not taught at conservatories, there is no such thing as a major degree in bagpipe, and most people learn to play them by ear in traditional Celtic music ensembles and not by learning Mozart's repertoire from music sheets. Had La Polla Records included violins or a piano, the sound would have probably sent a different message.

---

38 My little friends, in this world everything is under control... Everything? No!

39 A village inhabited by indomitable Gauls resists the invader now and always with a magic potion that makes them invincible: their brains.

Through the inclusion of bagpipes, La Polla Records is identifying itself as part of the Spanish lower classes, which will help connect the song with a republican and anti-Francoist position. A few bars after this, Evaristo comes in, revealing the main theme of the song: "Somos los nietos de los obreros que nunca pudistéis matar / por eso nunca, nunca votamos para Alianza Popular / ni al PSOE ni a sus traidores ni a ninguno de los demás / Somos los nietos de los que perdieron la Guerra Civil."[40] Through these lyrics, La Polla Records creates a "we versus you" dichotomy in which the descendants of the republicans are still opposing the current politicians because, as the band seems to suggest, they are the same as those who tried to kill their grandparents. In other words, La Polla Records claims that Francoism still prevails in the new governments of the Transición. Afterward, the whole band shouts the chorus: "No somos nada."[41] Through this chorus they seem to be denouncing the amnesia suffered by a great percentage of the Spanish population regarding their country's past. In other words, what they seem to be suggesting is that republicans are nothing because the consequences they suffered after the Civil War and the dictatorship have not been repaired and because they are still forgotten across the over 2,500 mass graves. Immediately after this, they repeat the very first line after the bagpipe arrangement ("Somos los nietos de los obreros que nunca pudistéis matar . . .") and then add that they are not "punk, ni mod, ni heavy, rocker, ni skin, ni tecno," perhaps pointing out that the amnesia with the Spanish republicans is not a matter of a specific subculture and that they do not believe in the working-class division that subcultures establish. Then they talk to this Francoist "you" again, stating that they will not be deceived by them, and repeat the first lines, saying several times that they are the children of those who lost the Civil War. At the end of the song, all the members of the band come together and shout that if "quieres identificarnos, tienes un problema."[42] In connection with not being part of any specific subculture and claiming that they are nothing, this could also be interpreted as saying that they do not relate with any of the political parties, or that they do

40 We are the grandchildren of those workers you could not kill / that's why we never ever vote for Alianza Popular / neither for the PSOE nor for their traitors or any other party / We are the grandchildren of those who lost the Civil War.

41 We are nothing.

42 You want to identify us, you have a problem.

not feel represented by any of the current leading political forces in Spain. But within the context of the amnesia of the Francoist past, one could also interpret being difficult to identify as part of republicans not being recognized and given the deserved reparation. We could even go further and talk about identifying the bodies of the executed republicans. Finally, the song closes with a military rhythm on drums accompanied by a melody that resembles a military bugle call, which could be interpreted as a call to fight or even as an aural reminder of the Civil War.

That same year, 1987, Olor a Sobako (Armpit Smell) and Tarzán y su puta madre buscan piso en Alcobendas released a joint album: *Madrí, qué bien resistes!* (Madrid, you resist so well!). This is a line from a song with multiple lyrics that the republicans sang during the Civil War. Probably the most famous version is the one called "El puente de los franceses" (The bridge of the French). In this song, the republicans sang about Francoists trying to take over Madrid during the Civil War and how the republicans resisted. The bridge is used to say that the Francoists cannot make it anywhere beyond it. Additionally, the lyrics mention that the republicans laugh at Francoist bombs because they are incapable of passing through. The melody of "El puente de los franceses" is based on that of "Los cuatro muleros" (The four muleteers), a traditional Andalusian song whose most famous recording is probably Federico García Lorca's version with the Argentinita. In Olor a Sobako and Tarzán's joint album, the latter conduct a punk cover of another version of this song titled "Los cuatro generales" (The four generals). In this case, the song talks about Francisco Franco, José Sanjurjo, Emilio Mola, and Gonzalo Queipo de Llano. These four people were the colonels in charge of the 1936 coup that ultimately imposed Franco's dictatorship, after the three-year Civil War. The lyrics mention that the four colonels have risen against the government and will be hanged by Christmas Eve, and these figures are included in the cassette's inner booklet in a picture along with what appear to be bloodstains. This constitutes both an exercise of historic memory through the recuperation of the melody and lyrics of popular republican songs and an update by playing them in a punk style.

Another band that is notorious for their reflections on historic memory is Habeas Corpus. Although they released their first album in 1995, they are inheritors of the punk culture developed during the

**Figure 18. "Los cuatro generales" in *Madrí, qué bien resistes!***

1980s, as their album *Subversiones* (2005), in which they recorded five renditions of previous Basque punk songs, shows. In this sense, they are evidence of the continuation of punk's discourse of memory throughout the years, and they will allow me to establish a connection between early punk's politics of memory and those of more contemporary productions such as Barricada's *La tierra está sorda* (The earth is deaf) (2009) and *En la memoria* (In memory) (2010). The first song of Habeas Corpus's debut album, *Sociedad mecanizada* (Mechanized society), is titled "Historia, memoria" (History, memory), and in it they reflect upon the relationship between history and memory from a general perspective: "Si el hombre posee escasa memoria / aún esconde peores intenciones [. . .] Llega entonces el momento de la exclusión cuando solo los más aptos sobreviven [...] Historia, memoria."[43] With lines such as these, Habeas Corpus addresses the construction of history and its memory as spaces in which power and hegemony are disputed and, hence, also spaces in which hegemony can be contested.

This stance on history connects with Walter Benjamin's "Theses on the Philosophy of History." Benjamin criticizes historicism by differentiating it from historical materialism. According to Benjamin, historicism's "method is additive: it musters a mass of data to fill the homogeneous, empty time," whereas "materialistic historiography, on the other hand, is based on a constructive principle" (Benjamin 1968, 262). In this way, while "historicism contents itself with establishing a causal connection between various moments in history" (263), a historical materialist thinks through history, "stops in a configuration pregnant with tensions [and] it gives that configuration a shock, by which it crystalizes into a monad." In this crystalized moment of tensions, the historical materialist aims to "seize hold of a memory as it flashes up at a moment of danger" (255). Consequently, it is in these crystalized monads, in these memories flashing up at a moment of danger, that the historical materialist can reconstruct a "revolutionary chance in the fight for the oppressed past" (263). Put differently, history does not occur in a homogeneous continuum of consequences; history is the result of moments of tension in which things could have been different and the whole history of the human race could have gone in a different direction. Freezing these moments to analyze them and identifying these alternative directions in which history could have gone, as well as acknowledging all those forgotten individuals who never became part of the official history of the victorious, is a must for the historical materialist. When in "Historia, memoria" Habeas Corpus states that "llega el momento de la exclusion, solo los más aptos sobreviven"[44] or that "se olvidan que hubo un frente que se cobró más vidas que todos los desembarcos de Normandía,"[45] they place themselves in this way of understanding history and memory.

In fact, Habeas Corpus seems to embody the role of this historical materialism in several different ways. In addition to "Historia, memoria,"

---

43 If man has limited memory / he hides yet worse intentions [...] That's when the moment for the exclusion comes when only those most fit survive [...] History, memory.

44 The moment for the exclusion comes when only those most fit survive.

45 There was a front that claimed more lives that all the Normandy landings.

their first album includes a song called "Miseria," in which they talk about the working class's passivity in the face of social injustice and speak of history and memory as the main factors that foster such passivity:

> La peor versión de los más bellos sueños
> engorda los libros de historia
> dictados por todos los asesinos que
> en este mundo han existido
> Ante tal hipocresía
> el carácter se destempla
> y me traiciona la memoria[46]

What Habeas Corpus state here is that those who have killed the most people in the world—equating this to Benjamin's idea of the "victorious" and "barbarous" in history—have been those who have written the history books and filled them with "beautiful dreams" to which the working class aspires, forgetting their past struggles and only seeing the possibility of a brighter future. This is the same idea that Benjamin discusses in his thesis XII, stating that "social democracy thought fit to assign to the working class the role of the redeemer of the future generations" and that, by doing so, the working class forgot "both its hatred and its spirit of sacrifice, for both are nourished by the image of enslaved ancestors rather than that of liberated grandchildren" (Benjamin 1968, 260). In this way, the working class, by forgetting the past and aspiring to the "bellos sueños" (beautiful dreams) they might be able to achieve in the future, turns into a passive mass in the face of injustice and inequality. Throughout Habeas Corpus's discography we can find other songs that present a similar discourse, such as "Eso que ellos llaman paz" (That which they call peace) and "Bajo un manto de olvido" (Under a layer of oblivion). In "Eso que ellos llaman paz," Habeas Corpus denounces the manipulation of history and memory to make the current state of things appear as the best possible and most peaceful reality, as well as its role in fostering passivity:

> Investigar sobre el sufrimiento
> viene a ser una constante de nefasto recuerdo

46 The worst version of the most beautiful dreams / fill up the history books / dictated by all the assassins / that have existed in this world / Before such hypocrisy / the character weakens / and memory betrays me.

Es un extremo que plantea iguales
dudas al querer ser explicado
y al pretender que sea aceptado
Son demasiadas las voces
que partiendo de ese fatal razonamiento
no tardarán nada en abandonar cualquier aspiración
por corregir los errores que demuestra
este mundo agotado en sí mismo[47]

In these lines, Habeas Corpus states that trying to understand suffering is limited by a bad memory and that, as a result, it poses as many doubts as those created by people who argue that we should simply accept the world as it is. After this, they claim that those doubts and confusion result in many people not understanding the origin of such suffering and abandoning any aspiration they had to change the state of things. A bit later in the song, they argue that "la historia del hombre incluye todas las mentiras / capaces de ser ideadas por su mente, / y por verdad puede entenderse el / que hasta hoy es el mayor ejemplo de hipocresía."[48] The word "hipocresía" here refers to defining our current world as the best possible and most peaceful reality, which seems clear again when they say that "eso que ellos llaman paz es otra forma de muerte."[49] For its part, in "Bajo un manto del olvido" we find a very explicit denunciation throughout the entire song:

El tiempo pasa y juega . . . juega y pasa a vuestro favor
La historia pasa y juega . . . juega y pasa. (x2)
Enterrad la historia bajo las ruinas de la desmemoria
Bajo un manto de silencio y otro de revisionismo
Sepultad la memoria en la fosa común del olvido
donde no alcance la luz ni el recuerdo de los vivos
Enterrad a los muertos

---

47 Researching the suffering / turns into constant awful remembering. / It's an extreme that presents the same / doubts when one tries to explain it / and when it's expected to be accepted / There are too many voices that / taking that fatal thought as a starting point / won't wait for too long to abandon any aspiration / to amend the mistakes that show / this self-exhausted world.

48 Man's history includes all the lies / his mind is capable of coming up with, / and it can be thought of as truth / what until today is the greatest example of hypocrisy.

49 That, which they call peace, is another form of death.

y también enterrad a los vivos
¿Bajo qué? Bajo un manto de olvido
Hasta que todo pierda sentido
¿A quién le importa saber quiénes fuimos
cuando hoy ni siquiera sabemos quién somos?
[...]
Reinventad la historia. Dadle vuestra propia forma
Escribidla de tal modo que no se os escape nada
Convertidla en mito o en pasto de las llamas
Borrad sus testimonios, y reducidlos a cenizas
Enterrad a los muertos
y también enterrad a los vivos[50]

In relation to Spain's Francoist past, Habeas Corpus also presents a clear discourse of resistance. In their 2000 album *A las cosas por su nombre* (Say it like it is), they include a song of the same name that is probably their best-known number. In it they start by questioning the construction of history and memory from a general perspective as in the previous songs:

Sabemos que las buenas palabras
son el maquillaje más habitual utilizado
por la mentira para de este modo mostrarse atractiva
Sabemos que esos a los
que llaman creadores de opinión, expertos tertulianos
rigurosos historiadores son la voz de su amo
la voz de la que nos sentimos esclavos[51]

---

50 Time passes and acts... acts and passes in your favor. / History passes and acts... acts and passes. / Bury the history under the ruins of oblivion. / Under a layer of silence and a layer of revisionism. / Bury memory in oblivion's mass grave / where neither light nor the memory of the living can reach. / Bury the dead / and bury the living too. / Under what? Under a layer of oblivion. / Until everything loses all sense. / Who cares about knowing who we were? / When today we don't even know who we are? / [...] / Reinvent history. Give it your own shape. / Write it in such a way that leaves no gaps. / Turn it into a myth or into burning ashes. / Erase its testimonies and reduce them to ashes. / Bury the dead / and bury the living too.

51 We know that kind words / are the most common makeup used / by lies to, in this way, appear more attractive. / We know that those whom we call / opinion makers, expert scholars, / rigorous historians are their master's voice / the voice by which we feel enslaved.

In this song, Habeas Corpus begins by calling attention to the relationship of the media and historians to those in positions of power. The Madrilenian band is denouncing what Althusser referred to as the "ideological state apparatus," which is also the backbone of the cultural framework represented by the CT and what makes the latter become the dominant culture in Spain. As is well known, according to Althusser there are two ways in which the dominant power maintains its hegemony: by violence and by ideology. With this in mind, he establishes a distinction between the state institutions that work through violence, the RSA (repressive state apparatus), and those who do it by ideology, the ISA (ideological state apparatus). The RSA would include institutions such as the police, the army, the prison, and the courts, among others. The ISA, on the other hand, includes institutions such as school, the media, the culture industry, and others. By stating that the "creadores de opinion," "expertos tertulianos," and "historiadores" are "la voz de su amo," Habeas Corpus is identifying them as part of the ISA and denouncing that they work to perpetuate the dominant power's hegemony. After a few more general lines like these, the band focuses specifically on the Francoist past of Spain and the new democratic state after Franco's death, stating that we should "say it like it is":

> A las cosas por su nombre
> La monarquía española es
> la más directa herencia del franquismo
> La transición a la democracia
> el ejemplo perfecto del fiel continuismo
> Adaptarse a los nuevos tiempos
> exigía esa amnesia que llaman consenso
> Los partidos de izquierda dejaban de serlo
> Los de derecha decían ser de centro
> Los sindicatos mayoritarios, culpables de la mayor
> de las traiciones cometida a los trabajadores
> pasaban a convertirse en funcionarios
> Y la constitución española
> cadena que aprieta, cadena que ahoga
> Cadena del todo todopoderosa
> La norma suprema

La ciega obediencia[52]

From here onward, the song reflects on the transitional process to denounce the subjective character of the construction of Spain's recent history in a way that resembles the message seen in Guerrilla Urbana's "Transición mierdocrática." In this case, however, and since Habeas Corpus wrote this song at the end of the twentieth century, they had greater temporal perspective and provided a significantly deeper analysis. They started by denouncing that the monarchy was a Francoist inheritance and that the Transición represented a continuity with Francoism.[53] Then they brought up the idea of Spain's general "amnesia" in order to achieve what the architects of the Transición would refer to as "consenso"—which chimes with Aguilar's idea of the need for a collective memory or, at least, individual memories that "do not contradict each other" (Aguilar 2002, 2) for the stability of a political regime. Such amnesia would imply not only the construction of history but also other things, such as the general amnesty granted in 1977. Along these lines, the band also refers to the Spanish constitution as "norma suprema" and "ciega obediencia" that connects with a long-standing tradition of questioning the constitution's legitimacy and its necessary modification to adapt to contemporary Spain. Such questioning originates because the constitution was written and voted on in exceptional conditions due to the conflictive and unstable scenario of Spain immediately after Franco's death and the lack of a process for constitutional amendments through general voting or for another referendum ever since. By the end of the song, Habeas Corpus focuses on even more specific things and, after saying that we should "say it like it is," they make their final statements:

La bandera española es la bandera fascista.
El ejército español, el ejército fascista.

---

52 Say it like it is / The monarchy is the most direct heritage of Francoism / The transition to democracy / is the perfect example of a loyal continuism / Adapting to new times / demanded that amnesia they called consensus / The left-wing parties stopped being left-wing / The right-wing parties would say that they are "center" / The majority unions, guilty of the biggest / betrayal ever committed against workers / they became governmental civil servants / And the Spanish constitution / chain that tightens, chain that chokes / Almighty chain of everything / The supreme law / The blind obedience.

53 Juan Carlos I, king of Spain, was elected by Franco before his death to continue his regime.

> La policía española, la policía fascista.
> La clase política, la clase fascista.
> Por su nombre. A las cosas por su nombre. (x2)[54]

Additionally, Habeas Corpus has also composed songs about the republicans and other victims of the Francoist regime and the Civil War as a way to contribute to their remembrance. In "Fascismo nunca más" (Fascism never again), for instance, they start the song with a sample of the famous last "parte oficial de Guerra" read on the radio to declare the end of the Civil War in 1939:

> Parte oficial de Guerra del cuartel general del generalísimo correspondiente al día de hoy 1º de abril de 1939, tercer año triunfal. En el día de hoy, cautivo y desarmado el Ejército Rojo, han alcanzado las tropas nacionales sus últimos objetivos militares. La guerra ha terminado.
> Burgos, 1º de abril de 1939, año de la victoria.
> El Generalísimo Franco.[55]

Then, after this intro, they state that what the victory of the fascist brought was "miseria" (misery), "dolor" (pain), and "death" (muerte) and that in order to honor those "defeated" they shout: "fascismo nunca más" (fascism never again) and "no pasarán" (they shall not pass). Additionally, they add several lines in Galician-Portuguese, Basque, and Catalan, as, perhaps, a more inclusive way to remember all those repressed individuals during Francoism whose main language was not Spanish. In the song "Una cuenta pendiente" (Unfinished business), for its part, the band states that leaving the past behind in order to move forward is not an option when they say that "claro que no, no basta con decir que aquello ya pasó / que el tiempo cierra las heridas, porque no / que hay que mirar hacia el futuro / porque es insultante y

---

54 The Spanish flag is the fascist flag. / The Spanish army, the fascist army. / The Spanish police, the fascist police. / The political class, the fascist class. / Like it is. Say it like it is.

55 Official war notice from the generalissimo's headquarters regarding today 1 April 1939, third victorious year. Today, the Red Army is captive and disarmed, the national troops have reached their last military objectives. The war is over.
Burgos, 1 April 1939, year of the victory.
Generalissimo Franco.

resulta sangrante ver que no."[56] And they demand "dignidad, memoria y verdad"[57] because "tenemos aún pendiente una cuenta que saldar, / dignidad, memoria y verdad, / con la España victoriosa, con la España triunfal."[58] Similarly, they have a song called "Ay de los vencidos" (Oh, the defeated ones) in which they remember those defeated in the Civil War and they demand reparations. Additionally, they state that those republicans defeated during the Civil War were killed twice, first literally, and second because they were unacknowledged in the new democratic state:

> Nunca habrá reconciliación
> mientras desde las cunetas
> se oiga el grito desgarrador
> de los muertos que las pueblan.
> Nunca hubo paz ni piedad ni perdón.
> Si hablaran los paredones . . .
> Nadie como ellos conoce el dolor
> de los malos españoles.
> [. . .]
> Dos veces muertos,
> dos gritos, dos lamentos.
> Los dos cobardes, los dos crueles, los dos en silencio.
> Primero el fuego, luego el olvido[59]

In addition, there are many other punk bands that wrote songs about the republicans, the Civil War, or the dictatorship, such as Benito Kamelas's "Fue mi abuelo" (My grandfather), Reincidentes's "Gracias por venir" (Thanks for coming) and "La republicana," Xenreira's "Mil nove 36" (1936), Sin Dios's "1936, un pueblo en armas" (1936, a People in Arms), Envidia Kotxina's "Historias en blanco y negro" (Stories in black and

56 Of course not, it's not enough to say that those times are over / that time heals wounds, because they are not over / that we must look at the future / because it's insulting and painful to see that they are not over.

57 Dignity, memory, and truth.

58 We still have to put a proper end to this unfinished business, / dignity, memory, and truth, / with the victorious Spain, with the triumphant Spain.

59 There will never be reconciliation / while the harrowing cry / of the dead who inhabit the ditches can still be heard. / There was never peace, mercy, or forgiveness. / If the firing line's walls spoke . . . / Nobody knows the pain of the bad Spaniards / better than them. / [. . .] / Killed twice, / two shouts, two laments. / Both cowards, both cruel, both silent. / First fire, then oblivion.

white), and Los muertos de Cristo's "Miliciano anónimo" (Anonymous militiaman), among many others.

As we have already seen with Olor a Sobako's "Los cuatro generales," another crucial trademark of Spanish punk regarding historic memory is the abundant work conducted to recuperate republican or anti-Francoist songs by adapting them to a punk style. In addition to Olor a Sobako's song we can cite other numbers such as Habeas Corpus's rendition of "El Quinto regimiento" (The Fifth Regiment), El Último ke Zierre's "Ay Carmela," 37 Hostias's "Gallo rojo, gallo negro" (Red rooster, black rooster), Los muertos de Cristo's "A las barricadas" (Let's go to the barricades), and many more.

Just like "Los cuatro generales," "El Quinto regimiento" is based on the melody of the traditional song "Anda jaleo jaleo," made famous by Lorca's recording with La Argentinita in 1931. Habeas Corpus's rendition starts with a classical guitar intro that resembles the sound it would normally have when played and sung by the republican troops as well as the many other singer-songwriters who have interpreted this same song. By doing so, they connect not only with the republicans but with a long-standing tradition of popular anti-Francoist singer-songwriters. After this intro, the sound changes completely, introducing a distorted guitar, a bass, and a drum pattern that resembles a military march. After a few bars, the singer comes in singing one of the verses of "El Quinto regimiento" once and again all throughout the song:

> Con el quinto, quinto, quinto
> Con el quinto regimiento, madre yo me voy al frente
> Hacia las líneas de fuego, madre yo me voy al frente
> Hacia las líneas de fuego. Anda jaleo, jaleo.
> Suena la ametralladora y ya empieza el tiroteo.[60]

At the end of the song they simply repeat the last line, "Suena la ametralladora y ya empieza el tiroteo," repeatedly as the sound fades in. This slow disappearance of the song, followed by the silence between tracks, can be interpreted as an aural metaphor of the deadly character of the Civil War. By making the sound increasingly quiet until it disappears,

60 With the fifth, fifth, fifth / with the fifth regiment, Mother I'm going to the front / toward the fire line, Mother I'm going to the front / toward the fire line. There's a racket, racket. / The machine gun rattles and the shooting begins.

while shouting that they are in the middle of a shooting, the band seems to aurally emulate the dying process of those individuals in the shooting.

In "Ay, Carmela," the band from Castellón, El Último ke Zierre, follows a similar formula. They start the song with a classical guitar intro and different people singing in unison, connecting with the way the republicans would sing and the way these songs have been interpreted through the years as hymns against fascism. Then, after this intro, they add the distorted guitars, bass, and drums. The lyrics are almost exactly the same as those in the traditional republican song "Viva la XV Brigada," which shares its melody with another traditional song also called "Ay Carmela." The only difference is that, in a line where the original says "luchamos contra los moros," referring to the Moroccan people whom the Francoists forced to fight on their side in the Civil War, they say "luchamos contra los curas." This is most likely a way to avoid singing a line that could be interpreted as racist and demeaning for Moroccan people of today, as well as to stress the church's decisive contribution to Francoist repression during the Civil War and the dictatorship.

In the case of 37 Hostias's "Gallo rojo, gallo negro," we find a rendition of singer-songwriter Chicho Sánchez Ferlioso's famous protest song with the same title. This song was released during the Francoist regime and recounts a fight between two roosters of different colors. The meaning of these two colors is open for interpretation, but it has been traditionally understood as a representation of the Francoist government and the anti-Francoist forces. The song starts by saying that "cuando canta el gallo negro es que ya se acaba el día"[61] and that "si cantara el gallo rojo, otro gallo cantaría."[62] These lines present an opposition between a black rooster that sings to announce that the day is ending and a red one that is not singing but, if it did, everything would be different. Similarly, one might also interpret this as a way of saying that fascism—which has often been represented by the color black—kills life and finishes the day, and that communism—usually represented by the color red—would make everything different. In any case, "Gallo rojo, gallo negro" is a clear anti-Francoist song. For its part, in Los muertos de Cristo's "A las barricadas," we would have a

61 When the black rooster sings, it means that the day is ending.
62 If the red rooster sang, everything would be different.

punk cover of the traditional song of the same name sung by Spanish anarchists during the Civil War, calling people to join the fight.

Finally, there have also been a few concept albums about the Civil War, such as Canallas's *¡Nunca más!* (Never again) (2000) and Barricada's *La tierra está sorda* (The earth is deaf) (2009) and *En la memoria* (In memory) (2010).[63] I now want to focus on the last two for their importance not only as music albums but as a whole project of recuperation of historic memory that involves a book, a documentary, and a *concierto-charla* (concert-discussion) tour around schools and high schools to discuss Spain's past with students all around the country. *La tierra está sorda* was released in 2009 and has eighteen songs. In each song, Barricada tries to recover the memory of the Civil War in several different ways, such as by telling the stories of different republican people, narrating different important historical events, or denouncing the crimes against humanity and war crimes conducted by Francoism. There are songs about the church's decisive role in Francoist repression, such as "Sotanas" (Cassocks); others about the biographies of specific republicans, such as "Matilde Landa," "Las siete de la tarde" (Seven o'clock in the evening), and "Pétalos" (Petals); and even three songs dealing with Francoist prisons and concentration camps, like those in "Trilogía Ezkaba" (Ezkaba trilogy). Additionally, the album includes a booklet of over 175 pages with a great amount of information regarding the Civil War and the Francoist dictatorship. In this book, the band starts by conducting a historical tour through the development of the war based on a large number of books and several interviews they carried out. After this, they provide a space for different intellectuals, historians, journalists, and other people involved with the recuperation of historic memory to discuss different topics regarding the Civil War in several short articles. Then they provide a twelve-page bibliography organized thematically to learn more about the war and the dictatorship and, after this, they devote

---

63 Musically speaking it is often discussed whether Barricada is or not part of punk subculture. In *Rock Radikal Vasco: El invento de la Euskadi Alegre* Juan Pardo Laguna states that Barricada confuses people because, while having a harder sound that is sometimes closer to hard rock or heavy metal, they do discuss ideas connected to anarchism, antimilitarism, squatting, and others that are traditionally connected to the punk subculture (n.p.). For the purpose of this book I believe they are as an important as any other Spanish punk band.

the rest of the book to contextualizing and explaining the meaning of each of the songs on the album. In order to do so, they use a great number of quotes and information from documentaries, testimonies, and books such as *Esclavos por la patria* (Isaías Lafuente), *Las fosas del silencio* (Montserrat Armenogu and Ricard Belis I Garcia), *Los niños perdidos del franquismo* (Montserrat Armengou, Ricard Vinyes, and Ricard Belis), and they even borrow lines from Dulce Chacón's novel *La voz dormida* (The dormant voice) and Carlos Fonseca's *Trece rosas rojas* (Thirteen red roses).

*En la memoria*, for its part, was published a year later, in 2010, and it is a live album recorded during Barricada's unplugged tour performing *La tierra está sorda*'s songs at social centers, theaters, and high schools. Additionally, the album includes the documentary *La tierra está sorda*, in which the members of the band visit Zafra (Extremadura) for one of their unplugged concerts. Zafra is a village that represents one of the most bloodthirsty episodes of the beginning of the Civil War, since it was one of the places in which Francoist troops went and killed every single person who had a leftist political inclination, without asking any questions, and even when they did not face any kind of resistance. This massacre was part of the Francoist objective to not only win power but also, as Franco said, to eradicate the spread of any Marxist ideas around Spain "at whatever the cost"[64] (Cazorla Sánchez 2013, 74). In this documentary we can see the members of Barricada meeting with people whose relatives were killed and then performing at the local theater and discussing several topics regarding the Civil War with the audience. We could say that the documentary shows an example of the outreach the band carried out with the unplugged tour.

As we have seen, these two Barricada albums were released in the twenty-first century, long after the Transición, but I believe that they represent the culmination of many other exercises in historic memory conducted by numerous bands and individuals within punk subculture since Franco's death. Ultimately, punk subculture represents a culture in which there was not such a generalized amnesia about Spain's recent past as in other sectors of society, as well as a movement that, contrary to the studies that have focused on the movida, proves that

64 This is what Franco said when Jay Allen, a journalist from *News Chronicle*, asked him if he was willing to kill half of Spain to eradicate Marxist ideas from the country.

there was a Spanish population that did not fall into a state of stasis and that remained critical toward the political affairs of the Transición. Furthermore, by doing this, punk subculture became part of the cultural sediment that resulted in the 15-M movement in 2011 and that opened up a new political scenario in twenty-first-century Spain.

CHAPTER 4

# SECOND NEGATIONIST TOPOS: PUNK AS ANTICAPITALISM AND ANTINEOLIBERALISM

On December 7, 1984, Boliche (Subterranean Kids' and Sentido Común's drummer), Ángel (GRB's singer), Tina (Sentido Común's singer), Rosa (Último Resorte's keyboard/synthesizer player), Joni D (Antidogmatikss's singer and author of the punk fanzine *N.D.F.*), and other punks, anarchists, and activists broke into an old medical center on Torren de l'Olla 18, Gràcia, Barcelona. They were all part of the Colectivo Squat Barcelona—in which Jordi Roca, "el Gos," singer of L'odi Social, also took part—and they had the intention of turning the old abandoned medical building into a public cultural center with rehearsal facilities for their bands (Bernal 2015, n.p.). An article published in *El Público* on May 31, 2015, echoes the words of Joni D, who justifies the occupation by saying that his punk band did not have anywhere to rehearse or perform and that they needed a place to do so. He states that it is for this reason that, after having tried to find institutional support and always being rejected, they decided to occupy the abandoned building and turn it into a cultural center with a space for bands to practice (Torrús 2015, n.p.). In another article, from August 9, 2015, in *El Periódico*, Joni D explains the need for the space:

> Estábamos unidos en torno a la estética y la música punk y teníamos una fuerza creativa que no teníamos dónde desplegar. Sentíamos que necesitábamos un espacio para desarrollarnos como artistas y como personas, y para aprender de una manera

EL PERIÓDICO de CATALUNYA

AÑO VII/1984. – Número 2.030 75 ptas.

Director: Enrique Arias Vega

Nacen en Barcelona los "ocupa-pisos"

La Policía saca a veinte chicos de una casa que habían tomado de forma ilegal

PRETENDEN ORGANIZAR UN MOVIMIENTO. – Una veintena de muchachos y muchachas de 16 a 20 años ocuparon en la noche del viernes una vivienda sin habitar del barrio de Gràcia. La Policía los desalojó y ayer dieron una rueda de prensa.

(Página 3)

Figure 19. *El periódico de Catalunya* cover about squatting in 1984

> libre, lejos del paternalismo de los locales sociales que gestionaba el ayuntamiento. Nuestra demanda era: no es posible que mientras hay un montón de casas vacías nosotros no tengamos un espacio donde desarrollar nuestras vidas.[1] (Bernal 2015, n.p.)

Even though none of this materialized and the building was evicted that same night, this action paved the way for many later occupations

1 We were all connected through punk music and aesthetics and we had a creative strength that we didn't know where to unleash. We felt that we needed a space to develop ourselves as artists and individuals, and to be able to learn in a free way, far from the paternalism of the social centers run by the council. Our demand was: it is not possible that, while there are plenty of empty houses, we have no place to develop our lives.

**Figure 20. Pro-squat concert poster**

in Catalonia and could be considered the trigger for the current *okupa* movement in Barcelona, one of the cities with the most occupied buildings in Europe.

Prior to the occupation, the Colectivo Squat Barcelona had organized different events and was actively publishing articles discussing their philosophy and objectives in different punk fanzines—which they continued doing together after the occupation and individually or as part of other collectives after their dissolution in 1985. One of the events they organized was the "pro-squat" fundraising punk show on October 27, 1984, in Barcelona. This concert was held at the Casal de Joves dels Transformadors, a public social center the local government had developed, which—despite Joni D's words—was open to hosting a punk concert. The bands that took part in this event were GRB, Antidogmatikss, Napalm, Shit.SA., Voices, and L'odi Social, and the collected money paid for the tools with which they broke into the medical facilities as well as the publication of more fanzines and informative flyers about the collective. In the poster for the event, they defended occupying abandoned buildings as a way to give the homeless a place to sleep. In addition to this, they presented the fictitious example of an abandoned building scheduled to be demolished in order to build a new police station as a way to criticize the lack of social projects and the mismanagement of public funds on the part of the government. Through this example, they criticized the unwillingness of the government to assign abandoned buildings a social role—such as giving shelter to the homeless—and its preference for using public funds to demolish them and create what in their opinion were less useful buildings, such as police stations. In other words, they present a problem (homelessness), provide an immediate possible solution (using abandoned buildings to house homeless people), and then state that the institutions do not want to help and that they would rather misuse public funds to take the abandoned building down and build an unnecessary police station. With regard to the fanzines, the main ones in which the Colectivo Squat Barcelona discussed their philosophy and objectives were Joni D's *N.D.F.* and some other short-lived fanzines of which only a few numbers were published, such as *Bacteria*. In fact, the first number of *Bacteria* is dedicated entirely to the occupation movement and provides a very informative historical study of the development of the movement in Spain.

While all this was occurring in Catalonia, in the Basque Country different groups of young people had also been occupying different buildings that belonged to the OJE (Organización Juvenil Española)[2] "con el objetivo de conseguir locales de ensayo para grupos de música rock y punk, y de reunion de jóvenes en general"[3] (González et al. 2022). Among these occupations, in November 1984, Andoain's important gaztetxea was occupied. Located in an abandoned school, it became a crucial reference as one of the most active social centers of the time when it came to organizing shows with national and international punk acts. In *Istorio bat kameraren atzean*, Andoain's gaztetxea collected thousands of pictures taken by Aitor Arregi "Txisto" and showed the plethora of punk gigs organized by this social center. Among many others, one can see pictures of Catalan bands L'odi Social, Tropel Nat, and Subterranean Kids; Dutch bands such as Indirect, Pamdemomium, and God; German bands such as Jingo de Lunch, Lethal Gospel, and

2 The OJE is an organization created during the dictatorship that provided leisure and educational activities aligned with the ideas of the Franco government. It was a complementary institution to that of the school to indoctrinate children through the spread of Francoist values and ideals.

3 With the objective of finding rehearsal spaces for rock and punk bands and a place for the youth to get together.

Mottek; Italian bands such as Kina, Negazione, and Dirty Joy; and many more. Even the later enormously popular band Green Day played there in 1993.[4] Due to all this, Andoain's social center became a reference for many of the countercultural and self-governed social centers to come. As the people from the gaztetxe themselves state in *Istorio bat kameraren atzean*:

> Andoaingo gaztetxea, aitzindaria izan zen, kontzertu antolaketan, garaian sortzen hasi ziren gune okupatu eta autogestionatuen artean. Garaiko udaletxe eta instituzioetatik eskaintzen zuten potean sarturiko kulturaren aurrean, musika ulertzeko eta bizitzeko beste era bat bilakatu zen. [...] Azken batean DIY (Zuk zeuk egin) filosofian oinarrituriko bizi filosofia muturrena eramana.[5] (*Istorio bat kameraren atzean* 2009)

Similarly, in 1985, this time in Madrid, a group of punks and some other youngsters broke into another abandoned building located on Amparo 83, in the Lavapiés neighborhood. They were all part of the KOKA collective (Kolectivo de Okupantes de la Kasa Amparo)[6] and they wanted to create a cultural center to provide people with alternative cultural activities to those offered by the institutions or other private corporations. Five days after the event, an anonymous member of the collective stated in the pages of *Diario 16* that they wanted to create a cultural center "que no forme parte de las estructuras institucionales, sino que sea algo propio, donde podamos desarrollar nuestras facultades creativas sin ser dirigidos por nadie."[7] And even though most of the members were self-proclaimed punks, they stated that the cultural center "estará abierto a todo tipo de gente, para que sea el

---

4 For the entire concert, see "Green Day Andoain 1993," YouTube, uploaded by mazinger z, February 10, 2018, https://www.youtube.com/watch?v=FdalnSRY-kQ&t=1399s.

5 Andoain's gaztetxea was a pioneer in the organization of concerts among the occupied and self-managed and self-financed centers of the time. Before the culture offered by the institutions and the councils, the gaztetxe became a different way of understanding and living music. [...] All in all, a life philosophy based on the DIY (do-it-yourself) philosophy at its greatest exponent. See also: http://istoriobatkamararenatzean.blogspot.com.

6 Collective of the Amparo house squatters.

7 That is not part of the institutional structure and that is our own thing, where we can develop our own creative skills without being directed by anyone.

EFE

**CINCO DIAS.** Treinta jóvenes madrileños ocupan desde el pasado viernes un edificio abandonado en el barrio de Lavapiés. Los jóvenes, que afirman no pertenecer a ningún partido ni asociación o colectivo, están limpiando y arreglando los más importantes desperfectos para transformar el inmueble en centro «cultural y de actividades alternativas de la juventud».

En la calle del Amparo, 83, del barrio de Lavapiés, de Madrid

# Un grupo de jóvenes punkies continúa la ocupación de un local que quieren convertir en centro cultural

**Fernando Lusson**

**Lid/Diario 16**

MADRID.—«*Squat dulce squat*» puede leerse en un cartel pegado en una de las habitaciones del edificio de la calle del Amparo, 83, del barrio de Lavapiés, de Madrid, que fue ocupado por una treintena de jóvenes el pasado día 1. La Policía aún no ha recibido ninguna denuncia por este hecho.

La actividad de los jóvenes para limpiar el local de los escombros y chatarras acumulados durante los quince años en los que ha estado deshabitado era intensa a primeras horas de la mañana de ayer.

Las labores de limpieza y vigilancia ocupan la mayor parte de las horas del día de estos «*squaters*», que pretenden instalar en el local ocupado un centro cultural «*que no forme parte de las estructuras institucionales, sino que sea algo propio, donde podamos desarrollar nuestras facultades creatívas sin ser dirigidos por nadie*», según uno de los ocupantes.

Estos jóvenes afirman que «*el local no está puesto a nombre de nadie en el Registro de la Propiedad y lleva dos años sin pagar la contribución urbana*».

El local ocupado albergó hasta su cierre, en 1969, un economato. Está dividido en tres plantas, con un gran patio interior que sus actuales ocupantes piensan destinar a salón de actos, donde realizarán exposiciones, conciertos y proyecciones de películas.

La ocupación del local se llevó a cabo mediante la acción de varios grupos autónomos que se pueden identificar preferentemente como *punks*, aunque manifiestan que el local «*estará abierto a todo tipo de gente, para que sea el centro cultural del barrio*».

El grupo de ocupantes de la casa de Lavapiés funciona de modo asambleario y autogestionario. La mayoría de estos jóvenes viven con sus padres y tienen alrededor de veinte años.

Aunque «*cada gente tiene sus motivos para estar aquí*», en el ánimo de todos ellos está «*buscar salidas a su situación*». «*No queremos locales para drogarnos ni hacer el gamberro, precisamente las razones de esto son siempre que la gente está tirada en la calle y sin sitios a donde ir*», dicen en un panfleto que «*de esta forma, tendremos también locales para ensayar*», comenta otro de los ocupantes que forma parte de uno de los cuatro grupos musicales cuyos integrantes han colaborado en la ocupación del local.

La casa ocupada servirá también de alojamiento a aquellos jóvenes que no tengan donde vivir «*y que se identifiquen con el proyecto global que supone la ocupación de esta casa, de carácter alternativo, al margen de las instituciones*».

Entre los vecinos del barrio, las reacciones son contrapuestas. Algunos han ofrecido a los «*squaters*» materiales de limpieza, comida y, en algunos casos, dinero. Otros, por su parte, se muestran contrarios a la ocupación. En la fachada de la casa existen dos pancartas que explican la nueva situación del local y se solicita al vecindario su colaboración para cubrir las necesidades más imperiosas, «*necesitamos un serrucho para hacer mesas y bancos, y alguien que tenga furgoneta para descombrar*», puede leerse en un cartel en la fachada.

La Policía, por su parte, no tiene noticia aún de que se haya denunciado la ocupación del local, por lo que no ha procedido al desalojo de los nuevos ocupantes que, en asamblea, decidieron ofrecer una resistencia pasiva en el caso de una posible intervención policial.

Figure 21. *Diario 16* article on a squat in Madrid

centro cultural del barrio."[8] Along with this, and in the same vein as the occupations in Barcelona and the Basque Country, another anonymous member speaks on behalf of the four punk bands that took part in the occupation and states that "de esta forma, tendremos también locales para ensayar."[9] Among the people who participated in the occupation we can cite Alberto Eiriz, the author of the fanzine *Penetración*; Kurdo from Tarzán y su puta madre buscando piso en Alcobendas and Olor a Sobako; and Canino, Olor a Sobako's and Sin Dios's drummer.[10] As a matter of fact, in the documentary *Lo que hicimos fue secreto*, it is Canino himself who states that, after having had problems to find places to perform, they decided to occupy an abandoned building on Amparo 83 to create a social center where they could organize shows and also have a space to rehearse.

All these occupations were triggered by the DIY ethos of punk culture and the determination of these young people to carry out projects lacking the funds and the institutional support from which movements such as the movida madrileña benefited. In this sense, the DIY ethos of punk is probably the most empowering and effective anti-capitalist element of punk culture. By adopting a constructive positive attitude within the already-established capitalist system, punk's DIY ethos helps construct valuable affirmative alternatives that go beyond simply showing a negationist oppositional attitude. Put differently, instead of simply being critical toward capitalism, following a DIY ethos allows one to adopt a positive attitude and create the forms of life one wishes they had. The rest of this chapter will focus on Spanish punk's opposition to capitalism and neoliberalism through the ways of life that resulted from its DIY ethos, through a close reading of various sections of a DIY manual published by the Spanish FAP (Federación Anarco Punk) that establishes connections with various other cultural elements.

## 1. DIY Punk in Spain

In 2008, the Spanish FAP published a DIY manual titled *Hazlo tú mismo: Recupera tu vida* (Do it yourself: Get your life back) that was a collaboration by several punk and anarchist associations across Spain. The book's cover

8 It will be open for all sorts of people, so that it can serve as the neighborhood's cultural center.

9 In this way, we will also have a rehearsal space.

10 They all tell the story of that day in *Lo que hicimos fue secreto*.

Figure 22. Cover of the manual *Hazlo tú mismo: Recupera tu vida*

shows a person with a clear punk style who has a mohawk and is wearing a T-shirt with the anarchy symbol. He has six hands and he is holding a guitar, a pencil, a pair of bolt cutters, a hammer, a carrot, and a Molotov cocktail. All these symbols anticipate some of the topics discussed in the book. In the introduction, they defend a DIY lifestyle because "estas prácticas nos enfrentan cara a cara y día a día contra el consumismo salvaje y destructor, que impera en los mercados capitalistas" (FAP 2008, 5).[11] In this sense, the book's primary message is clear: "Queremos crear nuestras propias condiciones de vida para dejar de ser individuos pasivos encadenados al trabajo y al mercado. Nuestras pasiones creativas quieren ser totales y enfocadas a la destrucción del sistema mercantil, como medio a su vez de construir unas formas de vida nuevas" (5).[12] In other words, they aim to become self-sufficient to take the fate of their lives into their own hands and not depend on the capitalist system that alienates them. The book covers a great variety of topics about how to achieve that goal.

### *1.1. Propaganda*

The first chapter of the book, "Propaganda," encourages us to create alternative means of counterinformation by explaining how to develop a homemade serigraphy studio, how to start a pirate radio station, or how to establish an alternative distribution network to share the news and culture that mainstream media does not cover. They also explain how one can recycle paper and create the glue paste used to put up posters on street walls. In addition to all this, the last section of the chapter discusses the important concept of "copyleft," to ensure that everything they create is distributed for free and nobody can monetarize it. As they state in the book, copyleft

> es una técnica que utiliza los derechos de autor como medio para subvertir las restricciones impuestas tradicionalmente por el copyright sobre la diseminación y desarrollo del conocimiento. Con este enfoque, el copyleft es principalmente una herramienta en una operación de mayor envergadura: la intención es invertir

---

11 These practices confront us face to face and every day with the wild and destructive consumerism that prevails in capitalist markets.

12 We want to create our own life conditions in order to stop being passive individuals chained to work and the market. Our creative passions want to be total and focused on the destruction of the mercantile system as a way to, at the same time, create new ways of life.

> permanentemente dichas restricciones. A través de diversas licencias copyleft se puede enfocar este concepto no sólo al software, como originariamente surgió, sino también al ámbito musical, literario, y artístico/cultural en general.[13] (FAP 2008, 27)

Taking literature or music as an example, a copylefted album, track, or book cannot be sold for any money by anyone in the world, and if they wanted to create compilations, or use the cultural product in any way, it would be illegal to make any profit from it. In other words, while copyright limits the right to use something and forces those who use it to pay for its usage, copyleft forces those who use the product not to make any profit from it. On the one hand, since distributors cannot make any money, a copyleft license can result in a more limited distribution of the work. On the other, however, it can also force companies working in the cultural market to give away albums or books for free if they want to benefit from the cultural producers in other ways—live concert tickets or merchandising, for example. In this sense, a copyleft license can be a powerful tool to effect a change on the music industry's modes of production. Moreover, a copyleft license can also democratize access to culture and information by encouraging its free distribution. The punk-influenced flamenco/fusion Spanish band Canteca de Macao can serve as an example to understand how copyleft works. This band published their albums with a copyleft license. The anomaly, however, is that, while they published their first album independently through their own means, they published the rest with several major labels. Despite this significant change of strategy, Canteca de Macao could subvert capitalism and affect the music industry's modes of production in a significant way, as they signed the record deal with the major labels only after reaching an agreement for their albums to be available for free downloading on their website under a copyleft license. Thus, they were able to work with very good producers, at very good studios, and created a high-quality cultural product that they gave away for free to

---

13 It's a technique that uses copyright as a way to subvert the restrictions imposed by it regarding the dissemination and development of knowledge. From this perspective, copyleft is mainly a tool in a greater operation: the goal is to reverse permanently the restrictions imposed by copyright. Through various copyleft licenses, one can apply this concept not only to software, as it was originally applied, but also in the musical, literary, and artistic/cultural fields in general.

the general public. In fact, they not only gave their work away for free, but they also allowed people to use their music for free without having to pay any royalties to the band or the record company—at bars or small businesses, for instance—which is a significant sacrifice on the part of the record label. In spite of everything, some might claim that Canteca de Macao distanced itself from a pure DIY ethos by taking part in the music industry and the capitalist system because there were concerts, merchandising, and other things from which the major labels benefited. While limited, it is still a significant subversion to get these labels to give away a high-quality and expensive-to-make album for free on the internet and to democratize access to culture by allowing everyone to freely download their music (*Europa Press* 2007). In this sense, publishing their work with a copyleft license was indeed a useful and powerful strategy.

Nonetheless, the purely DIY way to do it would be developing one's own distribution network that relies on mutual cooperation with other people involved in punk culture. *Hazlo tú mismo*'s "Propaganda" chapter gives some advice on how to do so. They mention things such as trying to work with bands or DIY labels and publications on a sell-pay basis, that is, paying them once you have sold their products and not in advance. Along the same lines, they also recommend reaching an agreement with them to be able to raise the price a little bit and make some profit to pay for the distribution expenses. In addition to these two ideas, they recommend looking out for punk fanzines and trying to arrange getting advertised in these publications. In fact, it is typical of punk fanzines to be full of advertisements and info on DIY distributors or publishers in order to create greater connections among different punks. Figures 23 and 24 give an idea of what these adverts look like. The first is a page from the sixth issue of *Penetración*, and it shows a list of different fanzines from all around the world with their names and contacts, when available, and the second is from the sixth issue of *N.D.F.* and presents a list of products from all around the world that the fanzine sells as "Distribuciones N.D.F."

One of the most representative examples among Spanish punk bands that followed a completely DIY distribution is the Madrilenean band Sin Dios. In the documentary *10 años de autogestión* (Ten years of self-management), Canino, Sin Dios's drummer, speaks in the following manner:

> Como Sin Dios nos consideramos una banda de difusión anarquista, pues, evidentemente, no podíamos delegar, pues, en sellos

> discográficos, managers, o promotores. Manejamos el concepto de la autogestión, que es llevar siempre tú todo adelante sin intermediarios, ¿no? Y sin lucrar a nadie. [. . .] Entonces, es un ejemplo claro, no el mejor quizás, pero es un ejemplo claro y real de que la autogestión es posible, y que desde nosotros mismos, o desde nosotras mismas, desde nuestra situación revolucionaria y nuestra ética, podemos sacar cosas adelante sin depender de los mercanchifles de la música o de, de lo que sea. Esto, por eso, es aplicable a la vida en general, nosotros lo hacemos con nuestro grupo, pero es que se podría hacer en cualquier ámbito de la vida. Por eso nos reclamamos anarquistas y por eso queremos llevar la autogestión a todos los ámbitos de la vida.[14] (Sin Dios 2000)

Similarly, if one takes a look at their website, they will find all their albums available for download free of cost and with the following message: "Esta es la discografía de Sin Dios desde 1990 hasta el año 2005. Pincha en las carátulas y accederás a la información de cada trabajo, letras de canciones y mp3 de cada una de ellas. Más abajo encontrarás las portadas de discos compartidos, videos, ep's y demás ediciones. Disfrútalo."[15]

In the "Biography" section of the website, the band also describes how they would exchange their albums at their shows for other materials and how they ended up storing so much material from other independent distributors and bands that they decided to create their own distribution association, "La idea" (The idea), and keep sharing all these materials. In addition to this, they also created a center for the distribution of alternative music and anarchist books in Madrid. This connects with one of the last pieces of advice in *Hazlo tú mismo*'s

---

14 Because in Sin Dios we consider ourselves a band of anarchist diffusion, well, obviously, we could not delegate to record labels, managers, or promoters. We follow the idea of self-management, which means that you are in charge of everything without intermediaries, right? And without profiting anybody. [. . .] So, it's a clear example, perhaps not the best, but it's a clear and real example that self-management is possible, and that on our own, through our own revolutionary situation and ethic, we can do things without the merchants of music or of any other thing. This, precisely for this reason, is applicable to life in general, we do it with our band, but it can be done in any area of our lives. That's why we consider ourselves anarchists and that's why we want to take self-management to all the areas of our lives.

15 This is Sin Dios's discography from 1990 to 2005. Click on the album covers and you will access each of our works, lyrics of the songs, and mp3 files. Farther down you will find the album covers of shared albums, videos, EPs, and other releases. Enjoy!

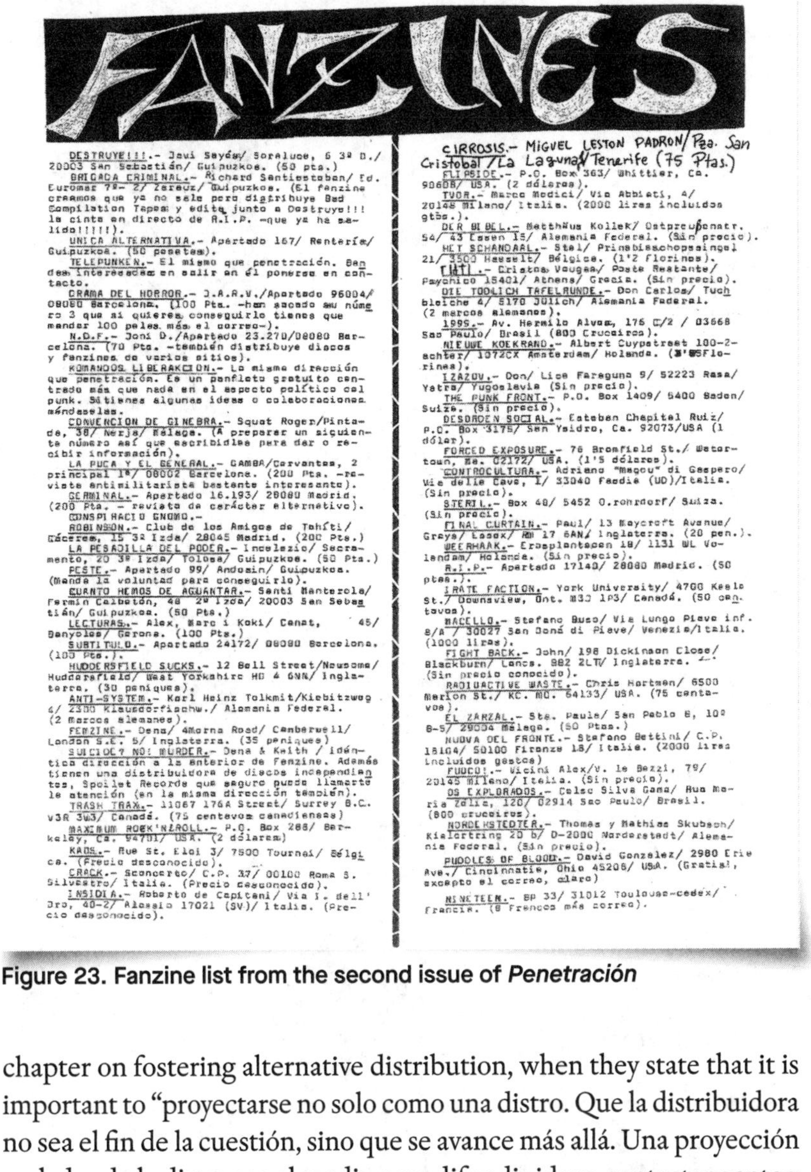

FANZINES

DESTRUYE!!!.- Javi Sayés/ Soraluce, 6 3º D./ 20003 San Sebastián/ Guipuzkoa. (50 pta.)

BRIGADA CRIMINAL.- Richard Santiesteban/ Ed. Euromar 7º- 2/ Zarauz/ Guipuzkoa. (El fanzine creamos que ya no sale pero distribuye Bad Compilation Tapes y edita junto a Destruye!!! la cinta en directo de R.I.P. -que ya ha salido!!!!!).

UNICA ALTERNATIVA.- Apartado 167/ Rentería/ Guipuzkoa. (50 pesetas).

TELEPUNKEN.- El mismo que penetración. Sean interesados en salir en él ponerse en contacto.

DRAMA DEL HORROR.- J.A.R.V./Apartado 96004/ 08080 Barcelona. (100 Pts. -han sacado su número 3 que si quieres conseguirlo tienes que mandar 100 pelas más el correo-).

N.D.F.- Joni D./Apartado 23.270/08080 Barcelona. (70 Pts. -también distribuye discos y fanzines de varios sitios).

KOMANDOS LIBERAKCION.- La misma dirección que penetración. Es un panfleto gratuito centrado más que nada en el aspecto político del punk. Si tienes algunas ideas o colaboraciones mándaselas.

CONVENCION DE GINEBRA.- Squat Roger/Pintada, 38/ Nerja/ Málaga. (A preparar un siguiente número así que escribidles para dar o recibir información).

LA PUCA Y EL GENERAL.- GAMBA/Cervantes, 2 principal 1ª/ 08002 Barcelona. (200 Pts. -revista antimilitarista bastante interesante).

GERMINAL.- Apartado 16.193/ 28080 Madrid. (200 Pts. - revista de carácter alternativo).

CONSPIRACIO GNOMO.-

ROBINSON.- Club de los Amigos de Tahití/ Cáceres, 15 3ª Izda/ 28045 Madrid. (200 Pts.)

LA PESADILLA DEL PODER.- Incelezio/ Secramento, 20 3º Izda/ Tolosa/ Guipuzkoa. (50 Pts.)

PESTE.- Apartado 99/ Andoain/ Guipuzkoa. (Manda la voluntad para conseguirlo).

CUANTO HEMOS DE AGUANTAR.- Santi Manterola/ Fermín Calbetón, 48 2º Izda/ 20003 San Sebastián/ Guipuzkoa. (50 Pts.)

LECTURAS.- Alex, Marc i Koki/ Canat, 45/ Banyoles/ Gerona. (100 Pts.)

SUBTITULO.- Apartado 24172/ 08080 Barcelona. (100 Pts.).

HUDDERSFIELD SUCKS.- 12 Bell Street/Newsome/ Huddersfield/ West Yorkshire HD 4 6NN/ Inglaterra. (30 peniques).

ANTI-SYSTEM.- Karl Heinz Tolkmit/Kiebitzweg 4/ 2300 Klausdorfischw./ Alemania Federal. (2 marcos alemanes).

FEMZINE.- Dena/ 4Morna Road/ Camberwell/ London S.E. 5/ Inglaterra. (35 peniques)

SUICIDE? NO! MURDER.- Dena & Keith / idéntica dirección a la anterior de Fanzine. Además tienen una distribuidora de discos independientes, Spoilet Records que seguro puede llamarte la atención (en la misma dirección también).

TRASH TRAX.- 11067 176A Street/ Surrey B.C. V3R 3W3/ Canadá. (75 centavos canadienses)

MAXIMUM ROCK'N'ROLL.- P.O. Box 288/ Berkeley, Ca. 94701/ USA. (2 dólares)

KAOS.- Rue St. Eloi 3/ 7500 Tournai/ Bélgica. (Precio desconocido).

CRACK.- Sconcerto/ C.P. 37/ 00100 Roma S. Silvestro/ Italia. (Precio desconocido).

INSIDIA.- Roberto de Capitani/ Via I. dell' Oro, 40-2/ Alassio 17021 (SV)/ Italia. (Precio desconocido).

CIRROSIS.- MIGUEL LESTON PADRON/ Pza. San Cristobal /La Laguna/ Tenerife (75 Ptas.)

FLIPSIDE.- P.O. Box 363/ Whittier, Ca. 90608/ USA. (2 dólares).

TVOR.- Marco Medici/ Via Abbiati, 4/ 20148 Milano/ Italia. (2000 liras incluidos gtos.).

DER BIBEL.- Matthäus Kollek/ Ostpreußenstr. 54/ 43 Essen 15/ Alemania Federal. (Sin precio).

HET SCHANDAAL.- Stal/ Prinsbisschopssingel 21/ 3500 Hasselt/ Bélgica. (1'2 Florines).

[illegible].- Cristos Vougas/ Poste Restante/ Psychico 15401/ Athens/ Grecia. (Sin precio).

DIE TODLICH TAFELRUNDE.- Don Carlos/ Tuchbleiche 4/ 5170 Jülich/ Alemania Federal. (2 marcos alemanes).

1995.- Av. Hermilo Alves, 176 C/2 / 03668 Sao Paulo/ Brasil (800 Cruceiros).

NIEUWE KOEKRAND.- Albert Cuypstraat 100-2-achter/ 1072CX Amsterdam/ Holanda. ([illegible] Florines).

IZAZOV.- Don/ Lice Faraguna 9/ 52223 Rasa/ Yatra/ Yugoslavia (Sin precio).

THE PUNK FRONT.- P.O. Box 1409/ 5400 Baden/ Suiza. (Sin precio).

DESORDEN SOCIAL.- Esteban Chapital Ruiz/ P.O. Box 3175/ San Ysidro, Ca. 92073/USA (1 dólar).

FORCED EXPOSURE.- 76 Bromfield St./ Watertown, Ma. 02172/ USA. (1'5 dólares).

CONTROCULTURA.- Adriano "Magou" di Gaspero/ Via delle Cave, 1/ 33040 Faedis (UD)/Italia. (Sin precio).

STERIL.- Box 48/ 5452 O.rohrdorf/ Suiza. (Sin precio).

FINAL CURTAIN.- Paul/ 13 Maycroft Avenue/ Grays/ Essex/ RM 17 6AN/ Inglaterra. (20 pen.).

WEERHAAK.- Eroseplantsoen 18/ 1131 WL Volendam/ Holanda. (Sin precio).

R.I.P.- Apartado 17140/ 28080 Madrid. (50 ptas.).

IRATE FACTION.- York University/ 4700 Keele St./ Downsview, Ont. M3J 1P3/ Canadá. (50 centavos).

MACELLO.- Stefano Buso/ Via Lungo Piave inf. 8/A / 30027 San Doná di Piave/ Venezia/Italia. (1000 liras).

FIGHT BACK.- John/ 198 Dickinson Close/ Blackburn/ Lancs. BB2 2LT/ Inglaterra. (Sin precio conocido).

RADIOACTIVE WASTE.- Chris Hartman/ 6500 Marion St./ KC. MO. 64133/ USA. (75 centavos).

EL ZARZAL.- Sta. Paula/ San Pablo 8, 10º B-5/ 29004 Málaga. (50 Ptas.)

NUOVA DEL FRONTE.- Stefano Bettini/ C.P. 18104/ 50100 Firenze 18/ Italia. (2000 liras incluidos gastos)

FUOCO!.- Vicini Alex/V. le Bezzi, 79/ 20145 Milano/ Italia. (Sin precio).

OS EXPLORADOS.- Celso Silva Gama/ Rua Maria Zelia, 120/ 02914 Sao Paulo/ Brasil. (800 cruceiros).

NORDERSTEDTER.- Thomas y Mathias Skubsch/ Kielortring 20 b/ D-2000 Norderstedt/ Alemania Federal. (Sin precio).

PUDDLES OF BLOOD.- David Gonzalez/ 2980 Erie Ave./ Cincinnatie, Ohio 45208/ USA. (Gratis!, excepto el correo, claro)

NINETEEN.- BP 33/ 31012 Toulouse-cedex/ Francia. (8 Francos más correo).

**Figure 23. Fanzine list from the second issue of *Penetración***

chapter on fostering alternative distribution, when they state that it is important to "proyectarse no solo como una distro. Que la distribuidora no sea el fin de la cuestión, sino que se avance más allá. Una proyección real, donde la distro sea el medio para difundir ideas, contactar gente y organizar acciones" (FAP 2008, 25).[16] Through their music and their work as distributors of punk and anarchist culture, Sin Dios

16 Not work only as a distributor. Distribution shouldn't be the only goal, one should go further. A real outreach in which distribution is a way to spread ideas, contact people, and organize actions.

Aqui tienes el segundo catalogo de "Distribuciones N.D.F.", no es mas amplio que el anterior, pero si mas interesante.

HOLANDA

LP... B.G.K. ..."Jonestown Aloha‡"...20 temas...600 ptas.
EP...Frites Modern..."Veel, vet, goor en duur"...13 temas...700 ptas.
SG... B.G.K. ..."White male dumbinance"...8 temas...300 ptas.

ITALIA

LP...Wretched..."Libero di vivere"...17 temas...700 ptas.
SG...CCCP..."Ortodossia"...3 temas...300 ptas.
SG...Stigmathe...3 temas...300 ptas.
SG...Crash Box..."...Vivi!"...6 temas...300 ptas.
FZ...Stato di polizia...nº 4...150 ptas.
FZ...Attack...nº 1...100 ptas.
FZ...Nashville skyline...100 ptas.

ALEMANIA

LP...Razzia..."Tag ohne schatten"...15 temas...800 ptas.
LP...Torpedo Moskau..."Malenkaja rabota"...14 temas...800 ptas.
LP...Blut and Eisen..."Schrei doch!"...16 temas...800 ptas.
LP...Varios..."Keine Experimente"...18 temas...800 ptas.
LP...Varios..."Keine Experimente vol. 2"...18 temas...800 ptas.
SG...Cretins, Blut and Eisen..."Dachau disco"...2 temas...300 ptas.

ESPAÑA

SG...Codigo Neurotico...5 temas...200 ptas.
SG...Kangrena..."Terrorismo sonoro"...5 temas...225 ptas.
K7...Anti-dogmatikss..."Rompan filas!"...11 temas...250 ptas.
FZ...Subtitulo...nº 1...100 ptas.
FZ...Destruye‡‡!...nº 11...30 ptas.
RV...Germinal...nº 4...200 ptas.
RV...Robinson...nº 8...200 ptas.
FZ... N.D.F. ...nº 6...50 ptas.

RESTO DEL MUNDO

SG... M.D.C. ..."Multi-death corporations"...4 temas...250 ptas.
SG...Faction..."You've got the fire"...4 temas...200 ptas.
LP...Kaaos, T. Kadet..."So much fun"...14 temas...800 ptas.
LP...Varios (de todo el mundo)..."Life is a joke"...18 temas...800 ptas.

Se ha de tener en cuenta que las cantidades son bastante limitadas, a parte, estamos esperando material de Inglaterra, Estados Unidos, Mexico y España.
Para hacer cualquier pedido se debe hacer un giro a:

J. SAHUN CASTET
Apdo. 23.270
08080 BARCELONA

Este giro debe incluir el importe del pedido, mas los gastos de envio que son los siguientes:
LP...125 ptas.
SG... 85 ptas.
K7... 85 ptas.
FZ... 50 ptas.

ESTE FANZINE VA ESPECIALMENTE DEDICADO AL COLECTIVO SQUAT DE BARCELONA
Y AL
KATACRAK (COLECTIVO KRAKER DE IRUÑA).
DESDE AQUI DENUNCIAMOS A "GRABACIONES ANFETAMINICAS" POR DEDICARSE A ROBAR EL EQUIPO DE LOS GRUPOS QUE ESTAN EMPEZANDO Y POR IR DE ANARCOS, CUANDO SON APRENDICES DE FELIPE GONZALEZ. JODIDOS BASTARDOS!

Figure 24. Distribuciones N.D.F.

embodies such a stance and helps develop an underground DIY network that poses resistance to capitalism and proposes alternative ways of interaction between culture producers and consumers.

Yet even if this DIY ethos is something that impregnated most punk to a greater or lesser extent, one should not conclude that every punk band followed such a pure DIY distribution as Sin Dios. In fact, such important punk bands as La Polla Records, Kortatu, and Eskorbuto all sold many—if not all—of their albums at record stores through different record labels. It is true that they did this mainly through independent record labels and not major labels but, nonetheless, labels that profited from taking part in the music industry. At the same time, one should not think that Sin Dios employs such a DIY distribution strategy because they are part of the anarcho-punk branch, since there are non-anarcho-punk bands that follow a purely DIY ethos as well as anarcho-punk bands that are signed to major record labels—for instance, the US band Anti-Flag. Taking all this into account, instead of falling into the never-ending discussion about which band is really punk or not depending on whether they follow a completely DIY ethos, I propose looking at the DIY ethos as a spectrum and a place for negotiation. In this sense, a DIY ethos would not necessarily have to be the goal or the rule through which everyone should act but rather a solution to not having any other way of doing things. Therefore, if one produces an album, a book, or any other cultural artifact that someone wants to commercialize even if that means they are going to make profit from it, it might also be a positive thing if they make a specific message reach more people. The Madrilenean ska-punk band Ska-P, for instance, has always been criticized for releasing their albums with major record labels, and when a journalist asked them about it in an interview, this is how they replied:

> Mira, nosotros estuvimos con una independiente y ya sabemos lo que es eso (1000 copias, mala distribución . . .). En RCA nos ofrecieron libertad absoluta, ni se pasaron por el estudio cuando estábamos grabando. Estar en una multinacional tiene sus ventajas, por ejemplo ahora no estaríamos haciendo esta ronda de entrevistas. Si Kortatu hubieran fichado por una multinacional, hubieran sido la bomba. Pero hay una serie de cosas por las que no queremos pasar, por ejemplo, no queremos entrar

> en radiofórmulas. En una llegaron a decir que si cambiábamos cojones por pelotas, saldríamos. ¡Ridículo! La maldita hipocresía . . . Lo importante es hacerse fuerte para poder imponer tus condiciones.
> *Entrevistador:* ¿Participar en el sistema para luchar contra él?
> Sí, de hecho es utilizar el sistema porque sabes que puedes llegar a mucha más gente. Es ridículo negarse a participar porque lo haces cada día inevitablemente: desde ver la televisión a coger el autobús.[17] (La Falcata, n.d.)

All Ska-P's songs discuss different political issues, and they have never written any apolitical lyrics. From a revolutionary perspective, it is advantageous to reach more people and share their message, regardless of whether they do it independently. Therefore, using DIY distribution when there is no other way to distribute one's work is a powerful strategy, but insisting in never engaging with other groups in order to remain independent while struggling to reach people with your work can also be counterproductive.

It is useful here to refer to Walter Benjamin's work "The Author as Producer." In this text, Benjamin reflects on the way an author can contribute to the proletariat revolution. In order to do so, he starts by referring to two key concepts: tendency and quality. Benjamin argues against considering an author revolutionary because the character of their work (tendency) favors revolution, regardless of the work's literary characteristics (quality). By doing so, he is not stating that there is a specific quality standard one should adhere to, but he is rather claiming that there is also revolutionary potential in the literary aspect of the

---

17 Look, we worked with an independent record label and we know what that means (1,000 copies, bad distribution . . .). At RCA they offered us complete freedom, and they didn't even come to the studio when we were recording. Working with a multinational has advantages. For instance, we wouldn't be doing this interview right now. If Kortatu had been signed by a multinational they would've been huge. But there are several things we won't do; for instance, we don't want to be part of any radio format music. Once they told us that if we substituted *cojones* (bollocks) for *pelotas* they would publish us. Ridiculous! Damn hypocrisy . . . The important thing is to become stronger so that you can impose your own conditions.
*Interviewer:* Participate in the system in order to fight against it?
Yes, in fact it's using the system because you know that you can reach way more people. It's ridiculous to refuse to take part because you already do it every day inevitably: from watching television to taking the bus.

work. Following this same line of thought, he goes even further to state that "a work that exhibits the correct tendency must of necessity have every other quality" (Benjamin 2005, 769), and he proposes a dialectical revolutionary approach that includes more elements than simply the work's prorevolutionary tendency. Among these elements, there is one connected to the importance of DIY as a direct intervention in the capitalist modes of production that I want to stress: the work's position. Instead of asking, "What is the attitude of a work *to* the relations of production of its time?" he wants to ask, "What is its position in them?" (770). In this sense, he states that "a political tendency, however revolutionary it might seem, has a counterrevolutionary function so long as the writer feels his solidarity with the proletariat only in his attitudes, not as a producer" (772) and that "the place of the intellectual in the class struggle can be identified—or, better, chosen—only on the basis of his position in the process of production" (773).

From this perspective, the revolutionary potential of punk's cultural artifacts resides not in their tendency but in the way such works relate to the process of their production. In this sense, the DIY distribution of punk would be a bigger contribution to the anticapitalist struggle than any anticapitalist content in any punk cultural production. When Sin Dios refuses to sign with producers or record labels that would make profit from their albums, they are effecting a change in the capitalist modes of production that rule the music industry. By doing so, Sin Dios transforms themselves "from a supplier of the productive apparatus into an engineer who sees as his task to adapt this apparatus to the purposes of the proletarian revolution" (781). Yet this is not necessarily an either-or situation, and by viewing the DIY ethos as a spectrum that is relative to various contexts, one can also appreciate that, as Ska-P points out, we all take part in the capitalist system every day and it would be ridiculous to dogmatically reject taking part in it if it serves a revolutionary purpose—such as spreading a political message or generating political discussions on specific topics. Furthermore, since people consume all sorts of cultural products, one could equally buy Sin Dios's DIY albums at a concert or buy an album that Ska-P sells through a major label at the mall and listen to both at home. Ultimately, their combination will probably still be more helpful as part of an anticapitalist agenda than having to listen exclusively and dogmatically to bands that follow a pure DIY distribution.

### 1.2. *Vivienda*

The second chapter of *Hazlo tú mismo*, "Vivienda" (Housing), focuses on housing and, more specifically, on squatting. The first page of the chapter shows the famous "Blokes fantasmas" squat in Barcelona, which can be seen from Parque Guell showing a huge graffito that reads "Okupa y Resiste" (Squat and Resist) on the roof. Additional graffiti show other messages such as "No justice, no peace" or "Fuck the police," along with the symbol of anarchism. This chapter is basically a guide on how to occupy abandoned buildings in the most convenient way. They begin the introduction by explaining why they support squatting. The first thing they make clear is that they support squatting only in abandoned buildings:

> Ocupamos edificios abandonados y animamos a otros a ocuparlos. No ocupamos la casa de una pareja que se va a la montaña el fin de semana, no ocupamos ni siquiera la segunda vivienda de un urbanita de clase media u obrero acomodado. Ocupamos edificios abandonados de particulares y empresas que están incumpliendo las hipócritas leyes del gobierno, desde las inútiles leyes del suelo hasta la tan cacareada Constitución Española con su hipócrita derecho a una vivienda digna.[18] (FAP 2008, 30)

In addition to this, one of their main arguments to support squatting is that the real estate industry, as part of a capitalist system, invests in housing to speculate and make a profit, and not to meet the citizens' need for a place to live. As a result, real estate companies end up having unsold empty houses while they wait for "el momento propicio, es decir, cuando los beneficios de la operación inmobiliaria sean más cuantiosos"[19] (30) since they buy "viviendas como se invierte en bolsa, viviendas que no son para habitar sino para ser utilizadas como valor

---

18 We occupy abandoned buildings and we encourage other people to do the same. We don't occupy the house of a couple who is out in the mountains for the weekend, we don't even occupy the second home of an affluent middle-class or working-class person. We occupy the abandoned buildings of people and companies that are breaking the hypocritical laws of the government, from the useless land law to the much-vaunted Spanish Constitution and its hypocritical right to dignified housing.

19 The favorable moment, that is, when the benefit of the real estate operation is most profitable.

de cambio"[20] (29)—which connects with Marx's crucial concepts of "use value" versus "exchange value." According to Marx, "The utility of a thing makes it a use value" (27). In this way, houses are use values as material things that provide a place for people to live in. Exchange value, for its part, "presents itself as a quantitative relation, as the proportion in which values in use of one sort are exchanged for those of another sort, a relation constantly changing with time and place" (27). In other words, the amount of eggs a loaf of bread should be exchanged for in a commercial trade is relative and not intrinsic to the utility of eggs or bread and, therefore, it is subject to change depending on time and place. The same happens with houses and the prices imposed by the real estate industry: They are relative and conditioned by the profit that those involved in the sale of a house want to make. Therefore, houses are not built for people to have a place to live but to be exchanged for money as an investment when their value provides a certain profit. This is especially conflictive when those buying the houses are large corporations who buy dozens of blocks to speculate with and make profit from individuals in need of a house to live in. Often, this results in people having to spend significant amounts of money to live in a house—mainly due to the profit margins different people in the real estate industry need to make on that house—or having empty houses and homeless people who cannot afford a house. In *Hazlo tú mismo* they see these actions as blackmailing people with their fundamental right of having a place to live and, therefore, see occupying abandoned buildings as a way to recover what is, in their view, illegitimately taken from them—be this a house in itself because they do not have a place to live, or the overinflated cost of housing.[21]

After this introduction, the chapter presents the steps one should take to occupy a building. They inform the reader about the various

---

20 Houses as one invests in the stock exchange, houses that are not for people to live in but to be used as exchange value.

21 It is always important to remember that a great percentage of the people who occupy abandoned buildings still have a house they pay for and in which they live. They might use the occupied building as a social center, as a meeting point, or as a place for homeless people to live, but it would be wrong to assume that those who occupy abandoned buildings always use them as their own residence. In this sense, when using the abandoned building as a social center, they are also providing the community with more affordable cultural events, which is also a way of getting back what one is forced to pay to live in a house whose price has been inflated due to its exchange value.

ways in which they can find out if a building is abandoned, and they describe different techniques to opening the doors or the windows to get inside. Then they focus on how to refurbish the house and make it habitable. In this section, they also explain how one can get electricity in the building. They present different ideas such as manipulating the electric meter in place so that it lets the current go in without showing consumption or connecting a cable to a streetlight's electric system. The descriptions become rather sophisticated and include explanations on voltage, the usage of a voltmeter, and others, along with images and electrical diagrams. In addition to this, this chapter also gives legal advice. It includes two sections covering how to behave when dealing with the police or the owner of the building and a specific section explaining relevant information regarding the Spanish Penal Code. They explain, for instance, that once you are inside the building the police cannot get in without a court order and that you have no obligation to open the door even if they ask you to. Furthermore, the police will need to wait for the order to get inside legally—which can take several months—and you can stay in the building while they get it. Regarding the owner, and having in mind that they talk exclusively about squatting in abandoned buildings, they explain that "muchas veces el dueño, dado que suponemos que ha abandonado su propiedad por muchos años, no tiene ningún interés en recuperarla inmediatamente. En ocasiones, ni siquiera les interesa llamar la atención sobre el inmueble denunciándoos" (FAP 2008, 40).[22] This is especially true when the building is violating any kind of law. Additionally, it is also common that, if the owner is still interested in the building and one explains the reasons behind the occupation—such as creating a social center for the community—often they even grants the space to the squatters. In an episode of TeleMadrid's show *20 minutos* focused on the squat movement, for instance, a squatter from the Lavapies nº 12 social center describes their relationship with the owner of the occupied building in the following manner:

> Tuvimos una visita del propietario, que no sabemos si seguirá siendo él el propietario. Vino, vio el local y dijo que le parecía

22 Often the owner, since we suppose that they have abandoned their property for many years, has no interest in reclaiming it immediately. Sometimes, they don't even want to attract attention by suing us.

> bien lo que estábamos haciendo, que lo teníamos bien y que él lo había comprado para venderlo . . . y que mientras él no lo pudiera vender que no tenía ningún interés en desalojarnos, pero que desde luego no iba dejar de venderlo porque estuviéramos nosotros aquí.[23] ("Okupas")

In fact, since it is a common practice for squatters to refurbish buildings that are almost in ruins, many owners view this also as a good way to keep their property in good shape and do not mind the occupation. Furthermore, if the owner of the building is the council or any other institution, they might even propose an agreement to legalize the squat. For example, they might grant the building for a minimum rent if squatters are people with no other place to live or, in the case of social centers, they might legalize the space in exchange for squatters organizing and holding specific social events they would normally hold in institutional buildings, such as literary recitals, concerts, or art exhibitions.

Here it may be important to highlight that, despite punk's strong ties with squatting, occupying abandoned buildings is not exclusively a punk-related practice and it has a broader history with much deeper implications. With this disclaimer in mind, and in order to understand the specific nature of punk squatting, one must also understand that, while all squatters follow a DIY stance by simply taking over what they need to meet their needs, not all squatters have the same needs or reasons for occupying a space. In this sense, punk squatters have also had their own specific motivations, and it is precisely on discussing these specific motivations that I want to focus in the rest of this section.

In Hans Pruijt's study of the different squat movements in Europe, "Okupar en Europa" (2004), he lists five different reasons for occupations:

- Okupation due to poverty
- Conservationist okupation
- Political okupation

23 The owner paid us a visit. Well, we don't know if he is still the owner. He came, saw the place, and said that he thought it was a good initiative, that we were keeping the place in good shape and that he only bought it to sell it . . . and that while he wasn't selling it he didn't have any interest in evicting us, but that he obviously was not going to not sell it because we were there.

- Okupation as an alternative strategy for housing
- Entrepreneurial okupation[24]

Those who occupy buildings due to economic difficulties ("okupation due to poverty") would normally agree to leave if given another housing alternative. Similarly, they would normally also celebrate the government purchasing the space for them to stay in it—or simply granting it to them if it is a public building—even if asked to pay a nominal low rent in exchange. In Spain, many of this kind of occupation took place immediately after Franco's death, as a response to the demand by lower-income families for the right to housing. Such occupations were especially triggered by the political bureaucracy that left dozens of public housing projects on standby. Under such circumstances, many families decided to take action and move into these public houses and other abandoned ones. In 1976, the "asociación de vecinos"[25] of La Ventilla demanded of the government the adjudication of public housing for needy families and, after several unsuccessful and never-ending negotiations and bureaucratic processes, the December 11 "recorrieron las calles del barrio, abrieron las puertas de una serie de casas desocupadas propiedad del Ministerio de la Vivienda y del Ministerio de Gobernación, y, posteriormente, abrieron la puerta de un antiguo dispensario que se encontraba en estado de abandono completo desde hacía más de ocho años"[26] and occupied the premises (*País* 1977). Another notorious case was the occupation of a building on General Fanjul by fifty families that lived in a shantytown. According to Tomás R. Villasante—a sociology professor but also an activist who took part in this occupation—such action was justified because of

> las necesidades de vivienda de familias trabajadoras que tenían que recurrir a construirse una chabola, cuando había viviendas vacías en abundancia para la especulación, incluso bastantes

---

24 The word okupation with a 'k' here is normally used to refer punk squatting or other squatting that is part of a more communal project, establishing a distinction with other styles of 'occupation.'

25 Neighborhood association.

26 Walked around the streets in the neighborhood, opened the doors of several vacant homes that were property of the Housing Ministry and the Ministry of the Government, and, consequently, opened the door of an old dispensary that had been abandoned for over eight years.

> construidas con capital público. Los actores eran tanto sectores chabolistas como jóvenes de asociaciones, que se aliaban para conseguir la casa al tiempo que se denunciaba la especulación sobre todo de la vivienda pública.[27] (Martínez and García 2015)

Similarly, there have also been many "conservationist okupations" in Spain—that is, occupations conducted to avoid the demolition of specific buildings or the destruction of rural and natural areas. An example of these would be the occupation of the Gallecs in Catalonia. Throughout the 1970s, Gallecs was a rural area in which several people lived and worked on their lands. But due to the Francoist ACTUR (Actuaciones Urbanísticas Urgentes en Madrid y Barcelona) project, people living there were in the process of being expropriated. As a consequence of the 1970 law of soil extension (ampliación de suelo) to build more houses and entire new towns in Spain, the government ordered the expropriation of the people living in the Gallecs in order to build a new town for about 150,000 people. But people in the area showed their opposition to the plan swiftly. As a result, a whole social movement for the conservation of the Gallecs emerged, and one of the actions that they carried out was the occupation of the rural houses there and the development of temporary communes to prevent the construction from starting. With the passing of time, they engaged in many other activities and protests, and today the Gallecs is still there, while the new city for 150,000 people was never built. As in the case of "poverty okupations," however, this kind of "conservationist okupations" aims to tackle isolated problems, and once these problems are solved, the squatting ends and everyone goes back to their normal lives. Punk squatters, on the contrary, would normally seek to foster alternate ways of living that do not depend on capitalism rather than simply providing a one-off solution to single problems. Put differently, even if punk squatters justify their squatting by the lack of housing and the retail market's speculation, and even if they do provide shelter for those who have no other place to live, their ultimate goal is to create spaces for

27 The need for housing of working-class families who had to build a shack, when there were plenty of vacant houses to speculate with, which in many cases had been built with public funds. The participants were the inhabitants of the shantytowns as well as young people from different associations that would unite to get the houses as well as to denounce the speculation with housing and, especially, with public housing.

alternative ways of living to be practiced and not simply to solve a housing problem—even less a conservation one. This is precisely why many squatters in social centers occupy buildings for sociocultural reasons but still have a house they pay for and in which they live.

The political modality, for its part, would be that of the squatters who occupy buildings as a way to confront the state and the capitalist system and who under no circumstances would negotiate with the institutions to legalize the squat, because their final goal is not to occupy a building for cultural or housing reasons but rather to dismantle the current capitalist system, of which the retail market is just a part. Punk squatters have a crucial anticapitalist character, and calling out the contradictions of the current capitalist system is an important part of them, but they are also significantly different from political squatters. Instead of seeking a confrontation with the state and the institutions, punk squatters conduct their occupations as "despite-the-system" actions that seek to create spaces in which to essay alternative ways of life to those fostered by capitalism and neoliberalism. In this sense, the crucial element in punk-influenced occupations is to be able to create the conditions for such alternative ways of life to be essayed, not whether these were achieved after negotiations with the institutions. Therefore, just as in the case of the DIY distribution network in the previous section, we need to understand the independence from the capitalist system and the institutions not as the goal or a requirement but simply as a mindset that allows punks to keep moving forward even when there are no means. In other words, the goal is to create a space to foster alternative ways of life even if there is no institutional or economic support, but this does not mean that they would always categorically oppose negotiating with the institutions or accepting funding if it helps them achieve the goal of creating such a space.

From this perspective, punk occupations are more connected to squatting as alternative strategies of housing and as entrepreneurial projects. In the case of occupations as alternative strategies of housing, squatters are not necessarily unemployed, poor, or lacking a place to live. They may be living with their family or renting a place with other people and working regular jobs, but they want to experience other ways of living and move into an abandoned building with that objective. This perspective chimes with the view of Agatha, a squatter in

Madrid's Cenicientos 14 social center, shown in the *20 minutos* program on squatting:

> ¡No me gusta este sistema, no puedo vivir en él! Me siento discriminada, explotada en el trabajo, me veo atacada en todo momento. Entonces, yo no creo que es una opción que yo tome gratuitamente, el okupar y empezar a plantearme ciertas cosas y funcionar asamblleariamente. O sea, yo es que me lo creo, yo creo que así tienen que ser las cosas, así se tiene que funcionar. Y que no es una opción que yo tome porque tenga mucho tiempo libre. Es mi forma de vida y es cómo quiero vivirla. Intentar vivir dentro de lo que se podría llamar "nuestra utopía." Intentar demostrar y demostrarlo viviendo que se puede vivir sin que haya relaciones de dominación-sumisión, sin que haya discriminaciones entre nosotros ni por el sexo, ni por el color de la piel, ni por ningún tipo de práctica ... es demostrar la solidaridad de nosotros, una cosa realista y que se puede hablar de ella. Unas cosas dentro de las que se puede vivir y que nos podemos ayudar para solucionar nuestros problemas. Yo qué sé.[28] ("Okupas")

Here Agatha highlights the predominance of being able to essay alternative ways of living; the important thing is not that they need a place to live but that they can escape the forms of life inherent to the current socio-economic system. In this same episode of *20 minutos*, other squatters express similar feelings. A man who displays a stereotypical punk mohawk while playing a few power chords on a nylon-string guitar, for example, states that the occupied house

> termina siendo como una familia, sabes, pero sólo que no una familia autoritaria como son las de ahora, porque siempre en una

28 I don't like this system, I can't live in it! I feel discriminated against, exploited at work. I feel attacked all the time. So, I don't think that it is an option that I take unwarrantedly, occupying and starting to think about certain things and live an assembly-based life. I mean, I believe in it, I believe that this is the way things should be, this how we should function. And it is not an option I choose because I have plenty of free time. This is my way of life and it is how I want to live it. Try to live within what we could call "our utopia." Try to show and show it by living this way, that one can live without any kind of domination-submission relations, without being discriminated against for our sex, color of our skin, or for any kind of practice ... it's about showing solidarity among ourselves, something real and that we can talk about. Something we can live and that we can help each other to solve our problems. I don't know.

> familia el padre es el que manda ¿no? Aquí somos todos una familia pero somos todos los hermanos, aquí no manda ninguno. Somos todos los mismos, se hace todo por asamblea, sabes, y si hay que decidir algo para el bien de la casa lo decidimos todos, y si hay que hacer esto ... pues lo hacemos entre todos. Y así.[29] ("Okupas")

Regarding occupations as entrepreneurial projects, Pruijt includes in this category almost any project that turns the occupied space not into a place for people to live but into spaces for social projects such as "centros de vecindad, bares de okupas (con beneficios destinados a acciones y proyectos solidarios), tiendas de reparación de bicicletas, casas para mujeres, restaurantes, imprentas, teatros y centros de proyecciones de películas, servicios de préstamo de herramientas, escuelas alternativas, centros de día, espacios festivos, galerías de arte, librerías y centros informativos."[30] In this sense, the most defining characteristic of the occupations in this category is that, through the occupation, squatters can establish these projects "sin necesidad de poseer grandes recursos ni de arriesgarse a perderse en interminables trámites burocráticos"[31] (Pruijt 2004, 48). With this definition in mind, punk squatters would also fall into this category if we think of the social centers they establish in order to foster an alternative cultural agenda for the neighborhood or city in which the occupied building is located—as the examples given at the start of this chapter demonstrate. In this case, while there may be people who live in the occupied building, that is not the space's primary use, and many of the people involved with the center live somewhere else. Closely related to occupations as alternative ways of housing, these social centers aim to essay alternative forms

---

29 It ends up being like a family, you know, but not an authoritarian family like today's families, because in a family it is always the father who is in charge, right? Here we are all a family but we are all the siblings, here no one is in charge. We are all the same, everything is done through assemblies, you know, and if we have to decide anything for our common good we all decide it together, and if we have to do this ... well, we do it all together. Just like that.

30 Community centers, occupied bars (whose profit is used for solidarity projects and actions), bike repair shops, housing for women, restaurants, print shop, theaters and centers to screen movies, service of tool lending, alternative schools, daytime centers, festive spaces, art galleries, book shops, and computer centers.

31 Without either having great economic means or getting lost in never-ending bureaucratic proceedings.

of living that go beyond the occupied space and that hope to spread throughout the community as a way to create or strengthen the social fabric in the area. The following description of the activities conducted in the Madrilenean social center Muniesa, provided by Ángel, a squatter in the *20 minutos* episode on the squat movement in Spain, is useful for understanding how social centers affect the social fabric of the place where they are located. Ángel states that, before the Muniesa social center was demolished,

> había un comedor popular, que lo llevaba una cooperativa, había locales de ensayo para grupos de música, había un grupo de teatro, había colectivos políticos como Lucha autónoma o el Colectivo antifascista, el sindicato de solidaridad obrera, que trabajaban en el centro social. Había, prácticamente todos los fines de semana, actividades contraculturales, ya sean charlas, debates, exposiciones.[32]

Along the same lines, it is also noteworthy how squatters in social centers seek to interact with the community and engage them in the project so that they not only take part in the activities but also use the space in whichever way it might be useful for them. The Solidaridad obrera (Worker Solidarity) union that established its workplace in the Muniesa social center is an example of this, as well as the testimonies of all the squatters in the *20 minutos* episode that explain how they hold open assemblies every week and how they reach out to the neighbors in the area to get them involved so that they take advantage of the space. Similarly, if we take a look at the programs organized by different social centers in Spain, we can note that involvement with the community tends to be a common feature. In the poster pictured in figure 25 for Plentzia and Gorliz's social center, Danontzat gaztetxea, we find all sorts of public activities during the month of June. In fact, even the name of the social center, "Danontzat," means "for everyone" in Basque. Every Monday, they offer guitar classes in what they call "kitarra ikastaro kooperatiboa" (cooperative guitar courses). The

32 There was a public canteen, run by a cooperative, there were several rooms for bands to rehearse, there was a theater group, there were political collectives such as Lucha autónoma or the Colectivo antifascista, the Solidaridad obrera union, which was based in the social center. There were, virtually every week, countercultural activities such as lectures, debates, exhibitions.

Figure 25. Danontzat gaztetxea schedule

reference to them as "cooperative" suggests that they are probably run by people who play guitar and come to donate their time to teach other people who come because they want to learn. Therefore, there is likely no payment involved. The same could be said about the tae kwon do classes on Tuesdays, the African percussion session on Wednesday the 12th, and the "oinarrizko euskal dantza ikastaroa" (basic Basque dancing course) on Friday the 14th. It is possible that they charge a small cover and that it is simply not indicated on the calendar, but, even then, it would normally be a symbolic amount that would always go to fund other activities or cover other maintenance costs. Through initiatives like these, they offer classes at popular prices for those who cannot afford to attend music schools, gyms, or dancing schools. In addition to these classes, they also offer other cultural activities such as lectures and debates on specific topics, comedy theaters (antzerki komikoa), and storytelling events (ipuin kontalaria). On Tuesday 11, for example, they are holding a lecture/debate on "La violencia en México y la lucha de las mujeres indígenas en las iniciativas autonómicas,"[33] on Wednesday 5 they have

33 Violence in Mexico and the struggle of the Indigenous women in the autonomous initiatives.

Lola Alvarez from the SAT (Sindicato Andaluz de Trabajadores) talk about the occupation of lands in Andalusia, and on Thursday 20 they have a debate on alimentary self-sufficiency—another example of the importance of the DIY ethos in these centers. Along with all the activities they organize, it is equally important to highlight that they also open the space for other people to use it for whatever they might need. For instance, the calendar shows that on Friday 8 the theater group Gilkitxaro will be meeting there and that on Wednesday 12, 19, and 26, people on Erasmus[34] and local people meet there to practice speaking different languages with each other. Finally, it is also relevant that, as part of this social center's purpose of connecting with the community, they also encourage everyone to come and take part explicitly through their message in Basque, "animatu eta parte hartu!" (come and take part!).

In this sense, punk occupations have a clear antineoliberal character, if we understand neoliberalism not exclusively in economic terms but as a more general worldview in which the individual is the absolute center of everything. From this perspective, punk occupations would not only resist the more immediate material consequences of capitalism—lack of housing or funds to develop life projects—but also the spread of a dominant neoliberal identity that Christian Laval and Pierre Dardot conceptualized in their idea of "the neoliberal subject." In their work *La nueva razón del mundo: Ensayo sobre la sociedad neoliberal* (The New Way of the World: On Neoliberal Society), Laval and Dardot go beyond thinking of neoliberalism exclusively in economic terms, and they state that neoliberalism is

> también productor de cierto tipo de relaciones sociales, de ciertas maneras de vivir, de ciertas subjetividades. Dicho de otro modo, con el neoliberalismo lo que está en juego es, nada más y nada menos, la forma de nuestra existencia, o sea, el modo en que nos vemos llevados a comportarnos, a relacionarnos con los demás y con nosotros mismos.[35] (Laval and Dardot 2013, 14)

34 Erasmus refers to the European student exchange program in which university students study abroad in another European country for a specific amount of time, normally either a semester or a whole year.

35 Is also the producer of certain social relations, certain ways of living, certain subjectivities. In other words, at stake in neoliberalism is nothing more, nor less, than the form of our existence, that is, the way in which we are led to conduct ourselves, to relate to others and ourselves.

In this sense, the neoliberal subject is that individual who has absorbed the ways of life that emerged from neoliberalism and whose thinking is guided by these forms of life. Such ways of life are those that make everyone

> vivir en un universo de competición generalizada, impone tanto a los asalariados como a las poblaciones que entren en lucha económica unos con otros, sujeta las relaciones sociales al modelo del mercado, empujar a justificar desigualdades cada vez mayores, transforma también al individuo, que en adelante es llamado a concebirse y a conducirse como una empresa.[36] (14)

Therefore, the neoliberal subject is one who understands human relationships through a market-oriented invest/profit logic and commodifies people, subjugating all personal relationships "a la regla del máximo provecho"[37] (327). They also believe that from their own individuality, without cooperating with others, they can solve all their problems and see competing with others as a natural stage previous to achieving success. It is the capitalist idea of surplus value applied to every personal space and the logic of profitability and meritocracy establishing itself as the new way of understanding life. In this way, in addition to the strictly economic impact of its economic aspects, neoliberalism is also palpable in Spain when, instead of collectively demanding their rights, working-class people become "entrepreneurs" that create their own businesses, competing with each other under the meritocratic illusion that, if they work hard enough, one day they will also achieve work-related success and, as a result, happiness as well. Similarly, it is also noticeable in the attitude of those Spaniards who view immigrants or unemployed people as parasites because, once the idea of collectivity has been erased, it is their personal life choices that lead them to where they are; had they studied more or done things differently, they would not have to "rely on *us* workers who took the right decisions to pay taxes for *them* to enjoy the society *we* create"—not to mention that in almost every case immigrants produce more wealth through taxes

---

36 Live in a universe of generalized competition, it imposes on wage-labor workers as well as citizens to engage in economic struggle against each other, it aligns social relationships with a market model, it pressures us to justify ever-greater inequalities, it even transforms the individual, who starts to view him/herself and act as a company.

37 To the rule of maximum profit.

than what they are often accused of gaining from welfare. From this perspective, social centers have a crucial role by reclaiming a public space for everyone in the neighborhood and by helping to strengthen the social fabric damaged by neoliberalism by fostering mutual support and a great variety of communal projects. The creation of fanzines, magazines, newspapers, local pirate radio, theater groups, inexpensive courses for the community, spaces for musicians to rehearse, spaces for the neighbors to meet and discuss their problems, concerts, bars with low prices, and more, they all contribute to fostering a more united and less neoliberal community.

Additionally, it is crucial to understand that, practically in all cases, social centers are located in working-class neighborhoods—which connects with the classic idea of subcultures as working-class resistance to the dominant culture. According to Stuart Hall, subcultures

> win space for the young: cultural space in the neighbourhood and institutions, real time for leisure and recreation, actual room on the street or the street-corner. They serve to mark out and appropriate "territory" in the localities. They focus around key occasions of social interaction: the weekend, the disco, the bank-holiday trip, the night out in the "centre", the "standing-about-doing-nothing" of the weekday evening, the Saturday match. They cluster around particular locations. (Hall and Jefferson 2006, 35)

Here Hall refers to the ways in which subculturalists develop their rituals around their working-class urban context, but he does not mention the crucial role of squatting in this regard. Through the occupation of abandoned buildings, punk squatters do not simply win symbolic space—like the one described by Hall—they literally take over real buildings in which to essay the alternative rituals and forms of life that Hall saw only in subculturalists' life around the city. Furthermore, adopting the Marxist structural perspective employed by the School of Birmingham, squatting becomes a crucial tool for many working-class individuals to create their own culture and rituals instead of simply having to consume those imposed on them by the dominant culture. For example, thanks to many of the numerous social centers around Spain, working-class people who cannot afford to go to the city-center clubs, venues, or cinemas are able to enjoy dancing, listening to music, or watching movies in their own neighborhood. Moreover, they also do not have to consume the music or the films being screened in the mainstream venues and cinemas because they get to agree on the movies they watch at the social centers. In this same vein, these centers have been crucial for punk bands to tour around Spain when they could not perform in any other place. Therefore, they have also helped to create a national punk circuit for bands to share their music without having to depend on mainstream venues and management companies—again empowering punk musicians and working-class people through a determinant DIY ethos.

Finally, both occupation as alternative housing and occupation as social centers can also be seen as what Hakim Bey referred to as TAZs (temporary autonomous zones). According to Bey, "The TAZ is like an uprising which does not engage directly with the State, a guerilla operation which liberates an area (of land, of time, of imagination) and then dissolves itself to re-form elsewhere/elsewhen, before the State can crush it." Furthermore, he states that

> history says the Revolution attains "permanence," or at least duration, while the uprising is "temporary." In this sense an uprising is like a "peak experience" as opposed to the standard of "ordinary" consciousness and experience. Like festivals, uprisings cannot happen every day—otherwise they would not be "nonordinary." But such moments of intensity give shape and meaning to the entirety of a life. The shaman returns—you can't stay up on the roof forever—but things have changed, shifts and integrations have occurred—a difference is made. (Bey 1985, 80)

Spanish social centers are an excellent example of temporary autonomous zones. Punks in Spain refused all political grand narratives and the idea of a social revolution that would liberate us all. In the same vein, they also did not want to depend on any institution or political group. As in the occupations discussed in the beginning of the chapter, and driven by a DIY ethos, punks would simply go ahead and do what they had to—legal or not—in order to get what they believed they deserved. As Kurdo, Olor a Sobako's singer, states in the episode of *¿Dónde estabas entonces?* dedicated to the squat movement in Spain: "Es esta idea de no esperar a una revolución, a un cambio grande para hacer aquello que queríamos, sino ponerlo en práctica desde el minuto cero"[38] ("Ni banderas ni fronteras"). By doing this, they would create these TAZs until they were evicted, and then would go occupy a new building somewhere else or wait until the space was legalized. In the process, alternative ways of life were put into practice, consciousnesses were shaped in specific manners, and, ultimately, it made a difference.

### 1.3. Other Chapters

Reading through the rest of the chapters of *Hazlo tú mismo*, one can find an extensive array of strategies on how to follow a DIY ethos in many aspects of our lives. The third chapter focuses on alimentary self-sufficiency and begins by connecting punk's DIY ethos with what they refer to as food "recycling." The main argument of the first pages is that, even if it is normally assumed that one needs to engage in wage labor in order to have money to eat, that is not necessarily true if, among other things, we consider the idea of food recycling. The author defends his argument in a more enthusiastic way and expresses himself in the following manner: "Lo típico que te suelen decir los aburguesados es que quien no curra no come, ¡y una mierda! Yo no curro y como, y ahí es donde entra la importancia del recicle"[39] (FAP 2008, 47). Food recycling is nothing other than going to wholesale food markets or supermarkets and picking up all the unsold food that they throw away every day. Just as houses have become a commodity for speculation due to their exchange value, so has food—especially in big supermarket chains such as Sabeco, Alcampo, and Aldi. But if housing is a right and something necessary in order to have a dignified life, food is necessary for survival. In this context, the profit-driven food industry accumulates overstock commodities in the form of food every day because, as Marx noted, "the rate of profit is the motive power of capitalist production. Things are produced only so long as they can be produced with a profit" (Marx 1897, n.p.), and if there is anything in the world that will never cease to be in demand and therefore allow for a potential profit, it is food. In this sense, while the car industry needs to pay more attention to the rise or fall in demand in order to make sure that the investment—in terms of machinery and materials,

38 It is this idea of not having to wait for a revolution, for a great change, in order to do what we want, but starting to do it from the very beginning.

39 The usual thing that a bourgeois would say is that if you don't work you can't eat. Fuck that! I don't work and I eat, and that's where recycling is important.

but also number of employees and salary levels—does not outstrip the profit, the food industry can play it slightly safer and simply produce food because everybody needs to eat.

For this reason, in advanced capitalist countries such as Spain, there is normally a massive amount of food coming to the supermarkets almost every day. Yet unlike housing, food cannot be bought as a future investment because it goes bad, and this creates a conflictive situation for those investing in the food industry. On the one hand, while everybody needs food and, therefore, the demand is always high, not everyone can afford it. On the other, supermarkets cannot keep the food for when these people have the money to buy it, because it goes bad. As a result, just like societies with empty houses and homeless people, many supermarkets end up throwing away their food, creating a society with wasted food and starving people.

In 2016, France passed a law that prohibited supermarkets from throwing away food and forced them to donate it to charities and food banks (Chrisafis 2016). This measure sought to use wasted food in a more sensible way but, at the same time, it represented an intervention in the economy by the state that opposes the neoliberal logic of a free market, as well as businesspeople's right to do as they please with their businesses. Thus, forcing all supermarkets to do so in contemporary neoliberal societies is a complicated thing to achieve. In Spain, FACUA–Consumidores en Acción—a nonprofit organization for consumer rights—published a document that showed nine Spanish supermarkets' responses to a questionnaire regarding food waste. The questions in it asked them about their commitment to donating food and being sensible about food waste. The questionnaire was originally sent to twenty-eight supermarkets, but only nine replied, all of which showed a clear commitment to donating the food they do not sell—which probably means that the nineteen supermarkets that did not reply do not donate their food (FACUA, n.d.). In Spain, until recently at least, not only was there no law like the one in France that prohibits supermarkets from throwing away food but also people who look for food in rubbish bins could be fined for it. With all this in mind, the author of this part of *Hazlo tú mismo* proposes to use this contradiction of capitalism to one's advantage and gather food for those who do not want to work to pay for it, as well as for others who simply lack the resources. According to the author, many people could live on the food that is wasted every day, and they even state that, in the Casas Viejas Social Center of Seville, they have "llegado a hacer comedores para 100 personas con toda la verdura reciclada en tan solo un día yendo a los dos grandes mercados de Sevilla" (FAP 2008, 47).[40] They also claim that "la causa de la pobreza no es la falta de recursos pues estos acaban en los basureros todos los días"[41] and that "este sistema caerá por su propio peso, y [. . .] mientras tanto nosotrxs seguiremos siendo punks y recogeremos sus sobras para transformarlas en autogestión. D.I.Y. JODE AL SISTEMA"[42] (48). The rest of the chapter focuses on how to keep a vegetable garden and how to follow a vegan diet—a dietary option they strongly defend. Along with this, they provide various vegan recipes and some advice on how to maintain a healthy vegan diet, making sure to consume all the necessary nutrients.

The fourth chapter focuses on transportation and makes a point of using bicycles and public transportation not only to save money but also to avoid polluting the ecosystem. They also devote sections to explaining ways of riding public transportation illegally without paying—which links back to the cover of L'odi Social's album *Que pagui Pujol*—such as creating fake tickets. As shown in Figures 26 and 27 which demonstrate how to falsify metro tickets, the techniques they describe can be quite sophisticated.

The rest of the chapters follow a similar vein and talk about how to make your own clothes, hygiene products, and homemade remedies for different physical ailments. Additionally, they also talk about how to enjoy sex in nonnormative ways with references, for instance, to anal masturbation techniques for men regardless of their sexual orientation. Finally, they also develop a whole chapter to direct-action techniques, another one to explaining how to create cooperatives to avoid wage-labor-related work, and another one to justify theft and to explain different techniques for robbing—which they defend as a way to take back the surplus that the richer class steals from the working class.

---

40 Even organized public meals for over 100 people with all the food recycled, just by going to the two biggest wholesale markets of Seville on a single day.

41 The cause of poverty is not the lack of resources, since these end up in rubbish bins every day.

42 This system will fall due to its own nature and [. . .] meanwhile, we will keep being punks and we will pick up their leftovers to turn into self-financing. D.I.Y. FUCK THE SYSTEM.

**COMO FALSIFICAR TICKETS DE METRO**

Esto es válido para los sitios en los que en los billetes de metro o autobús, de varios viajes, te marquen con tinta los viajes que lleves gastados.

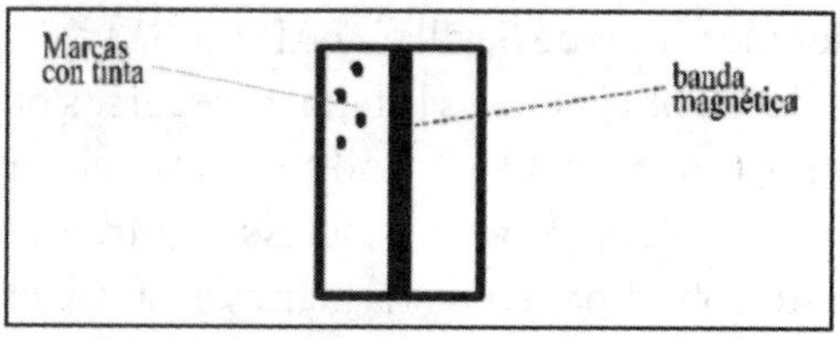


Bien, podemos ver en el dibujo, como tenemos un billete, del cual las medidas pueden varias, pero básicamente consta de un lado en el que pone información sobre el billete, la empresa, etc. y por el reverso, nos encontramos con la cara que nos interesa, aquí hay una banda magnética, que es la que lee la máquina para saber los viajes que te quedan, y dos costados en los que se nos marca con una tinta los viajes que llevamos gastados.
La falsificación consiste en poner un trozo de papel de liar, postick, celofán, etc. Algo que abulte poco y que tape la parte donde se nos marca la tinta, pero ojo, sin tapar la banda magnética.

Esta técnica la empezaremos a utilizar, por ejemplo, si tenemos un billete de 10 viajes, cuando hayamos gastado uno. Después de que este único viaje este marcado en el billete, colocaremos nuestro trozo de papel, para impedir que el resto de viajes queden marcados con la tinta en el billete. Podremos utilizar los otros diez viajes, hasta que agotemos el billete. Una vez que éste esté agotado, quitaremos el trozo de papel, con cuidado de no producir deterioro en el billete. Nos quedará un billete de diez viajes, en el que solo se ha marcado uno de ellos con tinta. Ahora, tenemos que pasarle un imán, normal y corriente, a la banda magnética para desimantar la información que viene en ella, y solo tendremos que acudir a una taquilla, alegando que lo hemos comprado hace nada, y solo hemos gastado un viaje, y no nos funciona. Esto es algo habitual, ya que lo puedes llevar cerca del móvil o algo con imán, y puede haberte pasado. La taquillera, lo comprobara, y lo examinara, así que ojo con dejar cualquier huella, y ojo con no pasarle el imán, ya que entonces nos habrán pillado in fraganti. Si todo ha salido bien, la taquillera, nos hará un billete con los viajes que faltaban del billete, es decir, con 9 viajes.

UN PAR DE CONSEJOS

No seas tan capullx de irte a cambiar siempre a la misma estación de metro. Aunque no te salga tan rentable, no lo entregues nuevo para hacer el cambio, al menos pica uno sin el "truquillo". Cuando te devuelvan otro metrobús nuevo, esta vez te pondrá la palabra CANJE, o sea que si con el cambiado también haces el truco, van a saber que anteriormente ya cambiaste el metrobús. Compañerx de viaje, sin más, te animamos a que lleves a cabo esta idea, y a que rule esta pequeña "solución" entre todxs tus colegas. Aunque siempre queda el modo de toda la vida, colarte por todo el morro sin tantas remilgaciones.

**Figures 26 & 27. How to make a fake metro ticket**

## 2. DIY as a Fluid Spectrum

The previous exploration of punk's DIY ethos in Spain and the ways of life derived from it provide various clues to understanding the value of punk as an anticapitalist and antineoliberal culture. First, the refusal to guide one's life based on the ways of life determined by capitalism provides multiple examples of nonnormative identity models that challenge the dominant culture. People involved in punk are generally people who do not want to have to engage in wage labor, follow specific time schedules, get married, have children, and so on. Second, through their DIY ethos, they get things done and solve immediate problems that institutions do not: They open spaces for public leisure through occupied buildings, they create communal food banks, they give the homeless shelter, and more.

But as in the first chapter, which discussed punk as a polymorphous subculture, those who take part in punk subculture today have very different profiles. These may include a banker who owns an independent punk label and helps punk bands promote their work, or a councilor who takes part in institutional politics and then works at an occupied social center in the evenings. In this sense, while it is common for punks not to engage in wage labor, follow specific time schedules, get married, and have children, they are also people who would do all of the previous if they wanted to. Therefore, it would be an error to believe that there is a homogeneous and always-coherent way of being part of punk subculture. For this reason, I want to close this chapter by viewing the anticapitalist and antineoliberal potential of punk's DIY ethos as a fluid spectrum that serves punk's multiple purposes in varied and contextual ways.

Canteca de Macao and Ska-P worked with major record labels, but the first forced the labels to give their album away for free, while the second have never written a nonpolitical song and have used the exposure granted by the label to spread their political ideals. In the case of some of the squatters shown in the *20 minutes* episode on squatting, they even had jobs and/or attended university, and they were there only because they wanted to live in a community that shared similar beliefs to theirs. Another illustrative example is that of Canino, Sin Dios's drummer, whose real name is José Couso Permuy and who was a member of the European Parliament with Izquierda Unida (United Left) from 2014 to 2019. These examples show that one needs to view punk's DIY ethos as a fluid spectrum in which people involved in punk culture follow independent and beyond-the-system ways in order to get things done, but without necessarily refusing to use institutional politics or capitalism to one's benefit when useful, as the example of food recycling has shown. Another pertinent example is the following response from Evaristo, the singer of La Polla Records, when in a Basque TV show in 2014 he was told that he had always sung against political parties but then has also openly supported several of them:

"Sí, no me parece contradictorio, yo puedo odiar a los partidos y tocar para ellos. Luego el precio que les haga yo es cosa mía. Si me llaman del PP pa' un concierto les cobro cien veces más y encima me oyen. No me parece nada contradictorio"[43] ("Entrevista completa a Evaristo en PFV de ETB2").

In this way, punk's DIY ethos is a tool for empowerment but not a dogmatic rule through which everyone involved in punk should operate at all times. Put simply, punk fosters ways of life alternative to those spread by capitalism but does so within capitalism and using capitalism in its favor if necessary. As I will discuss in the conclusion, it is precisely in this fluid idea of the DIY ethos that one can also trace the connection between many Spanish contemporary nongovernmental social movements and their commitment to participating in institutional politics through parties like Podemos. For example, a very punk and DIY-influenced movement such as the 15-M, which refused to define itself through the left wing versus right wing binary opposition and which was not part of any specific political party, was partially taken to the institutions by Podemos. As a result, a social movement that was, in principle, against institutional participation engaged in political activity to defend its goals while continuing to also work independently at the grassroots level. This is precisely what punks will do through their fluid idea of a DIY ethos. They will engage with whomever in whatever way necessary if it serves the purpose of fostering the ways of life they defend while also working independently, because the ultimate goal is to do precisely that: to put those alternative forms of life into practice, right now, right here, and in any way necessary.

43 Yeah, I don't think that's contradictory; I can hate political parties and perform for them. Then I decide the rate I charge them. If the PP calls me to play for them I charge them a hundred times more and, on top of that, they hear what I have to say. I don't think that's contradictory at all.

CHAPTER 5

# SÍ HAY FUTURO (YES, THERE IS A FUTURE)

## 1. Punk, Social Movements, and Antiestablishment Identities

On May 15, 2011, the popular movement commonly known as the 15-M, the indignados, or the Spanish revolution emerged in the streets of Madrid. This movement was formed by people across the political spectrum who gathered to protest the government's austerity measures as well as the more generalized increasing precariousness of life among the Spanish population. In addition to single individuals, the 15-M was also formed by recently established collectives such as Democracia Real Ya, No Les Votes, and Juventud Sin Futuro, among others. When talking about this movement, there is a tendency to speak of a sudden repolitization of the Spanish population after the long period of political apathy that followed the end of Franco's dictatorship. Hence slogans such as "Dormíamos, despertamos" (We were asleep. We woke up.)—as if before the 15-M they had all been asleep, meaning not politically engaged—or "Nobody expected the Spanish revolution"—which communicates some sort of immediacy and surprise. Similarly, if one watches the different documentaries or testimonies on the 15-M, expressions about the novelty and the sudden political awakening are a constant theme. As a result, many have come to view the 15-M as a spontaneous occurrence that emerged as something of a short circuit in the generalized political disaffection of the country—an unexpected spark that interrupted the apathy and reengaged politically an important part of the Spanish population. In a similar way, under such a perspective, that repolitization would have

**Figure 28. 15-M in Madrid**

necessarily been triggered by the current affairs of the country at that specific time, reiterating the idea that there was no political engagement before then. Yet both the form and content of many of the expressions that emerged from the 15-M, as well as its general modus operandi, have a clear background in previously existing movements, among which that of punk culture played a crucial role. At the end of the day, the 15-M and the occupation of the plazas are another clear example of TAZs in which the ways of life fostered in social centers are taken to even more visible spaces and are now put into practice in the center of the public square.

Cristina Flesher Fominaya (2015, 143) highlights the role of the Spanish autonomous movement in this regard and argues against the "spontaneous theory" by stating that it was thanks to previously established activist networks that the 15-M became so popular. Additionally, Flesher Fominaya borrows Verta Taylor's concept of "abeyance" to establish a theory of continuation within Spanish social movements that prevents us from viewing events such as the 15-M as one-off, disconnected occurrences. Taylor studies the women's movement in the US, and through her idea of abeyance she establishes "linkages between one upsurge in activism and another" (762). In this sense, "the term 'abeyance' depicts a holding process by which movements sustain themselves in nonreceptive political environments and provide continuity from one stage of mobilization to another" (761). Therefore, a social movement in abeyance is a social movement that has lost centrality in a nonreceptive context but that keeps working in many different ways from a marginal position until a favorable opportunity emerges and gains central importance once again. In this way, we could speak of a continuous activism in Spain that has reached the surface with higher intensity in specific moments, such as that of the 15-M. Other high-intensity moments could also be that of the anti-NATO mobilizations, the Nunca Mais (Never Again) movement, the No a la guerra (antiwar) movement, or that of the post 11-M demonstrations.[1] In other words, we could say that many varied and often disconnected social movements—anticapitalist, antinuclear, antimilitary, ecologist, feminist, antifascist, and others—have been working at an underground level and have converged and reached the surface at times when the context has become more receptive, with events such as the 15-M. With all this in mind, I want to close this book by showing that punk culture has been a decisive cultural glue that has held many of these movements together and a persistent cultural axis from which many other movements have emerged. Additionally, I will show that punk has been a crucial element in the development of critical and antiestablishment political identities among many Spaniards. I will list a number of examples that support my argument before presenting the final conclusions of this book.

"Lo llaman democracia y no lo es" was probably one of the most repeated chants all across Spain during the 15-M mobilizations.[2] Likely unknown to many, however, this chant is literally the same one with which Evaristo and La Polla Records had been opening their song "Ellos dicen mierda" years before the 15-M ("La Polla Records 'Ellos dicen mierda'"). The melody, rhythm, and lyrics are exactly the same as those in La Polla Records' song. In fact, the audience singing "Lo llaman democracia y no lo es" at La Polla Records concerts and those singing it in the occupied squares during the 15-M seem quite interchangeable. Long before that, punk had also been the soundtrack of the antimilitary and "insumiso" movement in Spain during the 1980s and early '90s. Bands such as Eskorbuto, La Polla, RIP, Barricada, and others were very active in the anti-NATO movement during the 1980s—regardless

---

1 "11-M" refers to the terrorist bombing of Madrid's Renfe trains in 2004.

2 To hear the chant, see "Lo llaman democracia y no lo es," YouTube, uploaded by Santico, May 19, 2011, https://www.youtube.com/watch?v=Q4Gp4rJ8KWo.

**Figure 29. Cover of *Rock Anti Mili***

of their personal commitment to the cause. Probably the best example of this is the anti-NATO festival held in Tudela in 1983 as part of the demonstrations organized all across Spain, in which these four bands and others performed. Strictly related to the "insumiso" movement, there are also several concerts and initiatives in which punk bands participated, such as the Koncierto Anti-Mili in 1988 in Madrid, in which the punk bands Radical H.C., 37 Hostias, Tarzán, and Hormigón took part, or the *Rock Anti Mili* and *Insumisión* tape compilations. *Rock Anti Mili* was self-produced and self-released in 1988 by the joint efforts of the Ateneu Llibertarti del Poble Sec, the CAMPI (Colectivo Antimilitarista y Pro-Insumisión), the graphic artist Carlos Azagra,[3]

3 Carlos Azagra has worked as a cartoonist in magazines such as *El jueves,* and he created the famous Pedro Pico and Pico Vena cartoon characters in 1984 for this magazine. The former is a skinhead, and the latter is a punk.

**Figure 30. Cover of *Insumisión***

Estudios Q-3, and each of the twenty-one punk bands that contributed a different song dealing with topics related to the antimilitary and "insumiso" movement. Regarding this compilation, it is important to note that all the bands and people involved in the recording donated the earnings to help the "insumisos." *Insumisión*, for its part, was released by Gato Salvaje, a DIY independent distribution company based in the occupied social center El Centro Social Seco[4] in Madrid.

In 1992, the year when Spain was celebrating the Olympic Games in Barcelona, the Expo in Seville, Madrid's designation as the "European City of Culture," and the five-hundredth anniversary of Columbus's arrival in the Americas, Spanish punk was also engaging with different social movements to show a different interpretation of these celebrations. One of the most outstanding pieces of evidence in this sense is

4 https://web.archive.org/web/20061004065647/http://www.cs-seco.org/.

probably the compilation *Kaña al 92*, which seeks to oppose all four of these celebrations in a single work. It is worth reading the statement on the first pages of its inner booklet to understand the scope of the project:

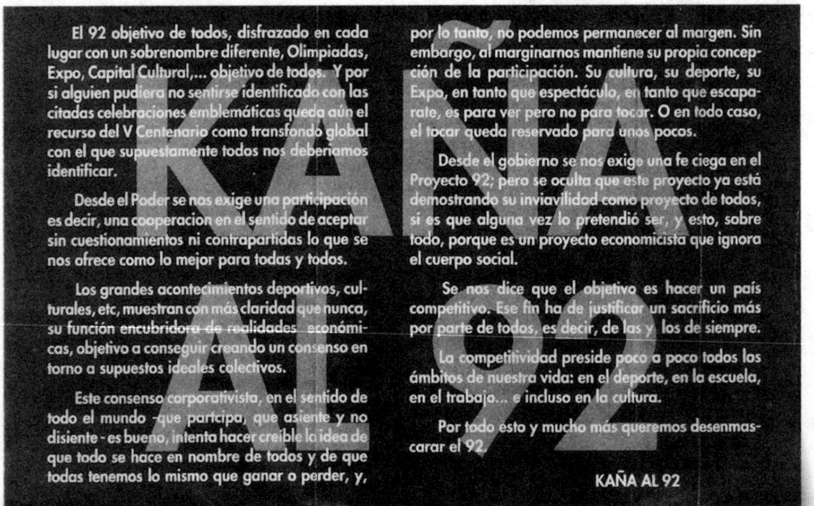

El 92 objetivo de todos, disfrazado en cada lugar con un sobrenombre diferente, Olimpiadas, Expo, Capital Cultural,... objetivo de todos. Y por si alguien pudiera no sentirse identificado con las citadas celebraciones emblemáticas queda aún el recurso del V Centenario como transfondo global con el que supuestamente todos nos deberíamos identificar.

Desde el Poder se nos exige una participación es decir, una cooperacion en el sentido de aceptar sin cuestionamientos ni contrapartidas lo que se nos ofrece como lo mejor para todas y todos.

Los grandes acontecimientos deportivos, culturales, etc, muestran con más claridad que nunca, su función encubridora de realidades económicas, objetivo a conseguir creando un consenso en torno a supuestos ideales colectivos.

Este consenso corporativista, en el sentido de todo el mundo -que partcipa, que asiente y no disiente - es bueno, intenta hacer creíble la idea de que todo se hace en nombre de todos y de que todas tenemos lo mismo que ganar o perder, y, por lo tanto, no podemos permanecer al margen. Sin embargo, al marginarnos mantiene su propia concepción de la participación. Su cultura, su deporte, su Expo, en tanto que espectáculo, en tanto que escaparate, es para ver pero no para tocar. O en todo caso, el tocar queda reservado para unos pocos.

Desde el gobierno se nos exige una fe ciega en el Proyecto 92; pero se oculta que este proyecto ya está demostrando su inviavilidad como proyecto de todos, si es que alguna vez lo pretendió ser, y esto, sobre todo, porque es un proyecto economicista que ignora el cuerpo social.

Se nos dice que el objetivo es hacer un país competitivo. Ese fin ha de justificar un sacrificio más por parte de todos, es decir, de las y los de siempre.

La competitividad preside poco a poco todos los ámbitos de nuestra vida: en el deporte, en la escuela, en el trabajo... e incluso en la cultura.

Por todo esto y mucho más queremos desenmascarar el 92.

KAÑA AL 92

**Figure 31. Inner booklet of *Kaña al 92***

The text makes a clear reference to the economic investment in the events organized in 1992 by the government and to the capitalist logic of competition that, as is the case in the current neoliberal society, "preside poco a poco todos los ámbitos de nuestra vida."[5] The songs included in the album mix anticapitalist messages with songs against the invasion of the Americas and are performed by bands such as Maniatika, La Polla Records, Reincidentes, Etsaiak, Negu Gorriak, and others. In addition to this, we could also list *NO 92*, a compilation of Catalan bands singing against the Olympic Games of Barcelona.

Similarly, punk in Spain has always been closely related to antifascist and antiracist movements. In addition to the numerous songs written by individual bands about both topics, we can also find a few different compilations, such as *Cinta antifascista* or *Cinta antirracista*. The former includes national and international punk bands that sing against fascism and neonazism, and the latter presents bands from Spain that perform antiracist songs such as "Tercer mundo" by Tarzán, "La del inmigrante" by 37 Hostias, and "Europa Café con leche" by Monstruación.

---

5 gradually dominates all areas of our life

**Figure 32. Cover of *NO 92***

Additionally, we can also find other situations in which punk has crossed paths with activism and politics, as when in 2014 Eneko Erreondo, a congressman of the Basque political party Amaiur, sang the chorus of Eskorbuto's "Mucha policía, poca diversión" in Congress to denounce the passage of the "Ley Mordaza" (gag law) or the fact that Sin Dios's drummer became a representative of IU in the European Parliament. Similarly, it is also symptomatic that in 2012 Podemos's secretary and former professor at the Universidad Complutense, Pablo Iglesias, spoke of Evaristo from La Polla Records, citing lyrics from the song "Delincuencia," in the following manner:

> Siempre he dicho que si un día llego a pintar algo en la Universidad, aunque me temo que ese día no va a llegar nunca, haré lo que pueda para que Evaristo, el cantante de La Polla Records sea investido como Doctor Honoris Causa. ¿Por qué? Escuchad al gran sabio

**Figure 33.** Cover of *Cinta antifascista*

punki: "Banqueros, unos ladrones sin palanca y de día. / Políticos estafadores juegan a vivir de ti. / Fabricantes de armamento, eso es jeta de cemento. / Las religiones calmantes y las bandas de uniforme. / La droga publicitaria, delito premeditado. / Y la estafa inmobiliaria. / Delincuencia, delincuencia, es la vuestra, asquerosos. / Delincuencia, vosotros hacéis la ley." En fin . . . Los que crecimos en los 80 y nos educamos con La Polla Records sabemos más de lo que significa el garantismo que esos hipócritas católicos hijos del franquismo que gobiernan en este país.[6] (Iglesias Turrión)

6 I've always said that if I ever have any power in the university, although I don't think that day will ever come, I will do my best to confer Evaristo, the singer of La Polla Records, an honorary doctorate. Why? Hear the great wise punk: "Bankers, thieves with no levers and during the day time. / Fraudster politicians live at your expense. /

Figure 34. Cover of *Cinta antirracista*

Along with this, another Podemos member, Ramón Espinar, used the lyrics of the La Polla Records song "No somos nada" (We are nothing) to protest impunity of the crimes committed during Francoism. In 2014 he tweeted the following message: "Somos los hijos de los obreros que nunca pudisteis matar, los nietos de los que perdieron la Guerra Civil. Impunidad, la vuestra" (@RamonEspinar May 23, 2014).[7] Regardless of the appropriate choice of words to express his protest—considering that his father was part of the PSOE government in Madrid during the

---

Weapon manufacturers, what a nerve. / Soothing religions and people in uniforms. / Advertisements, premeditated crime. / And the estate agents' fraud. / Delinquency, delinquency, is yours, filthy bastards. / Delinquency, you make the law." And that's it . . . Those of us who grew up during the 1980s and were educated by La Polla Records know more about the meaning of garantism than those hypocrite descendants of Francoism that govern this country.

7 We are the grandchildren of the workers you were never able to kill, the grandchildren of those who lost the Civil War. Impunity, that is what *you* have.

**Figure 35. Eskorbuto graffito during anti-G20 riots in Hamburg in 2017**

1980s, part of Caja Madrid's board of directors during the "black cards" affair, and sentenced to jail for this same matter—his tweet is evidence of the influence of punk in contemporary politics and antiestablishment identities. Along the same lines, and still connected to Podemos, we can also point out that Fernando Madina, Reincidentes' vocalist, is part of the Podemos circle in Carmona and was fourth on the list presented to the local elections in 2015 by the party.

In a more globalized context, it is also remarkable that, during the anticapitalist and anti-G20 riots in Hamburg in 2017, someone took the time to do a graffito with the name of Eskorbuto, as seen in figure 35.

Finally, I would like to mention the demonstration against the rally organized by the political parties Vox, PP, and Ciudadanos in Altsasua on November 4, 2018. The rally aimed to show support for the Guardia Civil in this town due to the incidents that had occurred in 2016, in which a group of people had a fight outside a local bar. What seemed to be a simple bar fight between several young people soon became defined as a terrorist attack by many, because two of the men involved in the fight were Guardia Civiles. According to some, the two Guardia Civiles and their girlfriends were attacked by local youth because of their occupation while they were off duty and having a drink at a bar. But others claimed that the incident had been instrumentalized to turn attention toward the fact that they were Guardia Civiles and to describe the fight as a terrorist attack. From this perspective, the dialectical connections between the alleged attackers and ETA had been constant, and the public prosecutor's office (Fiscalía) requested a sentence of fifty years in jail for terrorism. According to this office, the attack was a continuation of the repression against the Guardia Civil carried out by ETA. Others stated that one of the Guardia Civiles, who was drunk, used force against another young during a discussion, subduing him on the floor, and taking advantage of his power as a Guardia Civil to later have him arrested and tried. In summary, the Guardia Civiles were never tried, and the other young people were sentenced to up to thirteen years in jail—even when charges for terrorism were finally dropped. With this context in mind, the rally to support the Guardia Civiles organized by the PP, Vox, and Ciudadanos in Altsasua stirred things up for the friends and relatives of the convicted young people, and a counterdemonstration was organized. Now, let alone the controversy of the incidents, what I want to highlight is the influence of punk in this counterdemonstration. The video on *Naiz*, an online newspaper, shows different things that people were chanting at the demonstration, among which we find not one, but three, different punk songs (Zaldua 2018). At 1:28 we can hear the people sing Vomito's "Las fuerzas de seguridad" (Security forces): "Perros guardianes del orden y la ley / asesinos a sueldo, abuso de poder,"[8] and then, at 1:54, they sing Eskorbuto's "Mucha policía, poca diversión" (Lots of police, little fun). In addition to this, they had a punk concert on a mobile platform being driven all around town, and at 2:16 we can see them play "No somos nada" by La Polla Records while all the people in the counterdemonstration sing along. In addition to all this, Fermin Muguruza, former singer of Kortatu, played a show in a public square in the town center area as part of the counterdemonstration events.

But punk's influence and interactions with politics and activism in Spain are not limited to its cultural artifacts. We can also see the influence of punk's DIY ethos in many ways. An example of this would be its modus operandi and the practices conducted by the 15-M movement all across Spain. The occupation of the squares is almost identical to squatting an abandoned building. People involved in the 15-M occupied that space and began living there and organizing projects as they would have done when occupying an abandoned building. By doing so, they

8 Watchdogs of law and order / paid assassins, abuse of power.

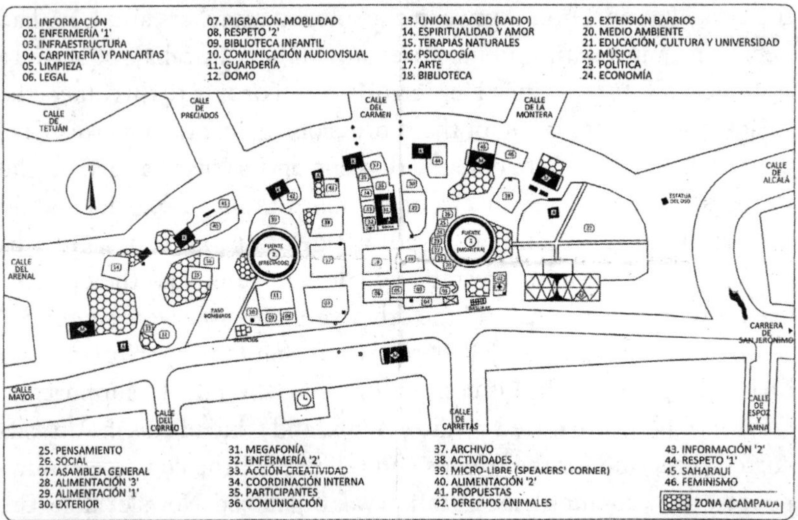


**Figure 36. Madrid 15-M camping plan**

reclaimed the public space, temporarily liberated a zone by turning it into a TAZ, and started to practice ways of life similar to those in the occupied social centers. In figure 36, for instance, one can see the organization and the different sections that they established around the Plaza del Sol in Madrid.

As we can see, there were small tents with all sorts of services all around the square. There were sections dealing with music, politics, economics, environmental issues, feminism, animal rights, and others, and even a kindergarten for children and a canteen for people to eat at. They also had a section dealing with communications, a library, and even a radio station. In addition to this, they held discussions, lectures, and assembly-based decision-making events to coordinate the movement. It was essentially an outdoor social center. The DIY practices that fostered the creation of their own radio, social media, informative videos, documentaries, brochures, live broadcastings, and more were decisive in the success of the 15-M. But one does not come to the square and suddenly improvise all these practices. These practices were being exercised in the social centers all around Spain since the very first punk occupations. Therefore, it would not be too far-fetched to say that, had people involved in the 15-M not experienced the DIY practices and the cooperative nature of the ways of life fostered at social centers, the 15-M would probably not have been half as successful.

Along with this, we can also see the influence of these ways of life in many of the practices carried out by the political party Podemos during its first years of existence—especially after viewing the connections with punk culture of several of its original members. When the party was created in 2014, they held open assemblies in town squares, social centers, local libraries, and other spaces, in which people would come to express their worries about their neighborhood or to organize and develop different actions for the people living there. In contrast with the typical party that meets with its affiliated members in a private local space, Podemos tried to affect the social fabric by bringing politics to the streets and by opening it for all residents to participate. In this same vein, when the time came to propose specific people for local, autonomic, and national governments, any citizen could run for office as a Podemos representative, and anyone could vote for that person online with their national ID. Therefore, the party would not develop a list of people based on the affiliated members' votes that the citizens would then vote for in the elections. Since there was no concept of "affiliated member" in Podemos, anyone could run and anyone could vote, in an attempt to truly represent the people's will as much as possible and with as little intervention of hierarchical powers as possible. Even the program for the elections was the result of proposals developed through discussions in local assemblies in which anyone could participate. In a similar vein, Podemos refused to use banks or any other private money for their campaigns during its first years. Every time there was a campaign, they followed a system in which citizens could lend the party money that they would get back afterward when the government paid Podemos the electoral subsidy. Through this somewhat DIY self-financing method, they avoided engaging with banks and other private interests.

Now, after this promising and exciting beginning, it is necessary to clarify that Podemos soon became a party with the same old practices as any other. By 2020, Podemos was not too different from any other traditional left-wing party. That year they became part of the Spanish government in coalition with the PSOE, and, although having been essential to push different progressive laws, the practices that aspired to create a nonhierarchical and anticapitalist model of direct democracy were long gone. Despite this, Podemos's beginnings are still illuminating to understand punk's scope of influence adequately.

## 2. Conclusions

In 2018, there were mass demonstrations and riots in France after the president, Emmanuel Macron, announced that the government was going to raise the price of fuel. Swiftly, these demonstrations became a more general denunciation of the precariousness of the French working class. While all this was going on, it was common to see memes and Facebook and Twitter statuses or to hear statements made by Spaniards depicting the Spanish working class as weaker than the French one. "While in France they complain about a 1,200 euros minimum wage, in Spain, with a minimum wage of 757 euros, you stay on your couch." Statements like these were constantly shared by Spaniards both on social media and in casual conversations. This became even more constant when, as a result of the demonstrations, Macron increased the minimum wage to almost 1,500 euros. But this is nothing new, as putting down their own neighbors without doing much about it is a trademark of many left-oriented people in Spain. In this way, in an overcritical exercise, it is normally those on the left who criticize most voraciously all the culture produced during the Transición for its alleged apolitical and hedonist character. Obviously, it is necessary to always maintain a critical attitude in order to avoid becoming complacent with the state of things. Yet I wonder whether ranting about the Transición and the culture produced during this time has become a practice that hinders us from looking deeper into the subject, contributing, as a side effect, to a paralyzing hopelessness. This might be the reason why the works around Francoism's cultural traces in contemporary Spain are far more prominent than those exploring the ways in which culture has opposed these very same Francoist traces. In this sense, it might be worth reflecting on whether "el mono del desencanto" (longing for disenchantment) is more present in the scholarship on the culture of the Transición than in the cultural producers of the Transición themselves.

But there are exceptions. Against the discourse of depoliticization and cultural apathy, scholars such as Germán Labrador have worked to provide an alternative narrative about the culture produced during the Transición. In his work *Culpables por la literatura: Imaginación política y contracultura en la Transición (1968–1986)*, he studies a completely different corpus to that normally represented in the works about this period (Labrador Méndez 2017). Labrador focuses on what he refers to as the culture of the losers of the Transición—in other words, the people who were imagining a different democracy to the one that was established and that never succeeded. In this vein, he also refers to the democracy that these people were imagining as the "democracy still to come." By doing this, he contributes to creating an archive of cultural producers that are normally ignored by most scholarship and that were neither apathetic nor hedonistic. Following Walter Benjamin's (2006, 402) idea of revolutions as "an attempt by the passengers on this train—namely, the human race—to activate the emergency brake" and in tune with punk's urgency to take action today since there is "no future," I believe it is important to identify the everyday revolutions that do contribute to a more equal world in our daily lives. In other words, the quotidian actions that activate the emergency brake and in which punk culture has played an important role since it came about. Punk's anticapitalist discourse, the spread of mutual-aid culture in social centers, and others might not have changed the base of society but have had relevant effects in several areas.

In the case of Spain, punk represents a culture that has been critical of the Transición and all the political happenings in the country while also showing a crucial anticapitalist and antineoliberal character in both its cultural artifacts and its ways of life. Regarding the Transición, it produced one of the most critical cultural corpuses, and it always questioned the process toward democracy and everything around it from a great number of perspectives. It did so explicitly by referring to the change of regime, showing a clear commitment to historic memory, and continuously questioning the politics of the time. In regard to its anticapitalist and antineoliberal character, it is crucial to refer to the ways of life fostered by punk's DIY ethos and the influence of these on Spanish social centers and contemporary social movements and politics. The DIY ethos empowers individuals to go and get what they want instead of having to wait for others to do it for them and, above all, to do it immediately and in any way necessary. Additionally, it also represents a clear opposition to capitalism by proving that, when we cooperate, we can achieve things for which money is not necessarily an obstacle. With this state of mind, punk has fostered the creation of innumerable alternative cultural artifacts, the creation of independent fanzines and record labels, pirate radio stations, festivals, cultural events, and more. Clearly, punk is not the ultimate revolution, and the earth has not risen on new foundations,[9] but it has had a decisive impact, especially at the grassroots level. Giving shelter to the homeless, feeding people through food recycling and community meals, fostering cheap and local leisure for the neighborhood, holding discussions, lectures, and more, punk has fostered a strong alternative to the culture promoted by the dominant political and economic class.

Today there are punk movements such as the queercore, riot grrrl, and Afropunk movements, and new underground cultural movements that keep emerging and mixing with older ones. Such movements seek to fight homophobia, sexism, and racism within the general political activism of punk culture. In the Spanish queercore and riot grrrl context, we can cite bands such as Genderlexx, Perra Vieja, Meconio, or Las Sexpeares. Additionally, there are other movements in Spain that are not necessarily framed within punk, such as the hip-hop movement, that also present interesting political cultures. I think it is important to explore the potentialities toward social change in all these phenomena. Instead of simply reading culture against the grain to explain where neoliberal or capitalist ideologies appear in the dominant culture, one must identify and socialize those cultures that seem to propose other positive alternatives. If, with Gramsci (1986, 247), we understand that "crear una nueva cultura no significa solo hacer descubrimientos 'originales', significa también y especialmente difundir críticamente verdades ya descubiertas, 'socializarlas' por así decirlo y por lo tanto hacer que se conviertan en base de acciones vitales,"[10] I believe that, in addition to being critical with culture, studying how cultures such as punk can effect a positive change is also imperative. If we had spent more time studying punk for its contributions than simply scorning the movida for its hedonism, we could have probably understood and socialized other very necessary ideas and ways of living. I hope this book can serve as a humble contribution to this goal.

9 Lyrics from "The Internationale": "The earth shall rise on new foundations."

10 To create a new culture does not mean to make "original" discoveries; it also and especially means to spread critically already discovered truths, "socialize" them, and therefore, make them the base of vital actions.

# WORKS CITED


Adorno, Theodor W. 1990. *Negative Dialectics*. London: Routledge. Print.

Aguilar, Paloma. 2002. *Memory and Amnesia: The Role of the Spanish Civil War in the Transition to Democracy*. New York: Berghahn Books. Print.

Alaska y los Pegamoides. 1982. "Bailando." *Grandes éxitos*. Hispavox. Vinyl.

Alfonso, José Antonio. 2001. *Hasta el final: 20 años de punk en España*. Zaragoza: Zona de obras. Print.

Alfonso, José A., and Alberto Bocos Oyarbide, dir. 2007. *No acepto*. DVD.

Allinson, Mark. 2000. "The Construction of Youth in Spain in the 1980s and 1990s." In *Contemporary Spanish Cultural Studies*, edited by Barry Jordan and Rikki Morgan-Tamosunas, 26–73. London: Arnold. Print.

Álvarez, David. 2017. *Lo que hicimos fue secreto*. Eleventh Floor. DVD.

Ambrose, Joe. 2001. *Moshpit: The Violent World of Mosh Pit Culture*. London: Omnibus Press. E-book.

Antidogmatikss. 1984. *Rompan filas!* Self-released. Vinyl.

Bakhtin, Mikhail. 1981. *The Dialogic Imagination*. Austin: University of Texas Press. Print.

Bakhtin, Mikhail. 2009. *Rabelais and His World*. Bloomington: Indiana University Press. Print.

Barricada. 1986. "Okupación." *No hay tregua*. BMG Ariola. Cassette.

Barricada. 2009. *La tierra está sorda*. Warner Music Spain. CD.

Barricada. 2010. *En la memoria*. Warner Music Spain. CD.

Bella Bestia. 1986. *Lista para Matar*. Nuevos médios. Vinyl.

Benjamin, Walter. 1968. "Theses on the Philosophy of History." In *Illuminations: Essays and Reflections*, edited by Hannah Arendt, 253–64. New York: Schocken Books. Print.

Benjamin, Walter. 2005. "The Author as Producer." In *Selected Writings Volume 2, Part 2, 1931–1934*, edited by Michael W. Jennings, Howard Eiland, and Gary Smith, 768–82. Cambridge, MA: Harvard University Press. Print.

Benjamin, Walter. 2006. "Paralipomena to 'On the Concept of History." In *Walter Benjamin: Selected Writings, Volume 4 (1938–1940)*, edited by Howard Eiland and Michael W. Jennings, 401–11. Cambridge, MA: Harvard University Press. Print.

Bernal, Mauricio. 2015. "La primera okupación." *El Periódico*, August 8. https://www.elperiodico.com/es/sociedad/20150808/la-primera-okupacion-4418898.

Berry, Chuck. "Johnny B. Goode." Chess Records, 1958. Vinyl.

Bestley, Russ, Mike Dines, Alastair "Gords" Gordon, and Paula Guerra. 2019. *The Punk Reader: Research Transmissions from the Local and the Global.* Bristol: Intellect. E-book.

Bestley, Russ, Mike Dines, Alastair "Gords" Gordon, and Paula Guerra. 2021a. *Trans-Global Punk Scenes: The Punk Reader Volume 2*. Bristol: Intellect Books. E-book.

Bestley, Russ, Mike Dines, Matt Grimes, Paula Guerra. 2021b. *Punk Identities, Punk Utopias: Global Punk and Media.* Bristol: Intellect Books. E-book.

Bey, Hakim. 1985. *T.A.Z.: The Temporary Autonomous Zone, Ontological Anarchy, Poetic Terrorism.* Uploaded April 16, 2009, by *The Anarchist Library.* https://theanarchistlibrary.org/library/hakim-bey-t-a-z-the-temporary-autonomous-zone-ontological-anarchy-poetic-terrorism.pdf.

Boikot. 2015. "Boikot en Rivas Rock 2015 Live." Uploaded May 22, by Boikot Oficial. Video, 3 min., 44 sec. YouTube. https://www.youtube.com/watch?v=JFUEleRHrdc.

Bourdieu, Pierre. 1996. *Distinction: A Social Critique of the Judgement of Taste.* Cambridge: Harvard University Press. Print.

Bray, Mark. 2017. *Antifa: The Antifascist Handbook.* Brooklyn: Melville House. Print.

Butler, Judith. 1988. "Performative Acts and Gender Constitution: An Essay in Phenomenology and Feminist Theory." *Theatre Journal* 40 (4): 519–31. Print.

Cañas, Gabriel. 1986. "El Ayuntamiento de Madrid Culpa al Grupo 'Punk' La Polla Records de no aplacar al público." *El País,* May 14.

Cardús i Ros, Salvador. 2000. "Politics and the Invention of Memory: For a Sociology of the Transition to Democracy in Spain." In *Disremembering the Dictatorship: The Politics of Memory in the Spanish Transition to Democracy,* edited by Joan Ramon Resina, 17–28. Amsterdam: Editions Rodopi. Print.

Casals Meseguer, Xavier. 2009. "La Renovación de la Ultraderecha Española: Una Historia Generacional (1966–2008)." *Historia y Política,* edited by Centro de Estudios Constitucionales, no. 22, 233–58. Print.

Cazorla Sánchez, Antonio. 2013. *Franco: The Biography of the Myth.* London: Routledge. Print.

Cerdán, Diego. 2001. *Eskorbuto: Historia triste.* Madrid: Ediciones marcianas. Print.

Chrisafis, Angelique. 2016. "French Law Forbids Food Waste by Supermarkets." *Guardian,* February 4. https://www.theguardian.com/world/2016/feb/04/french-law-forbids-food-waste-by-supermarkets.

Christgau, Robert. 2007. "New York Dolls." In *Stranded: Rock and Roll for a Desert Island,* edited by Greil Marcus, 132–47. Cambridge, MA: Da Capo Press. Print.

Cicatriz. 1986. "Horacio." *Inadaptados.* Oihuka. Reissued 1994. CD.

*Cinta antifascista.* n.d. Cassette.

*Cinta antirracista.* n.d. Cassette.

Clark, Dylan. 2003. "The Death and Life of Punk, the Last Subculture." In *The Post-Subcultures Reader,* edited by David Muggleton and Rupert Weinzierl, 223–36. Oxford: Berg. Print.

Clarke, John, Stuart Hall, Tony Jefferson, and Brian Roberts. 2006. "Subcultures, Cultures, and Class." In *Resistance Through Rituals: Youth Subcultures in Post-War Britain,* edited by Stuart Hall and Tony Jefferson, 9–74. London: Routledge. Print.

Cohen, Albert K. 1955. *Delinquent Boys: The Culture of the Gang.* Glencoe, IL: Free Press of Glencoe. Print.

Costa, Salvador. 1977. *Punk: Fotografías de Salvador Costa.* Barcelona: Producciones Editoriales S.A. Print.

Crass. 1978. "Punk Is Dead." *The Feeding of the Five Thousand.* Small Wonder Records. Vinyl.

Cruz, Juan. 2016. "Hicimos divertida la España de los 70 y 80." *El País,* March 27. Print.

Cuéllar, José M. 1986. "Obús levantó un concierto arruinado por los 'punkies.'" *ABC Madrid,* May 14. https://www.abc.es/archivo/periodicos/abc-madrid-19860514-82.html.

Danza Invisible. 1983. *Contacto interior.* BMG Ariola. Vinyl.

Dardot, Pierre, and Christian Laval. 2013. *La nueva razón del mundo: Ensayo sobre la sociedad neoliberal.* Barcelona: Gedisa. Print.

del Val Ripollés, Fernán. 2011. "Pasotismo, cultura underground y música pop: Culturas juveniles en la Transición española." *Revista de Estudios de Juventud* 95: 74–91.
Destruye, Joni, ed. 1983a. *N.D.F.*, no. 1. Barcelona. Print.
Destruye, Joni, ed. 1983b. *N.D.F.*, no. 6. Barcelona. Print.
"Detención de Punks en Bilbao Durante el Aste Nagusia 1985." Uploaded January 8, 2015, by Pepitas Editorial. Video, 5 min., 15 sec. YouTube. https://www.youtube.com/watch?v=oTRJ69MECCE.
Drogas Guais. 1990. "Baila al son del PSOE." *El encanto de la perversión*. Berlin Records.
Dunn, Kevin. 2016. *Global Punk: Resistance and Rebellion in Everyday Life*. New York and London: Bloomsbury. E-book.
Eiriz, Alberto, ed. 1985. *Penetración*, no. 6. Madrid. Print.
El Último ke Zierre. 1993. "Ay Carmela." *Que se repartan el mundo*. Discos Suicidas. CD.
"Entrevista completa a Evaristo en PFV de ETB2." Excerpt of the TV program *Por fin, viernes*, hosted by Jon Bilbao. Uploaded December 6, 2014, by Imanol Larraza. Video, 30 min., 33 sec. YouTube. https://www.youtube.com/watch?v=HERjslJX510.
Eskorbuto. 1983. *Jodiéndolo todo*. Self-released. Cassette.
Eskorbuto. 1986. "Cuidado." *Anti-todo*. Discos Suicidas. Reissued 1996. CD.
Eskorbuto. 1991. "No quiero cambiar." *Demasiados enemigos*. Oihuka. CD.
Etxarri, Tonia. 1985. "Limpieza Corporal Obligada para los 'Punks' en Bilbao." *El País*, August 22.
Etxeberria, Francisco, Carlos Martín Beristain, and Laura Pego. 2017. "Proyecto de investigación de la tortura y malos tratos en el País Vasco entre 1960–2014." https://www.irekia.euskadi.eus/uploads/attachments/10779/INFORME_FINAL_-_investigacion_tortura_y_malos_tratos_18-12-2017.pdf
*Europa Press*. 2007. "Crónica Música: Canteca de Macao empieza una nueva etapa con su primer disco, 'Camino de la vida entera.'" July 23. http://www.europapress.es/otr-press/cronicas/noticia-cronica-musica-canteca-macao-empieza-nueva-etapa-primer-disco-camino-vida-entera-20070723165224.html.
Exploited, The. 1981. "Punks Not Dead." *Punks Not Dead*. Secret Records. Vinyl.
FACUA. n.d. *¿Qué hacen los supermercados con la comida que no venden? Encuesta a 28 cadenas de distribución*. Accessed January 20, 2025. https://www.facua.org/es/tablas/InformeFACUA_despilfarroalimentos.pdf.
La Falcata. n.d. "SKA-P gana dinero vendiendo anarquismo y revolución." *La Haine*. Accessed January 20, 2025. https://www.lahaine.org/musica/lafalcataskap_comoganardinero.htm.
FAP (Federación Anarco Punk). 2008. *Hazlo tú mismo: Recupera tu vida*. FAP. Print.
Flesher Fominaya, Cristina. 2015. "Debunking Spontaneity: Spain's 15M/*Indignados* as Autonomous Movement." *Social Movements Studies* 14(2): 142–63.
Fouce, Héctor. 2002. "'El futuro ya está aquí': Música pop y cambio cultural en España, Madrid 1978–1985." 2002. Universidad Complutense de Madrid, PhD dissertation.
Fouce, Héctor. 2004. "El punk en el ojo del huracán: De la *nueva ola* a la *movida*." In "De las Tribus Urbanas a las Culturas Juveniles," edited by Instituto de la Juventud, special issue, *Revista de Estudios de Juventud* 64: 57–65. Print.
Fouce, Héctor, and Fernán del Val. 2013. "*La movida:* Popular Music as the Discourse of Modernity in Democratic Spain." In *Made in Spain: Studies in Popular Music*, edited by Silvia Martínez and Héctor Fouce. London: Routledge. Print.
Furness, Zack. 2012. Introduction to *Punkademics: The Basement Show in the Ivory Tower*, edited by Zack Furness, 5–24. Brooklyn: Minor Compositions. Print.
Gabinete Caligari. 1983. *Que Dios reparta suerte*. Tres cipreses. Vinyl.
Gara Jova, Olvido, and Nacho Canut, eds. 1977. *Kaka de Luxe*, no. 2. Madrid. Print.
González Lezama, Tomás. 2016. *Punk, pero ¿qué punk?* Madrid: La Fonoteca. Print.

González, Robert, Lluc Peláez, and Asier Blas. 2022. "Okupar, resistir y generar autonomía: Los impactos políticos del movimiento por la okupación." *Creadores de democracia radical*, coordinated by Pedro Ibarra, Salvador Martí, and Ricard Gomá. Barcelona: Icaria Editorial. Print.

Graham, Helen, and Jo Labanyi. 1995. "Democracy and Europeanization: Continuity and Change 1975–1992." In *Spanish Cultural Studies: An Introduction*, edited by Helen Graham and Jo Labanyi. Oxford: Oxford University Press. Print.

Gramsci, Antonio. 1986. *Cuadernos de la cárcel: Tomo 4*. Edited by Valentino Guerratano. México D.F.: Ediciones Era. Print.

Gras, Marc. 2005. *Punk: Tres décadas de resistencia*. Barcelona: Quarentena Ediciones. Print.

Guerrilla Urbana. 1989. *Razón de estado*. Jaja Records. Vinyl.

Habeas Corpus. 1995. "El quinto regimiento." *Sociedad mecanizada*. Potencial Hardcore. Cassette.

Habeas Corpus. 2000a. "A las cosas por su nombre." *A las cosas por su nombre*. Desobediencia. CD.

Habeas Corpus. 2000b "Eso que ellos llaman paz." *A las cosas por su nombre*. Desobediencia. CD.

Habeas Corpus. 2006a. "Bajo un manto de olvido." *Basado en una historia real*. K-Industria. CD.

Habeas Corpus. 2006b. "Fascismo nunca más." *Basado en una historia real*. K-Industria. CD.

Habeas Corpus. 2008. "Una cuenta pendiente." *Justicia*. Maldito Records. CD.

Habeas Corpus. 2014. "Ay de los vencidos." *A este lado de la crisis*. Potencial Hardcore, CD.

Hall, Stuart, and Tony Jefferson, eds. 2006. *Resistance Through Rituals: Youth Subcultures in Post-War Britain*. London: Routledge. Print.

Hebdige, Dick. 1979. *Subculture: The Meaning of Style*. London: Routledge. Print.

Herreros, Roberto, and Isidro López. 2013. *El estado de las cosas de Kortatu*. Madrid: Ediciones Lengua de Trapo. Print.

Iglesias Turrión, Pablo. "Hipócritas católicos, hijos del Franquismo, gobiernan este país." Excerpt of TV segment produced by La Tuerka. Video, 1 min., 46 sec. Uploaded October 31, 2012, by La Base. YouTube. https://www.youtube.com/watch?v=t56hePmYuDY.

*Insumisión*. 1994. Gato Salvaje. Cassette.

*Istorio bat kameraren atzean*. 2009. Andoain: Andoaingo Gaztetxea. Book.

Junquera, Natalia. 2013. "Jueces para la democracia acusa al Gobierno de incumplir la ley de memoria." *El País*, Oct 9. https://elpais.com/politica/2013/10/09/actualidad/1381322308_843838.html.

Kaka de Luxe. 1983. *Las canciones malditas*. El fantasma del paraíso. Vinyl.

*Kaña al 92*. 1992. Desenmascaremos el 92. Cassette.

Kortatu. 1985. *Kortatu*. Pamplona: Soñua. Cassette.

Kortatu. 1986. *El estado de las cosas*. Pamplona: Soñua. Cassette.

Kortatu. 1988. *Unzensuriert*. Switzerland: Agit Prop Edition Negra. Vinyl.

Labanyi, Jo. 2000. "History and Hauntology; or, What Does One Do with the Ghosts of the Past? Reflections on Spanish Film and Fiction of the Post-Franco Period." In *Disremembering the Dictatorship: The Politics of Memory in the Spanish Transition to Democracy*, edited by Joan Ramon Resina, 65–82. Amsterdam: Editions Rodopi. Print.

Labrador Méndez, Germán. 2017. *Culpables por la literatura: Imaginación política y contracultura em la Transición (1968–1986)*. Madrid: Akal. E-book.

Laclau, Ernesto. 2005. *On Populist Reason*. London: Verso. Print.

Laing, Dave. 2015. *One Chord Wonders: Power and Meaning in Punk Rock*. Oakland: PM Press. Print.

Lechado, José Manuel. 2005. *La movida: Una crónica de los 80*. Madrid: ALGABA Ediciones. Print.

Llach, Lluís. 1977. "Campanades a morts." *Campanades a morts*. Movieplay. Vinyl.

Llansama, Jordi. 2011. *Harto de todo: Historia oral punk en la ciudad de Barcelona 1979–1987*. Barcelona: BCore. Print.

Maffesoli, Michel. 1996. *The Time of the Tribes: The Decline of Individualism in Mass Society*. London: SAGE. Print.
Marcus, Greil. 1990. *Lipstick Traces: A Secret History of the Twentieth Century*. Cambridge, MA: Harvard University Press. E-book.
Marcuse, Herbert. 2009. *Negations: Essays in Critical Theory*. London: MayFly Books. Print.
Martínez, Guillem. 2012. “El concepto CT.” In *CT o Cultura de la Transición: Crítica a 35 años de cultura española*, edited by Guillem Martínez. Barcelona: Debolsillo. E-book.
Martínez, Miguel A., Angela García Bernardos, eds. 2015. *Okupa Madrid (1985–2011)*. Madrid: Seminario de Historia Política y Social de las Okupaciones en Madrid-Metrópolis. E-book.
Marx, Karl. 1884. *Capital Vol. 1*. Marxists Internet Archive. https://www.marxists.org/archive/marx/works/download/pdf/Capital-Volume-I.pdf.
Marx, Karl. 1897. *Capital Vol. 3*. Marxists Internet Archive. https://www.marxists.org/archive/marx/works/download/pdf/Capital-Volume-III.pdf.
Marx, Karl. 1988. *Economic and Philosophic Manuscripts of 1844 and The Communist Manifesto*. Amherst: Prometheus Books. Print.
Marx, Karl, and Friedrich Engels. 1998. *The German Ideology*. Amherst: Prometheus Books. Print.
MCD. 1987. “Squatters.” *Bilboko Gaztetxean*. Discos Suicidas. Reissued 1994. CD.
McKay, George. 1996. *Senseless Acts of Beauty*. London: Verso. Print.
Mecano. 1981. “Hoy no me puedo levantar.” *Hoy no me puedo levantar*. CBS Columbia. Vinyl.
Mekons, The. 1978. “Never Been in a Riot.” *Never Been in a Riot*. Fast Product. Vinyl.
Moon, Tony, ed. 1977. *Sideburns*, no. 1. London. Print.
Morán, Gregorio. 1991. *El precio de la transición*. Barcelona: Editorial Planeta. Print.
Los muertos de Cristo. 1995. “A las barricadas.” *A las barricadas*. Fobia duros sentimientos. CD.
Muggleton, David. 2002. *Inside Subculture: The Postmodern Meaning of Style*. Oxford: Berg. Print.
Muggleton, David, and Rupert Weinzierl. 2003. *The Post-Subcultures Reader*. Oxford: Berg. Print.
“‘Ni banderas ni fronteras’, así aterrizo en España durante 1985 el movimiento okupa.” Excerpt of the TV program *¿Donde estabas entonces?* Uploaded March 18, 2018, by La okupación como analizador Okupa Madrid. Video, 4 min., 19 sec. YouTube. https://www.youtube.com/watch?v=nOn4DdEWju8&feature=youtu.be.
Nichols, William J., and H. Rosi Song. 2014. “Back to the Future: Towards a Cultural Archive of *La Movida*.” In *Toward a Cultural Archive of La Movida: Back to the Future*, edited by William J. Nichols and H. Rosi Song, 1–15. Teaneck, NJ: Fairleigh Dickinson University Press. Print.
*NO 92*. 1992. El Lokal Distribuidora. Cassette.
Obús. 1986. *Dejarse la Piel*. BMG. CD.
L’odi Social. 1986. *Que pagui Pujol* Barcelona: Col·lectiu Matxaka. Vinyl.
O’Hara, Craig. 1995. *The Philosophy of Punk: More than Noise*. San Francisco: AK Press. Print.
“Okupas. Programa ‘20 minutos’, Telemadrid, 1994.” Episode of the TV program *20 minutos*. Uploaded December 9, 2016, by La okupación como analizador Okupa Madrid. Video, 25 min., 38 sec. YouTube. https://www.youtube.com/watch?v=xg3Nv2Y-1RE.
Olor a Sobako. 1988. *Madrí, qué bien resistes*. Sabotaje. Cassette.
*El País*. 1977. “El Ministerio de la Vivienda reconoce y acepta la ocupación de vivienda en La Ventilla.” February 11. https://elpais.com/diario/1977/02/11/madrid/224511862_850215.html.
Park, Robert E., and Ernest W. Burgess. 1921. *Introduction to the Science of Sociology*. Chicago: University of Chicago Press. Print.
Pascual, Jakue. 2015. *Movimientos de Resistencia: Años 80 en Euskal Herria; Contexto, Crisis y Punk*. Tafalla: Txalaparta. Print.

Pérez Serrano, Julio. 2004. "Experiencia histórica y construcción social de las memorias: La Transición española a la democracia," special issue, *Pasado y memoria: Revista de Historia Contemporánea*, no. 3. Print.

Petras, James. 2018. *Padres-Hijos: Dos generaciones de trabajadores españoles.* Confederación General de Trabajo. http://www.inventati.org/ingobernables/textos/anarquistas/informe-petras.pdf.

Philips, Barry. 2023. *In Search of Tito's Punks: On the Road in a Country That No Longer Exists.* Bristol: Intellect Books. E-book.

Piperrak. 1994. "Mi Primer Amor." *Arde Ribera.* Discos Suicidas. CD.

Piperrak. 1996. "A la mierda." *Los muertos de siempre.* Discos Suicidas. CD.

Polhemus, Ted. 2014. *Streetstyle.* London: PYMCA. E-book.

La Polla Records. 1984. "Txus." *Salve.* Oihuka. Reissued 1994. CD.

La Polla Records. 1987a. "No somos nada." *No somos nada.* Self-released. Vinyl.

La Polla Records. 1987b. "Odio a los partidos." *No somos nada.* Self-released. Vinyl.

"La Polla Records 'Ellos dicen mierda.'" Uploaded September 28, 2013, by MENTEdeunESCLAVO. Video, 15 sec. YouTube. https://www.youtube.com/watch?v=zW1Gl6wPOPE.

"La Polla Records – San Isidro 1986 (Concierto Completo)." Uploaded June 12, 2016, by Víctor Hugo Calderon Brizuela. Video, 55 min., 44 sec. YouTube. https://www.youtube.com/watch?v=R5rOlw7mk2I.

Porras, Juan. 2006. *Negación punk en Euskal Herria.* Tafalla: Txalaparta. Print.

Potato and Tijuana in Blue. 1986. *Potato + Tijuana in Blue.* Soñua. Vinyl.

Prego, Victoria, screenwriter. 1995. *La Transición.* RTVE. http://www.rtve.es/archivo/la-transicion-serie/.

Pruijt, Hans. 2004. "Okupar en Europa." In *¿Dónde están las llaves? El movimiento okupa: prácticas y contextos sociales*, edited by Ramón Adell Argilés and Miguel Martínez López, 35–60. Madrid: Los libros de la catarata. Print.

Quaggio, Giulia. 2014. *La Cultura en Transición: Reconciliación y política cultural en España, 1976–1986.* Madrid: Alianza Editorial. E-book.

*Radical FM*, no. 2, 1982. Print.

Radio Futura. 1980. "Enamorado de la moda juvenil." *Música moderna.* Hispavox. Vinyl.

Ramones. 1976. "Biltzkrieg Bop." *Ramones.* Sire/ABC. Vinyl.

Reincidentes. 1989. "Esa nueva oligarquia." *Reincidentes.* Trilita. Vinyl.

Reincidentes. 1991. "Odio." *Ni un Paso Atrás.* Discos Suicidas. CD.

Reynolds, Simon. 2005. *Rip It Up and Start Again: Postpunk 1978–1984.* London: Penguin Books. Print.

Rioboo, Francisco, dir. 1977. "El Punk: Dossier informe semanal 1977 - RTve." Uploaded August 12, 2014, by Paola Bathory. Video, 32 min., 2 sec. YouTube. https://www.youtube.com/watch?v=I135ZhtsDTw.

RIP. 1984. "No hay futuro." *Zona especial norte.* Spansul Records. Vinyl.

RIP. 1987. *No te muevas.* Basati Diskak. Vinyl.

RIP and Eskorbuto. 1984. *Zona especial norte.* Spansul Records. Vinyl.

*Rock Anti Mili.* 1988. Cassette.

Rodríguez-Ulloa, Olga, Rodrigo Quijano, and Shane Greene. 2022. *PUNK! Las Américas Edition.* Bristol: Intellect Books. E-book.

Sayes, Javier, ed. 1981. *Destruye!!!*, no. 1. Gipuzkoa. Print.

Sex Pistols, The. 1977. "God Save the Queen." *Never Mind the Bollocks.* Virgin. Vinyl.

Sham 69. 1979. "If the Kids Are United." *The Adventures of the Hersham Boys.* Polydor. Vinyl.

Shaw, Clifford R., and Henry Donald McKay. 1942. *Juvenile Delinquency and Urban Areas.* Chicago: University of Chicago Press. Print.

Silva, Emilio. 2016. "Emilio Silva, sobre la afirmación de Alaska en el País: 'Hicimos divertida la España de los 70 y 80.'" *Tercera información*. https://eldesperttador30.wordpress.com/2016/03/29/emilio-silva-la-afirmacion-alaska-pais-hicimos-divertida-la-espana-los-70-80/.

Sin Dios, dir. 2000. *10 años de autogestión*. DVD.

Sin Dios. 2019. http://www.sindios.net.

Skow, Marie Arleth. 2023. *Punk Art History: Artworks from the European No Future Generation*. Bristol: Intellect Books. E-book.

Soziedad Alkoholika. 1995. "Nos vimos en Berlín." *Intoxicazión Etílika*. Mil a Gritos Records. CD.

Stewart, Francis, and Laura Way. 2023. *Punk Pedagogies in Practice: Disruptions and Connections*. Bristol: Intellect Books. E-book.

Strange, Simon. 2022. *Blank Canvas: Art School Creativity from Punk to New Wave*. Bristol: Intellect Books. E-book.

Strauss, Fréderic. 1994. *Pedro Almodóvar, Un cine visceral: Conversaciones con Fréderic Strauss*. Madrid: Ediciones El País. Print.

Subterranean Kids. 1989a. "Amigo." *Hasta el Final*. La Isla de la Tortuga Discos. Vinyl.

Subterranean Kids. 1989b. "Has Llenado ese Vacío." *Hasta el Final*. La Isla de la Tortuga Discos. Vinyl.

Taylor, Verta. 1989. "Social Movement Continuity: The Women's Movement in Abeyance." *American Sociological Review* 54 (5): 761–75.

Thornton, Sarah. 1995. *Club Cultures: Music, Media, and Subcultural Capital*. Cambridge: Polity Press. E-book.

Torrús, Alejandro. 2015. "Movimiento 'okupa': 30 años de lucha urbana contra la economía de mercado." *El Público*, May 31. https://www.publico.es/politica/30-anos-movimiento-okupa-traves.html.

37 Hostias. "Gallo Rojo, gallo negro." *De Strepitus: Tratado sobre el ruido*. Potencial Hardcore, 1997. CD.

Triana Toribio, Nuria. 2000. "A Punk Called Pedro: *La Movida* in the Films of Pedro Almodóvar." In *Contemporary Spanish Cultural Studies*, edited by Barry Jordan and Rikki Morgan-Tamosunas, 274–82. London: Arnold. Print.

Trowell, Ian. 2023. *Throbbing Gristle: An Endless Discontent*. Bristol: Intellect Books. E-book.

Último Resorte. 1982. "Peligro Social." Último Resorte. Flor y Nata Records. Vinyl.

Vilarós, Teresa. 2018. *El mono del desencanto*. Madrid: Siglo XXI. E-book.

Vomito. 1986. "Las fuerzas de seguridad." *Skalherria Punk*. Discos Suicidas. Vinyl.

Walser, Robert. 2014. *Running with the Devil: Power, Gender, and Madness in Heavy Metal Music*. Middletown, CT: Wesleyan University Press. E-book.

Who, The. 1965. "My Generation." *My Generation*. Decca. Vinyl.

Williams, Raymond. 1977. *Marxism and Literature*. Oxford University Press. Print.

Worley, Matthew. 2012. "Shot by Both Sides: Punk, Politics and the End of 'Consensus.'" *Contemporary British History* 26 (3): 333–54. Print.

Zaldua, Beñat. 2018. "Campanas y música frente a la provocación de Ciudadanos y sus secuaces en Altsasu." *Naiz*, November 4. https://www.naiz.eus/eu/actualidad/noticia/20181104/altsasu-muestra-su-repulsa-al-acto-de-ciudadanos.

# INDEX

Page numbers in *italic* refer to illustrations. "Passim" (literally "scattered") indicates intermittent discussion of a topic over a cluster of pages.

# ABOUT THE AUTHORS

**David Vila Diéguez** is a musician, filmmaker, and scholar specializing in and around Hispanic popular music and cultural studies. He grew up between the Basque Country and Galicia. He is currently a university professor in California. He is one of the founding members of the cultural magazine *Furman217* and the singer of the Latinx alternative band the Rumba Madre. His album *Prisiones y Fugas* was chosen as one of the best albums of 2020 by AllMusic, and he actively plays all over the world. He wrote an award-winning script for a long-form musical film based on the Rumba Madre's second album, *Apropiaciones Culturales V.2*. Learn more about David at his website, davidviladieguez.com.

**Isabela Raygoza** is the associate editor for *Billboard Español* and a leading voice in Latin music, with nearly fifteen years of industry experience. Raised in the San Diego/Tijuana border region, she is based in New York City and joined *Billboard* full-time in 2022. She earned a bachelor's degree in interdisciplinary studies from UC Berkeley and a master's degree in media, culture, and communication from NYU.

# ABOUT PM PRESS

PM Press is an independent, radical publisher of critically necessary books for our tumultuous times. Our aim is to deliver bold political ideas and vital stories to all walks of life and arm the dreamers to demand the impossible. Founded in 2007 by a small group of people with decades of publishing, media, and organizing experience, we have sold millions of copies of our books, most often one at a time, face to face. We're old enough to know what we're doing and young enough to know what's at stake. Join us to create a better world.

**PM Press**
**PO Box 23912**
**Oakland, CA 94623**
**www.pmpress.org**

**PM Press in Europe**
**europe@pmpress.org**
**www.pmpress.org.uk**

# FRIENDS OF PM PRESS

These are indisputably momentous times—the financial system is melting down globally and the Empire is stumbling. Now more than ever there is a vital need for radical ideas.

In the many years since its founding—and on a mere shoestring—PM Press has risen to the formidable challenge of publishing and distributing knowledge and entertainment for the struggles ahead. With hundreds of releases to date, we have published an impressive and stimulating array of literature, art, music, politics, and culture. Using every available medium, we've succeeded in connecting those hungry for ideas and information to those putting them into practice.

*Friends of PM* allows you to directly help impact, amplify, and revitalize the discourse and actions of radical writers, filmmakers, and artists. It provides us with a stable foundation from which we can build upon our early successes and provides a much-needed subsidy for the materials that can't necessarily pay their own way. You can help make that happen—and receive every new title automatically delivered to your door once a month—by joining as a Friend of PM Press. And, we'll throw in a free T-shirt when you sign up.

Here are your options:

- **$30 a month** Get all books and pamphlets plus a 50% discount on all webstore purchases

- **$40 a month** Get all PM Press releases (including CDs and DVDs) plus a 50% discount on all webstore purchases

- **$100 a month** Superstar—Everything plus PM merchandise, free downloads, and a 50% discount on all webstore purchases

For those who can't afford $30 or more a month, we have **Sustainer Rates** at $15, $10, and $5. Sustainers get a free PM Press T-shirt and a 50% discount on all purchases from our website.

Your Visa or Mastercard will be billed once a month, until you tell us to stop. Or until our efforts succeed in bringing the revolution around. Or the financial meltdown of Capital makes plastic redundant. Whichever comes first.

## *The Spitboy Rule: Tales of a Xicana in a Female Punk Band*

Michelle Cruz Gonzales with a Foreword by Martín Sorrondeguy and Preface by Mimi Thi Nguyen

**ISBN: 978-1-62963-140-0**
**$15.95 160 pages**

Michelle Cruz Gonzales played drums and wrote lyrics in the influential 1990s female hardcore band Spitboy, and now she's written a book—a punk rock herstory. Though not a riot grrl band, Spitboy blazed trails for women musicians in the San Francisco Bay Area and beyond, but it wasn't easy. Misogyny, sexism, abusive fans, class and color blindness, and all-out racism were foes, especially for Gonzales, a Xicana and the only person of color in the band.

Unlike touring rock bands before them, the unapologetically feminist Spitboy preferred Scrabble games between shows rather than sex and drugs, and they were not the angry manhaters that many expected them to be. Serious about women's issues and being the band that they themselves wanted to hear, a band that rocked as hard as men but sounded like women, Spitboy released several records and toured internationally. The memoir details these travels while chronicling Spitboy's successes and failures, and for Gonzales, discovering her own identity along the way.

Fully illustrated with rare photos and flyers from the punk rock underground, this fast-paced, first-person recollection is populated by scenesters and musical allies from the time including Econochrist, Paxston Quiggly, Neurosis, Los Crudos, Aaron Cometbus, Pete the Roadie, Green Day, Fugazi, and Kamala and the Karnivores.

"The Spitboy Rule *is a compelling and insightful journey into the world of '90s punk as seen through the eyes of a Xicana drummer who goes by the nickname Todd. Todd stirs the pot by insisting that she plays hardcore punk, not Riot Grrrl music, and inviting males to share the dance floor with women in a respectful way. This drummer never misses a beat. Read it!*"
—Alice Bag, singer for the Bags, author of *Violence Girl: East L.A. Rage to Hollywood Stage, a Chicana Punk Story*

"*Incisive and inspiring, Michelle Cruz Gonzales's* The Spitboy Rule *brings the '90s punk world to life with equal parts heart and realism. Her story becomes a voyage of self-discovery, and Gonzales is the perfect guide—as she writes in rapidfire drum beats about epic road tours, female camaraderie, sexist fans, and getting accused of appropriating her own culture.*"
—Ariel Gore, *Hip Mama*

## *Orstralia: A Punk History 1974–1989*

Tristan Clark

**ISBN: 979-8-88744-039-2**
**$24.95 336 pages**

With appeal to more than just punk history obsessives, *Orstralia* offers an unprecedented snapshot of an underacknowledged segment of Australian life and history.

Far from punk's more modish North Atlantic core in the late 1970s, discontented youth in Australia were enacting similar musical and cultural reckonings. Yet in spite of the Australia's purported "laid-back" national demeanour, punks there were routinely met with insult, fist, or the police baton.

More subterranean than the national scandal that was punk back in "homeland" Britain, Australia's own bands nonetheless came to be heralded internationally. *Orstralia* represents the first definitive account of the country's initial years, from progenitors the Saints and Radio Birdman in the mid-70s, through the emergence of hardcore in the 1980s, to the stylistic diffusion that accompanied transition to the 1990s.

Based on over 130 interviews, *Orstralia* documents the most renowned to the most fleeting and obscure acts the nation produced. Included are equally engrossing and shocking personal narratives befitting such a passionate and intemperate cultural form, as well as punk's placement within broader Australian society at the time.

***"Australia has some claim to being a punk founder nation, most obviously through the influence of the Saints and Radio Birdman. In*** **Orstralia*****, Tristan Clark explores the wider terrain to recover a vibrant prepunk, punk, and postpunk history that captures the vibrancy and excitement of a culture brimming with ingenuity and teenage verve. A brilliant book and essential reading for all those interested in punk's cultural past."***
—Matthew Worley, author of *No Future: Punk Politics and British Youth Culture, 1976–84*

## *The Day the Country Died: A History of Anarcho Punk 1980–1984*

Ian Glasper

**ISBN: 978-1-60486-516-5**
**$24.95 496 pages**

*The Day the Country Died* features author, historian, and musician Ian Glasper (*Burning Britain*) exploring in minute detail the influential, esoteric, UK anarcho punk scene of the early Eighties. If the colorful '80s punk bands captured in *Burning Britain* were loud, political, and uncompromising, those examined in *The Day the Country Died* were even more so, totally prepared to risk their liberty to communicate the ideals they believed in so passionately.

With Crass and Poison Girls opening the floodgates, the arrival of bands such as Zounds, Flux of Pink Indians, Conflict, Subhumans, Chumbawamba, Amebix, Rudimentary Peni, Antisect, Omega Tribe, and Icons of Filth heralded a brand new age of honesty and integrity in underground music. With a backdrop of Thatcher's Britain, punk music became self-sufficient and considerably more aggressive, blending a DIY ethos with activism to create the perfectly bleak soundtrack to the zeitgeist of a discontented British youth.

It was a time when punk stopped being merely a radical fashion statement, and became a force for real social change; a genuine revolutionary movement, driven by some of the most challenging noises ever committed to tape. Anarchy, as regards punk rock, no longer meant "cash from chaos." It meant "freedom, peace, and unity." Anarcho punk took the rebellion inherent in punk from the beginning to a whole new level of personal awareness.

All the scene's biggest names, and most of the smaller ones, are comprehensively covered with new, exclusive interviews and hundreds of previously unseen photographs.

*"The oral testimony assembled here provides an often-lucid participant's view of the work of the wider anarcho-punk milieu, which demonstrates just as tellingly the diversity as well as the commonality by which it was defined. The collection hints at the extent to which—within a militant antiwar, anti-work, anti-system framework—the perception and priorities of the movement's activists differed: something the movement's critics (who were always keen to deride the uniformity of the 'Crass punks') rarely understood."*
—Rich Cross, *Freedom*

## *This Is a Message to Persons Unknown: The Story of Poison Girls*

Rich Cross with Alec Dunn and Erin Yanke

**ISBN: 979-8-88744-136-8 (paperback)**
**979-8-88744-144-3 (hardcover)**
**$34.95/$69.95 288 pages**

**Flesh and blood are what we are, flesh and blood are who we are, our cover is blown ...**

*This Is a Message to Persons Unknown* is the first full history of the legendary band Poison Girls. From their first gigs in Brighton in 1977 to years of DIY tours across Britain and Europe, the band forged a radical path through music, politics, and art.

Fronted by the uncompromising Vi Subversa—a singular lyricist, songwriter, and voice—Poison Girls challenged punk's Year Zero myth, weaving ferocity with wit, emotional depth, and inventive sound. Just as formative to anarcho-punk as Crass, yet defiantly their own, Poison Girls confronted misogyny, ageism, and authoritarianism with a passion and clarity that still resonates today.

Drawing on exclusive interviews, zines, contemporary accounts, and the personal archives of band members, this richly illustrated history documents Poison Girls' unforgettable songs, striking graphics, and fierce campaigns of resistance.

More than just a band biography, *This Is a Message to Persons Unknown* tells the story of a group of dissident artists who turned punk into both a protest and a possibility—an experiment in living, creating, and fighting for something new.

*"Why the fuck did I have a Crass shirt in high school but didn't hear about their peers, Poison Girls, until recently? When we do the meaningful work of digging back through the past and shining a light on women artists, we are making right past wrongs. Legendary all-male bands are only legendary because we gave them proper attention (sometimes exaggerated and undeserved) at the time, allowing their status to grow and their contributions to be oversold. But when women-centric bands are ignored or dismissed while active, their contributions not valued, it says less about their abilities in comparison to their peers and more about the insidiousness of sexism. Who else is missing from the history books?* This Is a Message to Persons Unknown *ensures Poison Girls will not be forgotten."*
—Shawna Potter, front-person for War On Women and author of *Making Spaces Safer: A Guide to Giving Harassment the Boot Wherever You Work, Play, and Gather*

## *One Chord Wonders: Power and Meaning in Punk Rock*

Dave Laing
with a Foreword by TV Smith

**ISBN: 978-1-62963-033-5**
**$17.95 224 pages**

Originally published in 1985, *One Chord Wonders* was the first full-length study of the glory years of British punk rock. The book argues that one of punk's most significant political achievements was to expose the operations of power in the British entertainment industries as they were thrown into confusion by the sound and the fury of musicians and fans.

Through a detailed examination of the conditions under which punk emerged and then declined, Dave Laing develops a view of the music as both complex and contradictory. Special attention is paid to the relationship between punk and the music industry of the late 1970s, in particular the political economy of the independent record companies through which much of punk was distributed. The rise of punk is also linked to the febrile political atmosphere of Britain in the mid-1970s.

Using examples from a wide range of bands, individual chapters use the techniques of semiology to consider the radical approach to naming in punk (from Johnny Rotten to Poly Styrene), the instrumental and vocal sound of the music, and its visual images. Another section analyses the influence of British punk in Europe prior to the music's division into "real punk" and "post-punk" genres.

The concluding chapter critically examines various theoretical explanations of the punk phenomenon, including the class origins of its protagonists and the influential view that punk represented the latest in a line of British youth "subcultures." There is also a chronology of the punk era, plus discographies and a bibliography.

*"A clear, unprejudiced account of a difficult subject."*
—Jon Savage, author of *England's Dreaming*

## *Queercore: How to Punk a Revolution: An Oral History*

Edited by Liam Warfield, Walter Crasshole, and Yony Leyser with an Introduction by Anna Joy Springer and Lynn Breedlove

**ISBN: 978-1-62963-796-9**
**$20.00 208 pages**

*Queercore: How to Punk a Revolution: An Oral History* is the very first comprehensive overview of a movement that defied both the music underground and the LGBT mainstream community.

Through exclusive interviews with protagonists like Bruce LaBruce, G.B. Jones, Jayne County, Kathleen Hanna of Bikini Kill and Le Tigre, film director and author John Waters, Lynn Breedlove of Tribe 8, Jon Ginoli of Pansy Division, and many more, alongside a treasure trove of never-before-seen photographs and reprinted zines from the time, *Queercore* traces the history of a scene originally "fabricated" in the bedrooms and coffee shops of Toronto and San Francisco by a few young, queer punks to its emergence as a relevant and real revolution. *Queercore* is a down-to-details firsthand account of the movement explored by the people that lived it—from punk's early queer elements, to the moment that Toronto kids decided they needed to create a scene that didn't exist, to Pansy Division's infiltration of the mainstream, and the emergence of riot grrrl—as well as the clothes, zines, art, film, and music that made this movement an exciting middle finger to complacent gay and straight society. *Queercore* will stand as both a testament to radically gay politics and culture and an important reference for those who wish to better understand this explosive movement.

*"Finally, a book that centers on the wild, innovative, and fearless contributions queers made to punk rock, creating a punker-than-punk subculture beneath the subculture, queercore. Gossipy and inspiring, a historical document and a call to arms during a time when the entire planet could use a dose of queer, creative rage."*
—Michelle Tea, author of *Valencia*

*"I knew at an early age I didn't want to be part of a church, I wanted to be part of a circus. It's documents such as this book that give hope for our future. Anarchists, the queer community, the roots of punk, the Situationists, and all the other influential artistic guts eventually had to intersect.* Queercore *is completely logical, relevant, and badass."*
—Justin Pearson, The Locust, Three One G

## *Sober Living for the Revolution: Hardcore Punk, Straight Edge, and Radical Politics*

Edited by Gabriel Kuhn

**ISBN: 978-1-60486-051-1**
**$22.95 304 pages**

Straight edge has persisted as a drug-free, hardcore punk subculture for 25 years. Its political legacy, however, remains ambiguous—often associated with self-righteous macho posturing and conservative puritanism. While certain elements of straight edge culture feed into such perceptions, the movement's political history is far more complex.

Since straight edge's origins in Washington, D.C., in the early 1980s, it has been linked to radical thought and action by countless individuals, bands, and entire scenes worldwide. *Sober Living for the Revolution* traces this history.

It includes contributions—in the form of in-depth interviews, essays, and manifestos—by numerous artists and activists connected to straight edge, from Ian MacKaye (Minor Threat/Fugazi) and Mark Andersen (*Dance of Days*/ Positive Force DC) to Dennis Lyxzén (Refused/The (International) Noise Conspiracy) and Andy Hurley (Racetraitor/Fall Out Boy), from bands such as ManLiftingBanner and Point of No Return to feminist and queer initiatives, from radical collectives like CrimethInc. and Alpine Anarchist Productions to the Emancypunx project and many others dedicated as much to sober living as to the fight for a better world.

*"Perhaps the greatest reason I am still committed to sXe is an unfailing belief that sXe is more than music, that it can be a force of change. I believe in the power of sXe as a bridge to social change, as an opportunity to create a more just and sustainable world."*
—Ross Haenfler, professor of sociology at the University of Mississippi, author of *Straight Edge: Clean-Living Youth, Hardcore Punk, and Social Change*

*"An 'ecstatic sobriety' which combats the dreariness of one and the bleariness of the other—false pleasure and false discretion alike—is analogous to the anarchism that confronts both the false freedom offered by capitalism and the false community offered by communism."*
—CrimethInc. Ex-Workers' Collective

# *The Fascist Groove Thing: A History of Thatcher's Britain in 21 Mixtapes*

Hugh Hodges with a Preface by Dick Lucas and a Foreword by Boff Whalley

**ISBN: 978-162-963-884-3**
**$22.95 384 pages**

This is the late 1970s and '80s as explained through the urgent and still-relevant songs of the Clash, the Specials, the Au Pairs, the Style Council, the Pet Shop Boys, and nearly four hundred other bands and solo artists. Each chapter presents a mixtape (or playlist) of songs related to an alarming feature of Thatcher's Britain, followed by an analysis of the dialogue these artists created with the Thatcherite vision of British society. "Tell us the truth," Sham 69 demanded, and pop music, however improbably, did. It's a furious and sardonic account of dark times when pop music raised a dissenting fist against Thatcher's fascist groove thing and made a glorious, boredom-smashing noise. Bookended with contributions by Dick Lucas and Boff Whalley as well as an annotated discography, *The Fascist Groove Thing* presents an original and polemical account of the era.

*"It's not often that reading history books works best with a soundtrack playing simultaneously, but Hugh Hodges has succeeded in evoking both the noises and the feel of a tumultuous 1980s. Proving that pop music is the historian's friend, he has here recovered those who help us best make sense of a scary, precarious, and exciting world."*
—Matthew Worley, author of *No Future: Punk, Politics and British Youth Culture, 1976–1984*

*"Those who think the 1980s were camp and fun clearly didn't live them. The Thatcher/Reagan era was grim as fuck. This tells the real story from the underground."*
—Ian Brennan, author of *Muse-Sick* and *Silenced by Sound*

*"Very interesting and timely indeed."*
—Anne Clark, spoken-word poet, *The Smallest Act of Kindness*

## *Argentina, A Tale of Two Utopias: Anarchism, Soccer, Neoliberalism*

Tomas Rothaus with a Foreword by Gabriel Kuhn

**ISBN: 979-8-88744-147-4**
**$22.95**

*A Tale of Two Utopias* takes us through the outsized and unexpected remnants of the influence of anarchist ideas and practice on modern-day Argentina—from the names of popular pastries to the foundation of numerous soccer clubs—until we arrive at the explosive intersection of anarchism, football, and the crisis of neoliberalism.

This is a thrilling first-person account of the December 2001 uprising in Argentina that marked the end of the neoliberal experiment of the 1990s, narrated by an anarchist participant in the clashes that laid siege to the presidential palace and forced the president to resign and flee on a rooftop helicopter. *A Tale of Two Utopias* weaves together two simultaneous yet seemingly unrelated events of those "days which contain decades" of Buenos Aires in December 2001: the uprising and the first championship in 35 years of the popular football club Racing Club de Avellaneda.

Alternating between urgent narration and historical account, and accompanied by over 150 photos and illustrations, *A Tale of Two Utopias* has the reader walking the streets of a Buenos Aires on fire, while finding the time to take us on a lovingly traced tour of the rich history of Argentina's anarchist movement of the early twentieth century (then among the largest in the world)—and it is also a compelling account of the trauma inflicted by Argentina's numerous dictatorships.

"A Tale of Two Utopias *weaves complicated histories of anarchism, football, resistance, and everyday life in Buenos Aires into an artful narrative of youthful exuberance and political turmoil. As opposition boils up again today in Argentina, this riveting snapshot of popular outrage from below presents readers with a fascinating point of inflection to connect general strikes and dreams of revolution, past and present.*"
—Mark Bray, author of *Antifa: The Anti-Fascist Handbook*

## *Collectives in the Spanish Revolution*

Gaston Leval
With a Foreword by Vernon Richards, and an Introduction by Pedro García-Guirao

**ISBN: 978-1-62963-447-0**
**$27.95 416 pages**

Revolutionary Spain came about with an explosion of social change so advanced and sweeping that it remains widely studied as one of the foremost experiments in worker self-management in history. At the heart of this vast foray into toppling entrenched forms of domination and centralised control was the flourishing of an array of worker-run collectives in industry, agriculture, public services, and beyond.

*Collectives in the Spanish Revolution* is a unique account of this transformative process—a work combining impeccable research and analysis with lucid reportage. Its author, Gaston Leval, was not only a participant in the Revolution and a dedicated anarcho-syndicalist but an especially knowledgeable eyewitness to the many industrial and agrarian collectives. In documenting the collectives' organisation and how they improved working conditions and increased output, Leval also gave voice to the workers who made them, recording their stories and experiences. At the same time, Leval did not shy away from exploring some of the collectives' failings, often ignored in other accounts of the period, opening space for readers today to critically draw lessons from the Spanish experience with self-managed collectives.

This classic translation of the French original by Vernon Richards is presented in this edition for the first time with an index. A new introduction by Pedro García-Guirao and a preface by Stuart Christie offer a précis of Leval's life and methods, placing his landmark study in the context of more recent writing on the Spanish collectives—eloquently positing that Leval's account of collectivism and his assessments of their achievements and failings still have a great deal to teach us today.

"Collectives in the Spanish Revolution *demonstrates clearly that the working class are perfectly capable of running farms, factories, workshops, and public services without bosses or managers dictating to them.*"
—Stuart Christie, author of *The Floodgates of Anarchy*

## *Lessons of the Spanish Revolution: 1936–1939*

Vernon Richards with an Introduction by David Goodway

**ISBN: 978-1-62963-647-4**
**$21.95    272 pages**

It was the revolutionary movement in Spain which took up Franco's challenge in July 1936, not as supporters of the Popular Front Government but in the name of the Social Revolution, and this book soberly examines the many ways in which Spain's revolutionary movement contributed to its own defeat.

Was it too weak to carry through the Revolution? To what extent was the purchase of arms and raw materials from outside sources dependent upon the appearance of a constitutional government inside Republican Spain? What chances had an improvised army of guerrillas against a trained fighting force? These were some of the practical problems facing the revolutionary movement and its leaders. But in seeking to solve these problems, the anarchists and revolutionary syndicalists were also confronted with other questions which were fundamental to the whole theoretical and moral bases of their organisation. Could they collaborate with political parties and reformist unions? Given the circumstances, was one form of government to be supported against another? Should the revolutionary impetus of the first days of resistance be halted in the interests of the armed struggle against Franco or be allowed to develop as far as the workers were able and prepared to take it? Was the situation such that the social revolution could triumph and, if not, what was to be the role of the revolutionary workers?

Originally written as a series of weekly articles in the 1950s and expanded, republished, and translated into many languages over the years, Vernon Richards's analysis remains essential reading for all those interested in revolutionary praxis.

*"The revolution that accompanied the outbreak of the Spanish Civil War was a high point in the history of working-class creativity, internationalism and self-activity. If it is to be a resource for present and future struggles, we must assess the strengths and weaknesses of the movement that propelled it. In this regard, the early endeavours of Vernon Richards remain indispensable."*

—Danny Evans, author of *Revolution and the State: Anarchism in the Spanish Civil War, 1936–1939*